# Queering Cold War Poetry

# Queering Cold War Poetry

## Ethics of Vulnerability in Cuba and the United States

ERIC KEENAGHAN

THE OHIO STATE UNIVERSITY PRESS / COLUMBUS

Library of Congress Cataloging-in-Publication Data
Keenaghan, Eric.
Queering Cold War poetry : ethics of vulnerability in Cuba and the United States / Eric Keenaghan.
p. cm.
Includes bibliographical references and index.
ISBN-13: 978-08142-0330-9 (cloth : alkaline paper)
ISBN-10: 0-8142-0330-2 (cloth : alkaline paper)
1. Stevens, Wallace, 1879–1955—Criticism and interpretation. 2. Duncan, Robert Edward, 1919–1988—Criticism and interpretation. 3. Lezama Lima, José—Criticism and interpretation. 4. Sarduy, Severo—Criticism and interpretation. 5. Cold War in literature. 6. Nationalism in literature. 7. Liberalism in literature. 8. Gays' writings—History and criticism. 9. Homosexuality and literature—United States—History—20th century. 10. Homosexuality and literature—Cuba—History—20th century. I. Title.
PS310.C6K44 2009
811'.5409358—dc22
2008021610
This book is available in the following editions:
Cloth (ISBN 978-0-8142-0330-9)
CD-ROM (ISBN 978-0-8142-9177-1)
Paper (ISBN: 978-0-8142-5732-6)
Type set in Adobe Minion Pro
Printed by Thomson-Shore, Inc.

# CONTENTS

# LIST OF ABBREVIATIONS

WALLACE STEVENS

| | |
|---|---|
| *CP* | *Collected Poems* |
| *LWS* | *The Letters of Wallace Stevens* |
| *NA* | *The Necessary Angel* |
| *SM* | *Secretaries of the Moon* (with José Rodríguez Feo) |

JOSÉ LEZAMA LIMA

| | |
|---|---|
| *CH* | *La cantidad hechizada* |
| *EA* | *La expresión americana* |
| *IP* | *Imagen y posibilidad* |
| *RI* | *El reino de la imagen* |
| *TH* | *Tratados en la Habana* |

ROBERT DUNCAN

| | |
|---|---|
| *FC* | *Fictive Certainties* |
| *GA* | *A Great Admiration* (with H.D.) |
| *HD* | *The H.D. Book:* Book and chapter numbers indicated (for example, as 1.2) |
| *LRD* | *The Letters of Robert Duncan and Denise Levertov* (with Denise Levertov) |
| *SP* | *A Selected Prose* |

SEVERO SARDUY

| | |
|---|---|
| *OC* | *Obra completa,* Volumes 1 and 2 |
| *WB* | *Written on the Body* |

# ACKNOWLEDGMENTS

Many people have supported the writing and research of *Queering Cold War Poetry.* The three chairs of my department at the University at Albany, SUNY—Gareth Griffiths, Steve North, Mike Hill—and their assistant, Liz Lauenstein, all helped secure small funds in the form of travel awards from the College of Arts and Sciences and the Department of English. The department also granted me a writing leave in fall 2006 that allowed me to complete the initial manuscript.

The now unrecognizable origin of *Queering Cold War Poetry* was my dissertation on passivity and the modernist baroque poetics of the authors discussed here, as well as a few others (Hart Crane, Reinaldo Arenas). Robert Caserio, Rachel Blau DuPlessis, and Larry Venuti enthusiastically supported that project. Although this book has moved far beyond that largely aesthetic study, their stamp still can be read here. Lázaro Lima served as the dissertation's outside reader, and I am indebted to him for his continuing encouragement.

Since those early days, many friends and colleagues have contributed to the project's evolution. My colleagues and students at SUNY Albany have offered valuable insights about, and encouragement of, my research; but I want to single out Branka Arsić, Bret Benjamin, Helen Regueiro Elam, and Tara Needham for graciously reading portions of this manuscript. Tom Cohen, Terri Ebert, and Charlie Shepherdson also offered strong advice at a critical stage. I am especially indebted to Rosemary Hennessy for several years of guidance, dear friendship, and strong criticism while she was at SUNY Albany. Pierre Joris and Don Byrd have joyfully shared their Duncan stories with me; and my conversations with Nicole Peyrafitte and Carol Mirakove about vulnerability, the role of the artist, and aesthetic politics continue to be a wellspring for me. Over many years, Angus Cleghorn, Ellen McCallum, Dana Luciano, Steven Bruhm, Scott Herring, and Laura Moriarty invited me to participate on various panels, colloquia, and symposia about queer theory and modernist poetry that have been useful, indirectly and directly, for shaping and revising the ideas explored here. This book's theoretical frame owes much to Susan Strehle, Ernesto Martínez, and Thomas Glave's lively engagement at my invited lecture for SUNY Binghamton's Department of English in October 2005. Thanks also to Paisley Currah, who invited me to offer a CLAGS public seminar in spring 2007, and to Sara Ganter, who took care of that operation's pragmatics. I am still learning much from my reflections on the eye-opening, stimulating, and challenging contributions by all the attending activists, artists, and academics; but I especially extend my thanks to Belkin Gonzalez, Patricia Meona-Picado, Ulrike Mueller, Oren Silverman, Josh Thorson, and Virgil Wong. Anonymous press readers offered invaluable suggestions that helped me streamline the manuscript, and the editorial guidance and enthusiasm of Sandy Crooms and Eugene O'Connor at the The Ohio State University Press have been heartening. Other friends and colleagues have supported me with food, drink, and intangibles: Rick Barney, Margie Byrd, Jason Cooke, Joanna Cooper, Sharon and James Danoff-Burg, Suzanne Gauch, Jen Greiman and Barry Trachtenberg, Glyne Griffith, Sue-Im Lee, Shelly and Alan Lependorf, Chris and Jenn McCreary, Shannon Miller, my extended Omi family (including Ruth Adams, John Davis), Anand Pandian, Jo Park and James Ker, Marjorie Pryse, Clare Robinson, Helene Scheck, Ed Schwarzschild, Stan Shire, Lisa Thompson, Lynne Tillman, Laura Wilder, and David Wills. All my other colleagues at SUNY Albany have been very supportive. And everyone who has populated my city life has offered reality checks and has shown reassuring signs of interest in my work: Lisa and Lucy Iacucci, Daniel Simmons, Bob Kirsch, Jay Nicorvo and Thisbe Nissen, Jamie Schwarz, Rob Casper.

Most important of all, though, is Jeffrey Lependorf. He patiently endured my prolonged disappearances into studies and libraries. When I reemerged, he grounded me with cocktails, treats, or gourmet meals while lovingly reading aloud poetry, Diana Vreeland's autobiography, Harry Mathews's short stories, or just pulpy smut. Jeff is the one who has taught me about vulnerability's personally transformative possibilities.

An earlier version of chapter 4 appeared in *Journal of Modern Literature* 28.4 (Summer 2005). I want to extend my gratitude to the editors of *JML* for permission to publish that article here, in revised form.

# PROLOGUE

*Queering Cold War Poetry* is a book about vulnerability: what it is, how it structures our lives, why it's imperative that queer theory and critical theory revalue its significance. Not only does it provide a key for reconstituting how we think about identity, difference, and community, but it also might ameliorate skepticism about theory's political potential. Although this study is the product of my longtime engagement with passivity in modern gay male writing from up to a half-century ago, only recently has the centrality of vulnerability to such literary passions become apparent to me. The post-9/11 preoccupation with the "security state" put a contemporary pressure on my growing interest in the political viability of vulnerability. In this book, I discuss four Cold War poets from Cuba and the United States—Wallace Stevens, José Lezama Lima, Robert Duncan, and Severo Sarduy—who struggled against similar state and cultural mandates that foreclosed any positive estimation of vulnerability so as to favor an attitude of nationalistic and identitiarian security. Their writings suggested to me that vulnerability can be appreciated as an ethical relation to one's world, a mode potentially viable for queer scholarship and activism today. Therefore, it seems appropriate to provide a few framing prefatory remarks that historically locate my reading of these writers in our contemporary moment, at the time of my own writing.

In the most colloquial of senses, queer subjects know all too well what it means to live "insecurely." Security also has a longstanding history in modern nation-states' political and ideological discourses. Those frames have structured, and continue to structure, how gay, lesbian, transgender, and other subjects have experienced their vulnerabilities differently, at specific historical junctures. The paradigm of security facing us today, in an age when globalized capitalism is in a standoff with international terrorism, is quite unlike the distinct schemas of national, collective, or human security emerging after the Second World War, schemas that affected how my literary subjects understood the idea of security.[1] Nonetheless, much can be learned from the past. During the protracted historical "moment" of the long Cold War, homosexual subjects in the Americas were constructed as outsiders, even traitors, to their national communities. At that time, risk and vulnerability bore much ideological weight. In his recent history of McCarthyism, David K. Johnson claims that U.S. governmental rhetoric rendered homosexuals and communists virtually coterminous. He even argues that the former may have been regarded as more of a "security risk" than the latter because homosexual citizens' politics were indeterminable, unreadable, and uncontainable (*The Lavender Scare*, 8–9). In Cuba, a parallel history of sexual and (trans)gender minorities' construction as counterrevolutionary security risks (the official term was *gusanos*, or "worms") was an explicit feature of the Castroist regime's Stalinism, especially in the early 1970s. That rhetoric continued an earlier, pre-Revolutionary moment's stereotyping of homosexual men. Ian Lumsden notes that during the 1940s and 1950s, one "factor contributing to the denigration of *maricones* [faggots] was their association with cowardice—*maricón* means coward as well as homosexual—in a country that has had to fight hard and long for its national liberation" (*Machos, Maricones, and Gays*, 53). Often living in urban centers where sexual tourism and queer culture were booming, homosexual men were imagined to be traitors who threatened the integrity of Cuban national culture because they consorted with *norteamericanos*.[2]

In more recent years, in the country where I write about and teach these issues, queer life increasingly interfaces with security primarily through neoliberal economics and a corresponding inflated sense of a need to protect and guard individuals' privacy. Lisa Duggan usefully describes this development as "a kind of right-to-privacy-in-public—a zone of immunity from state regulation, surveillance, and harassment" (*The Twilight of Equality?* 52). The U.S. Supreme Court decision *Bowers v. Hardwick* (1986) proved that queer citizens' private lives were vulnerable to the watchful eyes of the State and its enforcers. Since that decision, the condition of securing inviolable zones of privacy for queer subjects has continued to be a grave concern. "The legal tradition . . . tends to protect sexual freedom by privatizing it," as Michael Warner has noted; and those freedoms and "privacy protections" are secured only "for those whose sexuality is already normative" (*The Trouble with Normal*, 174). Warner cautioned about this predicament a few years prior to the Court's overturning of its earlier decision with *Lawrence v. Texas*

(2003); but, as Duggan notes, the situation has not abated due to the rise of "the new homonormativity," a conservative and mainstreamed gay and lesbian political movement that seeks to "redefine gay equality against the 'civil rights agenda' and 'liberationalism,' as access to the institutions of domestic privacy, the 'free' market, and patriotism" (*Twilight*, 50, 51). The vulnerable space of the home is extended into the public sphere. This fragile condition, wherein the public and the private overlap, must be secured at all costs, usually with the exclusion of those who can't pass for the norm.[3]

Since 9/11, *all* homes and *all* zones of privacy, whether they are domestic spaces or the neoliberal public's "complexly remap[ped] zones of collective autonomy," are imagined to be equally precarious (Duggan, *Twilight*, 52). Consequently, a quickly evolving sense of what constitutes privacy profoundly affects those structures that frame how all queer citizens—homonormative or not—imagine their relationship to the state and the nation. In a bold-faced subtitle, the U.S. Office of Homeland Security's *National Strategy for Homeland Security* (*NSHS*) proclaims that "Our Free Society Is Inherently Vulnerable." "The American people and way of life are the primary targets of our enemy, and our highest protective priority," the anonymous authors warn. "Our population and way of life are the source of our Nation's great strength, but also a source of inherent vulnerability" (*NSHS*, 7). Under the pressures of a perceived threat, this view reductively defines the nation as a population with a single "way of life" in order to promulgate a narrative justification of the state's invasions of Afghanistan and Iraq. Such stories wield a quite real historical and political force in shaping our experiences of nationhood. "A nation is not only a piece of land but a narration about the people's relation to the land," Donald Pease reminds us ("Global Homeland State," 5). Today's stories provide what Pease terms a "foundational fantasy" that reinforces a nationalist climate by stressing the "governing metaphor" of the homeland (6). It would do us well, though, also to remember the second term adding force to that metaphor and tempering that narrative. Conceived as a narrative constructing our collective experience of nationhood, Homeland Security actually functions as a *cultural effort* for which the American people are ultimately responsible. This cultural mode of defense is distinguished in the *NSHS* from its "twin concept" of state security (*NSHS*, 5). Citizens are called upon to tactically use identificatory narratives to counteract genuine fears about their vulnerabilities and to complement militaristic means of securing state sovereignty. In the process, nationalism has become something more than a jingoistic love of country. It is a state's and a culture's encouragement of egotism: *Care for your self, for the good of the population.* This biopolitical mandate has a corollary: *Be confident in your own identity, so as to ensure the stability and security of the collective with which you identify.*

What, then, does this nationalism ask of queer subjects, especially those who are activism-minded? In spring 2007, I had an opportunity to directly bring to my desired audience the ideas informing and growing out of my research for this book. I organized and led "Queer Nationalism and the Homeland Security State," a series of public lectures and seminar-style discussions sponsored by the City University of New York's Center for Lesbian and Gay Studies (CLAGS) and held between February and May 2007 at Greenwich Village's Lesbian, Gay, Bisexual, and Transgender Community Center. Those who attended varied from week to week. They came from many different backgrounds—activists, students, lawyers, artists. Despite the participants' changing faces and multiple interests, attendees at any given meeting were consistently committed to engaging one another's ideas thoughtfully. Repeatedly, many would confess that they were disillusioned by the present state of activism. The neoliberal context where queers must make themselves visible and heard has resulted in competition for scarce resources, volunteers, and contributions. This climate has had damaging effects on activism's coalitional possibilities. Seminar participants repeatedly complained about the particularly pernicious attention devoted to same-sex marriage, adoption, and partner-care rights. Even though almost everyone qualified their criticisms by noting how "important" these issues are, several also expressed frustration with how marriage and family rights are presumed to be the common political denominator for the so-called "community" (too often problematically described in the singular). These concerns have become mainstream gay and lesbian politics' spotlight issues because they can be easily pitched and sold. Working with a fair degree of financial security, middle- or upper-class gays and lesbians, most of whom are white and all of whom have economic resources at their disposal, seek to augment their relative safety at the expense of those in other queer communities (in the plural). Receiving less attention are problems concerning: sexual segregation of toilets and other facilities; transgender and transsexual subjects' access to reassignment therapies and surgeries; universal healthcare, housing, and job security; assistance for people living with AIDS, including partners and survivors as well as the infected and the ill; immigration and naturalization rights; and the intersectional inequities experienced by queers of color.

Several participants noted that they were drawn to political efforts outside "the community." Nearly unanimously, the seminar participants felt that the sociopolitical climate produced by the so-called "War on Terror" demanded a critical reappraisal of the possibilities for coalition and its anti-imperialist potential. Since interest in such coalition was found lacking in much queer politics, they opted to work in migration movements, citizenship rights organizations, and antiwar political groups. There they rediscovered the often forgotten anti-imperialist and antinationalist spirit of early Gay Liberation and later queer activism during the Persian Gulf War. They may feel more disconnected from direct action politics, but at least they knew that their new affiliations would let them advance their interests in working toward a general commonality that includes—but is not limited to—queer subjects. In such efforts, they explained, others are more open to differences as they look toward global horizons. To them, this quality seemed especially necessary in the face of *everyone's* ineluctable political vulnerability to an injurious capitalistic imperialism.

Over the months, our conversations about rethinking queer politics and culture had several breakthrough moments. One in particular stands out, though, and it set the tone for how I've recast the literary studies and the theoretic frame that follow. In the last hour of our second meeting, the group's self-identified activists concurred that how I delineated different historically overlapping constructions of security, from the Cold War to the present, was useful. But they asked a crucial question: If security is articulated in historically different ways, mustn't we distinguish between different forms of *vulnerability,* too? I had been promoting an idea of vulnerability as a laudable sort of de facto openness to others.One attendee cautioned, though, that in the heyday of Gay Liberation, vulnerability had less political and ethical gravitas. At that time it even read as symptomatic of the citizen's *failure* to act. Other members of our group proceeded to argue that that sense has changed over time, for they felt that some sense of vulnerability was at the heart of their experiences in the later coalitional politics of HIV/AIDS activism. In the same space of the Center where our seminar met, the AIDS Coalition to Unleash Power (ACT UP) was founded in 1987. That organization continues to reach across class, racial, sexual, and gender divides; and its pedagogical campaigns have done much to heighten citizens' consciousness of the interconnection of various domestic institutions (education, medicine, NGOs, government) on which our lives depend.[4] The political actions of the now-defunct Queer Nation, also originating in New York City's Center, sought to heighten, in different ways, consciousness about the networked nature of public space. By interjecting same-sex eroticism and queer visibility into the heteronormative public sphere at malls, restaurants, and other commercial spaces, activists attempted to bring queer bodies and queer desire into circulation as articles fit for consumption.[5] As these activists narrated it, participation in these organizations translated into exposing oneself to injury either by bringing same-sex eroticism into the public eye (Queer Nation) or by opening oneself to prioritize others' contextually defined needs (ACT UP). These quite different forms of vulnerability involved setting aside the immediate wants of oneself or one's group so as to demonstrate and act on the interconnectedness of North American life. Such an idea offset the equation of democratic living with competitive meritocracy and laissez-faire individualism. Coalitional openness is a kind of vulnerability growing out of a belief in the existence of a networked or ecological frame of mind, of the idea that everyone's actions are conditioned by, and contribute to the conditioning of, others' actions.[6]

The consensus was that politicized perceptions of vulnerability *have* changed. As two put it at that exciting March meeting, though, even when queer activists are interested in coalitional actions now, they tend to be wary of thinking about or expressing that necessary openness *as* vulnerability. However, this distrust is unlike gay revolutionaries and radicalesbians' suspicion of the term decades ago as symptomatic of an undesirable inaction and passivity. Now vulnerability is associated with a conservative nation-state's *intrusion* into queer life and affairs. A defensive identity politics has emerged at the levels of both national and minority communities, and one must fight to protect oneself against invasive policies and laws by securing group-specific rights and welfare interests. Alternatively, on the side of a conservative homonormativity that advocates the mainstreaming of the movement, one secures oneself from this exposure by disappearing into a national heteronormative cultural fabric.[7] Yet, if we reflect on how we differently experience our historically variable vulnerable condition, we can arrive at a new, less defensive attitude. We might turn exposure to possible harm into a political asset.

Collectively, we worked out three ways of understanding vulnerability today. First, it is a construct deployed by the state as an excuse for beefing up national security measures. Ultimately, these measures fuel the twin motors of an imperializing globalization: the state's military-industrial complex and corporate capitalism. There was some disagreement as to whether or not these vulnerabilities are real or imagined. After all, these New Yorkers could attest to the realities of 9/11 and its continuing material effects on their lives. Several, however, were also skeptical of official governmental rhetoric. They believed that a discourse sensationalizing the country's exposure to harm is used largely as a veil to facilitate a presidential administration's self-interest, as well as the interests of its corporate investors and lobbyists. Ironically, the second form of vulnerability we identified is produced by the security measures deployed to safeguard the nation-state. As a consequence of the suspension of civil liberties and the creation of a xenophobic climate, those who do not identify themselves with mainstream American values, or who are not identifiable as such, are more susceptible to injury. Queers of color are particularly subject to these developments, although white male queers, such as me, also feel unsettled by a pervasive loss of civil liberties and other personal securities. The third type of vulnerability enumerated by the CLAGS group is what I explore in *Queering Cold War Poetry*. Characterizing a particular sort of interpersonal relationship wherein one lets one's guard down, as in coalitional politics, it is an ontological—yet historically variable—condition of being open to others. If vulnerability now comes in three forms (at least), and two of those are injurious, it is worth reassessing the third's political viability. I concluded that meeting by noting that, even though we appreciate its merits, we now apparently lack a critical vocabulary for understanding vulnerability's progressive political potential.

Already existing theoretical investigations can help us begin to articulate such a politicized vulnerable attitude. Growing out of her writings about power and the necessity of conditionality, Judith Butler's recent work perhaps offers the most sustained engagement with questions akin to the ones we discussed in the CLAGS forum.[8] In similar ways, other theorists have reexamined passion or passivity, subjects' less guarded and less rational condition, to arrive at different understandings of the citizen-subject's agency. For example, Shane Phelan notes that "queering citizenship will require a refocusing of the passions of citizenship" and a blurring of the lines between the private and the public, the affective and the rational (*Sexual Strangers*, 17). With these shifts, she believes, we can more effectively challenge an entrenched liberalist tradition that privileges the private citizen who is self-contained and possesses inalienable rights. Similarly, Iris Marion Young argues that an inclusive democratic public cannot depend on rational deliberation and communicative action because certain groups, including but not limited to queers, lack or shun such discursive and social resources that are preconditions for full enfranchisement (*Inclusion and Democracy*, 52–80). According to these thinkers, new democratic possibilities are imaginable through an incorporation of passions, emotions, and affect into political discourse. These traits not only counter Western rationalism but, in drawing attention to bodies, they also heighten awareness of our connection with—and, consequently, our vulnerability to—others.

Because today's security tactics are "cultural," we can draw on cultural and intellectual predecessors to extend an already rich critical discourse about passion and passivity to enhance and update our vocabulary of vulnerability. Simply by emphasizing this often overlooked or shunned term, we can continue the critique of *a priori* agency carried out in the name of passion; yet, we can do so without wholly negating or dismissing citizens' need to act. Vulnerability provides a crucial key for countering the illogics of what I define in my introduction as "liberalism," the ontological condition defining biopolitical regimes that privilege individuals who care for themselves seemingly of their own accord in order to safeguard the security of the people. Too often maligned, vulnerability actually can ground a new language for rethinking and challenging the binary divide between identity and difference, an ethical project central to queer theory, much critical theory, and queer coalitional politics. *Queering Cold War Poetry* explores how two Cuban and two U.S. poets thought seriously about the ethicopolitical possibilities of different kinds of vulnerability. Their writings began as historicized and theoretic responses to their own epochs, but they crucially inform the general theory I elucidate below. These studies are my small contribution to what I hope will be a continuing revaluing of vulnerability as a remedy for past and present imperatives to maintain the state and its population's security, no matter the cost.

INTRODUCTION

# Toward a Queer Ethic of Vulnerability

While sitting in a theater, have you ever noticed an elderly couple exchanging discreet, barely visible touches, or whispering quiet words that actually don't say much? When in a train station, have you felt called by a baby burbling and cooing as she extends her hand? On the street, have you appreciated the kindness of a stranger who steps into your world with a simple hello, a look, a meaningful brush in passing? In such moments, others reach out to ask "Are you still alive?" or "Are you there?" or "Will you still be there when I finally touch you?" We take these ephemeral scenes of contact for granted, but they are significant because they illustrate how we locate our selves by verbally and physically touching what is outside. They are moments when we reflexively recognize we are at risk because the other may already have left us or may elude us in the future. Ironically, at those times we live affirmatively and presently. The other's being close by, now and in the future, is necessary. We need the other near so as to continually rediscover the joys of sharing and becoming, together.

Such a mode of living depends not only on a notion of corporeal or phenomenological proximity but also on an ontological principle residing somewhere between identity and difference: *similarity.* When we reach out to make contact, we do not look for what is the same or for what can replace us. Nor do we look for what is removed from our selves or for what is absolutely different. Instead, we look for what is *like* us, for what is metaphorically *close* to us. Because of our bodies, our trajectories of living intersect with others who, in the process, come to share their defining qualities with us. Such commonality makes new collectives imaginable. The recognition that we share in living—and that that allotment is predicated on existing somewhat vulnerably and in dependence on others—bears an ethical force. It can transform how we think about political collectives and how we imagine national possibilities. Subscribing to this kind of vulnerable and queer sense of nationhood entails moving between publics which intimate foldings that connect and invaginate our individual experiences with those of others. It is to search for intimacies that will redefine our public lives.

If similarity is the chief product of such intimacy, this condition should affect how we experience, if not always how we talk about, cultural identity. Not a language of *I am*; instead, a language of *I live like*. I live *like* a white American, *like* a gay man, *like* a professor, *like* a poet, *like* a theorist. What if we were to imagine identification as not occurring according to an individualized aspiration for equality? Equality, the rubric of a civil life and polity, is predicated on an arithmetical substitutability in which one doubles for or represents another, the generalized self or transparent citizen who is absent yet renders one's own identity legible. What if we imagined identification as occurring through similitude instead? Equity rather than equality, contact rather than parity. For you and me, so singularly dissimilar yet so humanly like one another, for us both to *live like Americans* in our embodied proximity to one another, through the narratives we exchange, is a metaphorical condition. To live in such a way depends on the juxtaposition of two singular entities. Such a mode permits us to figure—in both senses, *to imagine* and *to represent*—what the term "American" means now and how it can change. Such a future orientation depends on discovering the vital differences within our communities and our supposedly integral, contained selves.

To opt for a metaphorical existence is to inhabit a life of resemblance, not a life of identification or authenticity. Resemblances are risky, especially if we know that the condition we promote as "real" is just a figuration and thus is susceptible to change. Conceptualizing citizenship as a condition of living metaphorically moves us toward an ethical paradigm that remembers all bodies' vulnerable condition, a foundation of being that reinforces their similarity to one another. By thinking through this logic of resemblance, we can deconstruct predominant political fictions about identity, individualism, and security. Instead of living a completely individuated life, individuals are always multiple because they continuously open themselves to fellow citizens, with whom they share some likeness. Nation-state and global citizenship are thus conditions that need not be reduced to civil self-censoring in order to compel individuals' subscription to a homogeneous moral code.

They develop out of an ethical and publicly motivated sense of individual responsiveness to the privacies through which others imaginatively identify—or, better, liken—their selves to others.

Below I elaborate how this politicized ethic is a direct response to what Michel Foucault terms *liberalism,* a form of individualism that hampers the discovery of more equitable forms of democratic commonality. Liberalism prizes the identical and the contained self over other more vulnerable attitudes that could positively resignify difference. If we move away from liberalism's identificatory logics, we can promote a more coalitional, rather than communitarian or minority, understanding of commonality. In such a scenario, individuals rediscover themselves by finding likenesses to others with whom they presumably had none. A theoretical investigation of what liberalism is and how modern poetry disrupts it can spur queer theory to ethically reassess its rhetorical investments in those same rigid modes of identification and national belonging that it usually remonstrates against.

## Liberalism, One Half of a Democratic Faith

Michel Foucault's theory of biopolitics and its related technologies (population, security, governmentality) concerns the historical shifts in late modernity's dominant mechanisms of power. During the eighteenth century, the Western *polis* was based on a model of sovereignty, in which the head of state wielded absolute authority. This sovereignty was figured as a power over life, predicated on the ruler's sole ability to sentence subjects to death. With the rise of disciplinary structures (such as the clinic and the prison), and still later with the emergence of biopolitics proper, the sovereign's absolute control over life and death was no longer the preeminent form of power. The delinquent individual was now conditioned into a state of normalcy, thus giving rise to a normatively defined collective. With the advent of a biopolitical regime of power, however, individuals are not the subjects of a discipline aiming to create a moralistic, normative majority. The presumption is that a normative collective already exists. In this regime, the population is the object of power, more specifically of an administrative government's conservative management that aims to preserve and secure the collective's stability. Rather than a power over life, a right to life determines politics and social power. But this right is not, as is too often believed, a natural one belonging to the individual. Instead, only the population as a whole is entitled to it. Individuals are subjectivated in such a fashion that their first conscious priority is to care for their selves, to look out for their own well-being; however, they assume such a discipline primarily for the general population's benefit, not their own.[1]

Despite his seemingly schematic presentation of these three regimes' differences, Foucault never maintained that sovereignty or disciplinarity fully disappeared with the emergence of biopolitics. As has been reinforced by the work of theorists extending his thought, aspects of one regime are still present in the others.[2] For instance, Giorgio Agamben's work on exceptionality and the Nazi death camps underscores the close interrelation of sovereignty and governmentality in those systems where biopolitical strategies are deployed to the advantage of an exceptional class that operates with some degree of sovereign self-interest.[3] More recently, in federal responses to 9/11, we have witnessed what Wendy Brown calls "a transformation of American liberal democracy into a political and social form for which we do not yet have a name, a form organized by a combination of neoliberal governmentality and imperial world politics, shaped in the short run by global economic and security crises" (*Edgework*, 51). In her analysis of recent U.S. policies of preemptive war and indefinite detention, Judith Butler closely aligns the aforementioned governmentality with "petty sovereigns, unknowing, to a degree, of what they do, but performing their acts unilaterally and with enormous consequence" (Butler, *Precarious Life*, 65). Neither truly monarchical nor fascistic, new sovereign subjects are constituted by their own tactical speech acts. They selectively and performatively administer or suspend the law in the name of their duty to the nation's population, "to neutralize the rule of law in the name of security"; yet, their supposedly autonomous declarations, made "in the interests of the executive function of the state," actually cement their position as cogs in an impersonal administrative machine (ibid., 67, 83). This historical stage of antidemocratic sovereignty is distinct from past biopolitical forms insofar as it ushers in "an unprecedented generalization of the paradigm of security as the normal technique of government" (Agamben, *State of Exception*, 14).

Queer theory must redress this recently emergent, imbricated structure of the three regimes of power that produce heteronormative citizens and normalized populations. The accounts by Brown, Agamben, and Butler throw into relief the fact that queer theorists specifically need to scrutinize how *security* functions as the chief narrative device driving normalizing social processes and the management of populations.[4] The location of power at the juncture of sovereignty and biopolitics has historically led to the close association of late democracy with a laissez-faire paradigm that sustains capitalist economic forms and resultant distributive inequities. In the end, though, such "freedom is nothing else but the correlative of the deployment of apparatuses of security" (Foucault, *Security, Territory, Population*, 48). The seemingly antithetical terms of security (the maintenance of the status quo) and freedom (the permission or even encouragement of circulation and movement) are inextricably linked through administrating agencies' strategies of government and risk management. This "game" sets out to maintain the currently accepted order of things by "not interfering, allowing free movement, letting things follow their course" (ibid.). If the rules of the game are followed, the majority of the population should prosper, albeit at the expense of a dispensable few. What is more, the welfare and fortune secured by such a biopolitical strategy allows for only a rather limited—even illusory—mobility and freedom. Foucault dubbed this entire apparatus *liberalism*.[5]

For the purposes of this exegesis, though, I wish to extricate this concept from Foucault's reductively economic, laissez-faire definition. Instead, I wish to connect it to those modern democratic ideals that emerged alongside capitalism in the late eighteenth and early nineteenth centuries.[6] With the passing of a monarchical political sovereignty comes an institutionalized belief in the citizen-subject's individualized freedom. Although the pure sovereignty of that freedom is as illusory as Foucault notes, it would be deleterious to judge all freedom in a capitalistic-democratic system as utterly impossible. What is more, experiences of freedom are attached to some sense of autonomy, a rediscovery of a kind of sovereignty which disentangles that modality of power from its usual biopolitical constraints. For this reason, I prefer to approach liberalism not just as a particularly historicized economic force but also as a democratic first principle, a faith in the sovereign individual's inviolable integrity, self-sufficiency, agency, and privacy. I use the word "liberalism," rather than "liberal," in order to specify a *formal* condition not to be confused with a political attitude, partisan bias, or party alliance. Instead, I am interested in appropriating that idea of "comprehensive liberalism" which John Rawls summarily dispenses with in order to pursue its supposedly more historicized complement, "political liberalism."[7] However, my turn to a comprehensive or ontological logic is not intended to promote a neo-Kantian aesthetic theory or to stage an ahistorical recuperation of John Stuart Mill's utilitarian liberalism.[8] Rather, I wish to perform a deconstructive *re*historicizing of what Rawls calls a political liberalism. Rather than a trans- or ahistorical constant, liberalism is a polyvalent article of faith, inflected with different meanings in different epochs by different individuals. By putting that object of belief back into history, we can examine how various exclusions have been propagated through the unexamined embrace of notions of autonomy and privacy, as well as the associated principles of equality and freedom. Our objective should be to pluralize and historically reground, rather than simply reject, ontological fictions. Historicizing these fictions, somehow integral to democratic living, allows us to perceive their dynamic, shifting natures and thus generate a critical relationship to them.[9]

William Connolly's twin concepts of liberal individualism and liberal individuality, both of which "give the individual moral primacy over the interests of the collectivity," provide a useful parallel for my project's aim (*Identity/Difference*, 73).[10] For Connolly, the concept of liberal individuality is a more ethical, though not truly politicized, engagement with the question of the individual's status in democratic society. In contrast, liberal individualism subscribes to a normalizing logic that prescribes fixed identification and is pervasive in contemporary identity politics. With "ease," the "doctrine of the steadfast individual" becomes "a doctrine of normalization through individualization," a process often mediated by governmental apparatuses (ibid., 74). This danger is not easily skirted. In fact, it may be a necessary prerequisite that comes from how liberalism necessarily opposes the collective. These two distinct forms of liberalism "generate complementary strategies to evade the paradox of difference," namely that difference resides at the heart of identity itself instead of inhering in the relation between two supposedly self-same, integral entities (ibid., 92). "Identity is . . . a slippery, insecure experience, dependent on its ability to define difference and vulnerable to the tendency of entities it would so define to counter, resist, overturn, or subvert definitions applied to them" (ibid., 64). Both liberal individualism and liberal individuality allow us to overlook those political mediations that reveal how identity is contingent and mutable, rather than fixed. As Connolly interestingly puts it, they obscure how identity at its core is *vulnerable* because of the difference it contains.

Expanding on Connolly's conclusions, we might say that modern liberalism functions to normalize individuals, to render their senses of self more secure and less vulnerable by occluding the more destabilizing spaces and experiences of difference. Populations are able to emerge because individuals deploy narrative strategies that let them cling to secure forms of identity, rubrics that grant them some appreciable degree of sovereignty. Freedom necessitates individuals defend those boundaries that imbue them with some degree of social mobility. That sovereignty is limited, though, since it is tied to and circumscribed by the *state*, insofar as it relies on a stable or *static* identity that can be *statistically* measured. In this way, what is by nature an unpredictable freedom becomes a quite probabilistic quality.[11] The freedom associated with liberalist individualism is thus not an absolute sovereignty. Rather, it is a highly conditioned agency that is *recognizable* and *predictable* because the agent functions through an identificatory moniker (or intersection of monikers) chosen from an available assortment that lets the agent and the larger collective be administered and statistically assessed. That is, this highly qualified form of independence necessitates the individual's ultimate identification not just with recognizable identity groups and market niches but also with the categorical entity of the national population. Each of these units constitutes a collective whose unpredictable qualities can be treated as probabilities, like any other natural or pseudo-natural phenomenon.

Unlike a population, though, commonality—wherein difference resides—is a self-generative cultural construct that keeps alive individual members' differentiating singularities while establishing a shared ground. It does not subscribe to any rhetoric of identification, nor can it be easily categorized and fixed according to an undifferentiated mass identity. But political, even ethical, action does not come about simply by choosing commonality over liberalism or by disidentifying with the population. Liberalism and arguably even some understandings of population are necessary. Democratic living is unimaginable without *some* recourse to identifying our selves as individual actors within recognizable communities. An undemocratic danger, however, attends hyperbolic claims for the merits of liberalism and its attendant technologies (security, identity, population, stability, nation-state), at the *expense* of either commonality or historical consciousness. Liberalism and commonality are twin concepts: they are foundational principles existing *in tension* with one another, two agonistic halves of a democratic faith. Taking my cue from John Dewey's own assessment of liberalist individualism in the 1930s, I argue that this tension imbues liberalism with a dynamic historical life. Over time, an aporetic understanding of democracy—as necessarily both a condition of commonality and liberalism, of collective union and individualism—*becomes.*[12] Each of these terms of this paradox at the heart of democratic living is historically inflected and rearticulated even though each is too often *misread* as an ahistoric truth beyond examination, critique, or rearticulation.[13] To move critically toward commonality, then, we cannot simply ignore the liberalist portion of the equation. We must struggle with it and rediscover how often our very modes of critique depend on, and are invested in, forms of liberalist security and identification. Because queer subjects are both excluded from and persecuted by the biopolitical state and its strangely governmental liberalist paradigm, it is especially pressing that queer theorists reread those ideas of security believed to be emblematic of our own intellectual and civic freedoms.

## Ethically Redefining Queerness

Almost two decades ago, scholars began to rethink precepts of social justice and democracy through queer theory, a space located in the academy yet linked to extramural queer politics. The document that launched the field as such was Michael Warner's edited volume *Fear of a Queer Planet* (1993), which had appeared originally as a special issue of *Social Text* two years earlier. A glance at its contents gives a sense of the field's beginnings as an enterprise moving between and across several disciplines (gay and lesbian studies, Marxist studies, African American studies, sociology, literary and cultural studies). The contributors recognized that queer issues extend beyond the domain of sexuality since "queers live as queers, as lesbians, as gays, as homosexuals, in contexts other than sex" (Warner, introduction, vii). Following the lead set by Eve Kosofsky Sedgwick in *Between Men* (1985) and *Epistemology of the Closet* (1990), they proceeded with the assumption that, as Warner put it, "gay politics would be a starting point rather than the exception"; consequently, their inquiries "would not be limited to manifestly sex-specific problems" (ibid., xiv).

Routinely, queer theory still links issues pertaining to sexual and gender minorities to social and political matters beyond sex and minority identification. This concern partly accounts for this field's distinction from "queer studies," which is characterized more by sociological realism and a persistent tendency to describe already existing (or past) communities. Queer theorists conclude that such empiricism ultimately reinforces identity politics and a communitarian ethos. Drawing on Hannah Arendt's sense that modern society arises out of the unfortunate collapse of the cultural into the political, Warner's introduction to *Fear of a Queer Planet* boldly claims that "queer politics opposes society itself" (xxvii). Theorists pave the way for that resistance by focusing on what he dubs *queerness.* This is not a queer identity per se. Instead, it is a polymorphous entity usually read through antihumanist concepts, such as desire. In most theory, individuals are conceived as subjects acted on and constructed by outside forces, rather than as autonomous and agentic persons acting wholly on their own volition to represent themselves in a socially transparent way. Although queerness remains vague or even ill-defined, its alluring focus on passion seems to let thinkers sidestep the problems of egoistic inflation and seemingly unhindered agency associated with both politically liberal attitudes and comprehensive liberalism. "Queerness . . . bears a different relation to liberal logics of choice and will, as well as to moral languages of leadership and community, in ways that continually pose problems both in everyday life and in contexts of civil rights" (ibid., xviii–xix). By striking at the liberalist construction of the citizen-subject, queer theorists emphasize the importance of those forms of desire that are loosely linked to same-sex eroticism or sexual practices. In this way, they trouble how heteronormative sociopolitical orders limit and manage imaginings of political possibilities and individual experiences of difference.

It would do us well to remember that, since queer theory's inception, the term *politics* has signified for these scholars differently than we might presume. It is the domain of reflection, rather than direct action. "Queers do a kind of practical social reflection just in finding ways of being queer," Warner notes. The role of theory is to make such reflection less "reactive, fragmentary, and defensive," as well as less prone to being "misled by the utopian claims advanced in support of particular tactics." Theorists are charged with the objective of unearthing "the logic of the sexual order [which] is so deeply embedded by now in an indescribably wide range of social institutions, and is embedded in the most standard accounts of the world" (ibid., xiii). Because queer theory primarily analyzes the interface between queer subjects' social lives and their political and civic relations with others, we could posit that since its start it has been, strictly speaking, an *ethical*, rather than a political, field of inquiry. Instead of serving an immediately political function, queer theory is a *politicized* thinking about the conditions of relationality. Its "radical" nature depends on its production of crisis-provoking critique. When regarded as originating in ethical analyses, such crises do not necessarily result from a given theorist's outlaw or revolutionary stance in relation to the day's liberalist order. Rather, the order itself is resignified because the crisis *resituates* theorists in the present, from which they cannot extricate themselves. Critics must confront the difficult questions about how they are involved with, or folded into, the very norms and ideologies they resist.[14] Following the lead of Foucault's late essay "What Is Enlightenment?" I would say that such an ethic constitutes a praxis much like art. It "transfigures the world" and does so "not [through] an annulling of reality but [through] a difficult interplay between the truth of what is real and the exercise of freedom" (Foucault, *Essential Works*, 1: 311). If queer theory explicitly establishes itself as a kind of ascetic and aesthetic practice, then it can embrace its role as supplier of a new ethical imaginary. We can provide our activist colleagues with a new vocabulary about citizenry, autonomy, and difference that may aid their challenges to prevalent biopolitical modes of subjectivating citizens and constructing manageable populations.

Because it begins in a faithfulness to what is foreign to, and disruptive of, one's sensibilities, a kind of vulnerability is a precondition for a politicized queer ethic. Instead of securing and safeguarding an *a priori* self, an ethical subject emerges while pursuing an idea that captures and compels it to surrender the very sense of security usually afforded individuals through identificatory practices. The philosopher Alain Badiou postulates that such an ethical attitude rests on a single principle: "Do all that you can to persevere in that which exceeds your perseverance. Perseverance is the interruption. Seize in your being that which has seized and broken you" (*Ethics*, 47).[15] As he elaborates elsewhere, "All resistance is a rupture in thought, through the declaration of what the situation is, and the foundation of a practical possibility opened up through the declaration." Such declarative resistances are not heroic articulations of one's position in a given order. Rather, they follow an initial experience of "risk": "Not to resist is not to think. Not to think is not *to risk risking*" (*Metapolitics,* 8; emphasis in original). A politics begins only after one names the unknowable event that "breaks" one's self by disrupting the conventional narratives framing experience.[16]

If queer theory is to strategically rethink liberalism's biopolitical tenets, we must jettison frequent attachments to, and evocations of, revolutionary political attitudes. In their privileging of the security (or longed-for security) of an idealized, unflagging autonomy, too often many queer theorists reject vulnerability and true commonality.[17] Queerness itself is mistaken for the cause of ethicopolitical disruption, rather than its effect. This confusion is part of queer theory's political legacy. Before and during Gay Liberation, revolutionary theorists of queer subjectivity in the 1960s and 1970s claimed some power for themselves by embracing misperceptions about the threatening nature of nonnormative sexuality and by playing upon the illegality of sodomy and other same-sex acts.[18] Appropriating a homophobic discourse fearful and condemning of a supposedly dangerous eroticism, these authors aggravated Middle America's homophobic dis-ease by associating homosexuality with an asocial criminality which everyone was susceptible to being victimized by. By unsettling the supposed security of heteronormative conceptions of self and social mores, they hoped to advance their agenda of queer antipatriarchal and antisexist revolution. Theirs was "a total revolutionary movement," as Allen Young puts it in his essay for the epochal 1972 anthology *Out of the Closets* ("Out of the Closets, Into the Streets," 24). Gay liberationists sought to "offer a truly permanent peace"; ironically, the road to such yearned-after civil serenity would be modeled on the rejection of gender-normative roles, in both social life and sexual play, that made gays, lesbians, and transgender persons "'foreigners' in their own culture" (ibid., 20, 21). Thus, a misleading acceptance of their outlaw and outlawed positions was mistaken for a route to freedom.

Similarly, today's queer theorists often presume that political transformation begins with embodying or identifying as, rather than actually being seized by, the supposedly revolutionizing technologies of sex and the antihumanist (even depersonalizing or dehumanizing) force of desire. Lee Edelman's controversial anti-identitarian manifesto *No Future* (2004) exemplifies this trend.[19] Opposing the reproductive familial underpinnings of progressive and future-oriented ideologies, Edelman rejects a gay and lesbian minority politics dominated by civil rights rhetoric. Instead he assumes the position of the queer outlaw who chooses to be uncivil by embracing desire (in the Lacanian sense). He imagines this strategy to be a means of "enlarging the *inhuman*" (152; emphasis in original). Thus, his idealized queer theorist "situates his ethical register outside the recognizably human" and so undoes the presumed security of both personal identity and nationhood (ibid., 101). Echoing his forebears from the heyday of revolutionary politics and rhetoric, Edelman proclaims: "Fuck the social order and the Child in whose names we're collectively terrorized; fuck Annie [i.e., the Broadway character who adulates "tomorrow"]; fuck the waif from *Les Mis;* fuck the poor, innocent kid on the Net; fuck Laws both with capital *l*s and with small [i.e., Cardinal Bernard Law and the law]; fuck the whole network of Symbolic relations and the future that serves as its prop" (ibid., 29). Since Gay Liberation, queer thought's dual legacy has been the production of such a blatant "fuck you" attitude coupled with the cooption of queer subjects' demonized characterizations as the very embodiments of a living risk.

Such apocalyptic provocations of liberalist heteronormativity are not entirely surprising. In many ways, they attest to a realistic impetus for queer thought for decades. Since the Cold War, sexual minorities have occupied a place in the social imaginary in which they are thought to embody death in a variety of forms, ranging from a literal morbidity (HIV/AIDS-related afflictions) to figurative social constructs (the death of the family, the death of morality). Drawing on Agamben, we could say that queers in the United States have approximated the role of *homo sacer*, whose literal embodiment of bare life (itself contiguous with death) leads to their exclusion from the citizenry's metaphorical, civil body. In contrast, a fully enfranchised citizen is identified "as bearer of rights and, according to a curious oxymoron, as the new sovereign subject . . . can only be constituted as such through the repetition of the sovereign exception and the isolation of the *corpus,* bare life, in himself" (Agamben, *Homo Sacer*, 124). We are compelled to prove ourselves as entitled to full *habeas corpus,* the basis of democratic civil and civic existence; and we can only do so if we demonstrate enough sovereign volition to keep life in check. Queers who fully embody vitalist forces, such as an "uncontrolled" or "uncontrollable" sexual desire or polymorphous perversity, are judged not to have contained and isolated within themselves the unruly life force (often called "desire") threatening the heteronormative biopolitical order. In the early and mid-1980s the Reagan administration's deathly silence about the HIV/AIDS pandemic judged queers to be not just expendable but actually *worth sacrificing* so as to let the national majority's well-being remain intact. The coalitional politics of seropositive subjects and other persons living with AIDS that arose as a response to this situation was a wellspring for queer theory's original cross-disciplinary and ethicopolitical spirit.[20]

Even in today's supposedly more tolerant social climate, those of us who are recognizably sexualized or gendered as queer still live in close proximity to threat, self-endangerment, even death. Simply holding our partners' hands in public, walking too closely or displaying too much affection for one another, or expressing desire for a stranger may provoke an epithet, a threat, or a more violent response. For transgendered subjects, even banalities like choosing between sex-segregated public restrooms can incur bodily harm. Despite all the liberal cant, we are still judged by many to be high risks threatening the general population. A *social queerness* might be defined as that condition in which intimacy and the embrace of bodies and desires can become a death sentence. It is our ethical obligation to refuse to turn away from these realistic principles and the material actualities of loss, melancholy, threat, and vulnerability. These realities run through our lives, motivate our projects, and politicize our thinking. In Badiou's terms, they have seized us and have recreated our basic understandings of humanity, community, nation and world, health, and welfare. We must be cautious, though. There is a significant difference between acknowledging the vulnerable condition of our lives and appropriating the ideologically laden position of *homo sacer*, as many theorists and scholars have.[21] Seizing what has seized us is a matter of assuming an agency in naming an injurious ethical paradigm, so as to force its proponents to claim responsibility and participate in its transformation. Merely appropriating that paradigm to vanquish it or, worse, to dissolve our selves is not an ethical form of seizure.

Vulnerability can be realistically appreciated without reducing it to a painful or shameful condition. Edelman illustrates that some may reject this attitude out of hand because it seems to play into a heteronormative "fantasy" perceived to be the root cause for "the defensive structure of the ego" (*No Future*, 21, 14). Yet vulnerability does not just shore up heteronormative boundaries and liberalist egos. Actually, it is a multivalent condition and some of its forms might teach us surprising lessons about what is to be gained through our passions and our connections to others, our respective environments, and even language itself. To that end, it may be the key means of reimagining what is at the heart of queerness, that elusive idea so central to queer theory since Michael Warner first coined it in *Fear of a Queer Planet*. Queerness is more than a social experience of living in the biopolitical shadows. It is also an ethical attitude that resignifies the realistic circumstances of queer lives' vulnerability. Rather than align such a *critical queerness* with a radical, voluntarist dissolution of the liberal subject, we should approach it as an embodied vulnerability that resignifies liberalism by rediscovering its agonistic connections with the other side of the democratic paradox: *commonality*.

Biopolitics' glorification of liberalism and queer theorists' propensity for revolutionary posturing both foreclose openness because they similarly insist on antagonistically and defensively securing boundaries at any cost. In contrast, living with others demands that we accept the prospect of being hurt because of the inherent insecurities of life and freedom. This is an equally realistic and resistant attitude, even though it precludes the adoption of an adversarial stance. Most importantly, this realism lets queer subjects work through the material conditions defining them so that they may find new points of contact with one another. Exploiting those discovered contacts, they can then work outward and assume a future orientation to rebuild their social universes together. Thus, they may collectively rescript possibilities for freedom and autonomy. The queer Jamaican-American writer Thomas Glave describes this scenario most pointedly. Despite all the injury we face in a warmongering, racist, and homophobic culture, he admits: "I cannot imagine living without hope, without some sort of faith, in other people, no matter what color they are, no matter whom they love or desire. Such faith requires that one live slightly precariously here and there, with vulnerability; it requires that one constantly risk being terribly hurt by others' indifference to, and contempt for, one's personhood and the personhood of those for whom one cares" (*Words to Our Now*, 202). Our theoretic work must undo misbegotten ideas about sovereignty and security to find what Glave vulnerably—not naïvely—holds out for: *hope*. Therein begins a new queer ethic.

## The Embodied Joys of Similarity

We can begin to look for the hope attending a seemingly undesirable vulnerability by recognizing what is constructed as most at risk by the current regime of power: our private selves. At the heart of liberalism's celebration of the atomistic person and her sovereign agency is an embrace of privacy's mythic sanctity and security. Shannon Winnubst notes that, in the civil sphere, liberalism marks a particularly proprietary form of private relations. "The language of rights derives from the overarching model of ownership." Thus, "the modern project of liberal individualism thereby reads difference as that which can be, or ought to be, demarcated, delimited, enclosed—and owned" (*Queering Freedom*, 42).[22] The more one owns one's self, the more one can assume the privileged status, on both ontological and civic levels, of what Winnubst calls the "neutral individual." Such self-possession of a distinctive identity, one's full realization of private personhood, ironically allows one to claim a recognizable, disembodied status. Conceived as merely a husk, the body is imagined to block the view of the private mind that liberalist society exclusively privileges as evidence of a propertied, enfranchised citizen. That mind is culturally and ideologically conflated with the subject's identity, which, in turn, is metonymically attached to a desire she supposedly can own and control.

Privacy is thus the apparatus through which power is exercised over our most intimate experiences of our selves. Problems can arise because public space is always susceptible to being rescripted as a private domain. Contrary to what we might deduce from queer theory's outlaw legacy, however, this resignification of the public is not always a consequence of one's own willful introduction of one's "private" and sometimes "inappropriate" desires to a previously forbidden public space. Those who possess a normative authority and agency still engage what Phillip Brian Harper terms a "regularized manipulation of the public and private realms . . . in the myriad different contexts of our social life" (*Private Affairs*, 82). To our disadvantage, even when we do not wish it, we might be judged as imposing our private selves upon a public culture where we are regarded as foreign, estranging, uncivil, lewd, uncivilized, or treacherous.[23] An ethical reappraisal of liberalism should start with the recognition that the sacrosanct private sphere is not an abstract, metaphysical, or intellectual space removed from the civil or public spheres. Rather, embodiment itself blurs the line between the supposedly distinct spheres of public and private experience. *We are always public entities, even when we believe we're in the most intimate or private of situations.* A critical queerness emerges from the recognition or experience of this condition, and the consequential unveiling of liberalism's supreme fiction of private autonomy. "Although we struggle for rights over our own bodies, the very bodies for which we struggle are not quite ever only our own," Judith Butler reminds us. "The body has its invariably public dimension; constituted as a social phenomenon in the public sphere, my body is and is not mine" (*Undoing Gender*, 21). Through our bodies, our privacy is always being read by others . . . much like the content of a lyric poem. (I will return to the central role lyric plays in all this shortly.) If we cannot determine what parts of our "private" selves are so examined, then the censorious selectivity underpinning civil liberties' attachment to a propertied and proper existence of exclusive ownership and right should be regarded as utterly fictitious and disempowering.

Our private lives are folded into a public sphere, and that publicity is folded, in turn, into others' private realms through their own embodied living. The primary condition of civic life hinges on a paradox: what is an other's intrinsic privacy is also extrinsically ours to share. Our freedom, our very lives depend on the degree to which we respect others' differences not as absolute categories but as in-forming our senses of self. According to a liberalist logic of identity, we depend on others to define us as different and integrally singular individuals. I know that I can identify as "I" because "I" am not "you" because "you" are intrinsically different from "me." This is an idea of difference that, as Winnubst would say, we can *own*. Coupled with this rather commonsensical notion of the antonymous yet inevitable relation between identity and difference, though, is the sense that we depend on others because they facilitate our *changing* sense of our living selves. As Butler formulates it, another "makes a claim on me" by asking me for an account of myself (Who are you?). Simultaneously, this other raises my consciousness that I am a conditioned being because she asks that question "in a language that is impersonal and that belongs to historically changing horizons of intelligiblity." This language, shared between me and my other, brings to light "an enigma, a foreignness, that is ours without ever belonging to us" (*Giving an Account of Oneself*, 134). I want to emphasize that this "primary opacity to the subject," which Butler defines as dividing the subject and providing the ontological basis for an ethic, begins in an awareness of intimacy with, and a proximity to, others (ibid., 20). Such opacity is not only the product of a verbal or otherwise discursive address but is also *corporeal*.[24] Without our others' being-there, we would never have had the opportunity to discover the joy of who we are or who we will (or can) become. Some part of our "proper" intrinsic selves is folded into them. That is the difference from ourselves that we cannot own. Hence, that attribute is actually *im-proper* and folds into what "properly" defines, and supposedly wholly distinguishes, others from us. We cannot identify with or definitively appropriate the qualities of these simultaneously common properties and estranging improprieties. They are what Gilles Deleuze characterizes as the limits producing the very possibility of individuality. Rather than an atomistic, bounded being, the individual is a cluster effect, a multiple or a haeccity. We might trope the chief conceit of one of Deleuze's favorite American authors, Walt Whitman, to say that we should im-properly imagine our selves as *living multitudinously*. Individually, each of us exists as a process of becoming through one's foldings into and out of others, through the variability of our shifting connections.[25]

The promiscuous, recurrent production of those foldings is risky, for it renders our relations, and thus our selves, increasingly stranger. In our contacts with others and the outside world, we are always touching our selves *queerly*. In our encounters with what's outside, we rub up against and happen upon features similar to those constituting our selves. Such similarities are both familiar and unfamiliar because they are found *elsewhere* and thus are inflected with a difference that marks them as not ours. Because those attributes which we bodily communicate with the world around us also belong to some other, our contacts cause us to exit our selves (and do so joyfully, at that). As is the case with Badiou's subject, who claims fidelity to an idea that seizes it, we are captured by those objects that transport us beyond our limits by awakening in us a sense of our extensiveness and similarity with what we usually deem "alter." A paradoxically estranging likeness offers the inviting prospect of a life that approaches a better good. We touch a difference within our selves via similarities found elsewhere, and so an ethic emerges upon our becoming intimately familiar with—yet unable to wholly know or possess—what's "outside."

While the lessons we learn from vulnerability often do owe much to the grave circumstances conditioning us and supplying the limits for our own self-definition, this other mode of vulnerability that urges us to traverse lines of difference are *welcomed, desired, and invited.*[26] We long for that different body which joyfully brings a similarity that frees us from the bounded privacies mandated by a liberalist culture and a biopolitical state. This prospect of welcoming a risky condition brings to mind Hannah Arendt, that figure who influenced Michael Warner's early articulation of the ethics underlying the antisocial stance of queer theory. But the Arendt in my mind is quite different from Warner's. Mine is the one who finds vulnerability to be more than simply a condition attending romantic love (which she, perhaps problematically, believes is isolating). Instead, vulnerability can also produce a feeling for political collectivity. It is the root cause of *courage,* wherein all politics originates. In Greek antiquity, the individual's decision to enter the unpredictable space of the *polis* meant leaving behind the securities of the household's absolutely private space, the only place where one's power and sovereignty were certain. To be a citizen was to embrace a form of risk: "Only that man was free who was prepared to risk his own life" by taking leave of the home, that dominion where life was defined and secure (Arendt, *The Promise of Politics,* 122).[27] Oxymoronically, though, that privacy is now a feature of our political lives. Turning one's attention to the *polis* proper, to the nation-state, does not mark a courageous escape from the securities of a private bounded and sovereign home space. Since the Cold War, the chief problem of government has been that the nation-state figures itself as a macro-scale version of the home. Publicity recedes in the face of what Arendt terms a "society" that upholds a liberalist idealization of privacy and atomistic sovereignty. The right to a private and fully knowable existence is mistaken for acting responsibly. Political possibilities, however, arise in our critical reflection on our exposure to social institutions. Rather than look for a world apart, as Arendt tended to, we can look for an alternative ethos by embracing a hopeful courage, by regarding our bodies as instruments for redefining a social emphasis on privacy as an experience of a kind of publicity.

Vulnerability promotes such courageous public living. To appreciate it is to pursue an adventure in commonality, to sidestep the temptation of mourning the passing of a seemingly authentic (yet utterly illusory and ideological) privacy. Our public contacts with others bring vulnerabilities that do not just result in private injury; they can also bring publicly and personally transformative joys, an attitude that Spinoza characterizes as "always good" (*Ethics*, 258, proposition 42). Deleuze teaches us that Spinoza offers the basis of a "Postcartesian philosophy" (*Expressionism in Philisophy*, 335) wherein "adventitious affections," or those joyful passions arising from our embodied living, are the "occasional causes" of new forms of rationality and action (ibid., 307). Understood to be a passionate condition that will eventually realize an active joy, vulnerability can offer a degree of pleasure that—unlike any other pleasurably affective emotion—"consists in the fact that all parts of the body are equally affected. That is, it consists in the fact that the body's power of acting is increased or helped" (Spinoza, *Ethics*, 257–58, proposition 42). We can push our understanding of pleasure, then, beyond the self-shattering of *jouissance* cherished by many queer theorists as the chief means of rising above a compulsory cultural individuation. A Spinozist or Deleuzian sense of joy *augments* individuals. It reinforces singularities without egoistic inflation because it raises private beings' consciousness of their extrinsic connections to others.

Perhaps "joy" seems too individualizing for our purposes because it tends to promote the health and well-being of only *one* particular body. It would be better to cast this "joy" as a sense of possibility for collectivity, rather than a rejoicing at the opening of possibilities for the individual alone. If contact is the precondition for such joy, it is less individuating and isolating than even what Spinoza had imagined. What is more, we might more easily move beyond a notion of an affective joy found through corporeal contacts with objects. This quality is also bodily experienced through verbal contacts. A queerly common joy is *poetically voiced*, a textual grain hearkening back to the singular body from which it originated and affecting the auditor or reader who encounters the trace of that voice. For this reason, poetry reminds us of the possibilities for pursuing action through our passionate living, without necessitating that we surrender a realistic view of the dangers to which we are routinely exposed. "Without the unity prescribed by the poem," Badiou notes, "we are buffeted by waves of sadness. Thus, there is a principle of joy in the poem, an active principle" (*The Century*, 21).[28] It is in poetry, then, that we can find a means to articulate vulnerability not just as a cause for our sorrows and pains, but also as the beginning of common joys and newfound freedoms. Poetry can help us ethically re-vision and re-form liberalism.

## Lyric's Lessons about Living Metaphorically

Henry Abelove has argued that we have forgotten the anti-imperialism of Gay Liberation because social historians of gay and lesbian politics occlude how that movement appropriated the antinationalistic spirit of exilic queer North American literary writers such as Paul and Jane Bowles, James Baldwin, and Elizabeth Bishop (*Deep Gossip*, 70–88). Similarly, I believe that we can learn much about the past political histories and future possibilities of vulnerability if we explore poetry, that literary discourse veritably shunned by much queer theory and queer studies.[29] Poets past and present have resisted liberalism's various historical manifestations. Lyric is particularly equipped for such projects since it sets itself apart from other discursive modes through its renunciation of modernity's imperatives of rationality and its consequential blurring of the lines between public and private. As the contemporary poet Nathaniel Mackey reminds us, the importance of modern and contemporary poetry is owed to its ability to "other" its readers, to raise a general consciousness of "the dynamics of agency and attribution by which otherness is brought about and maintained." He continues, "Artistic othering has to do with innovation, invention, and change, upon which cultural health and diversity depend and thrive" (*Discrepant Engagement*, 265). Extending Mackey's thought, we could say that poetry's othering is a product of how lyric improperly draws the seemingly unrelated object even closer and thus resignifies understandings of the "proper" and "private." It lets differences discrepantly point to those similarities connecting us to others and does so without colonizing the other or overwriting crucial distinctions. That is to say, lyric puts into relief the inherent vulnerabilities of social conditions. "Cultural health and diversity," then, can be promoted through the study of how past poetries reject the stabilities of rigid modes of identification as they pursue dynamism and difference.

It might seem counterintuitive to align lyric with ethical efforts to disrupt liberalist imperatives that individuals secure integral, fixed selves. Doesn't it necessitate a subjective *I*, imbued with an unsurpassed linguistic agency? Doesn't such verse implicitly celebrate the private and self-possessed person? In his essay "On Lyric Poetry and Society," Theodor Adorno admits that the bourgeois and modern ideals of liberal individualism do, indeed, ground the genre; however, he also reminds us that poetry's linguistic material allows for a self-reflexive criticism of its liberalist basis. Because "language remains the medium of concepts," all lyric possesses an "inescapable relationship to the universal and to society," no matter how abstract or how individualistic it appears (Adorno, *Notes to Literature*, 43). In fact, it "is always the subjective expression of a social antagonism" (ibid., 45). In lyric, the irreconcilable contradictions of social structures speak through authors' voicing of their singular experiences. Often those expressions are not fully comprehensible: this is the basis of the aesthetic artifact's inscrutable nature. Nevertheless, social institutions' motivating presence remains legible even in texts' choked silences or mumblings. This echo or trace supplies the foundation of what Adorno terms elsewhere art's "immanent critique," its "double character" of attempting to reject empirical reality even though it is produced out of that same reality (*Aesthetic Theory*, 251, 227).[30] Even the seemingly most individualistic or asocial lyric aspires to transcend the liberalist idealizations enabling its production.

Others have noted how lyric has been used in the United States, specifically, to contest ideological constructions of privacy. In the decades before the New Deal, sometimes that resistance came in the form of poems explicitly advocating a socialist welfare state.[31] Later, during the Cold War, privacy would become, as Deborah Nelson argues, "an increasingly incoherent concept, which proved both troubling and, paradoxically, very valuable" (*Pursuing Privacy in Cold War America*, 4). It was the very idea on which the difference between "democracy" and "communism" depended, and government and law were devoted to preserving privacy as a sacrosanct foundation for democratic individualism. Many poets saw their work as contributing to more than individualistic or counterpublic interventions in some monolithic public sphere. Instead, they regarded poetry as a vehicle for what Nelson calls "the proliferation of privacies" (ibid., xiv). Rather than reject Romantic lyricism, confessional poets such as Sylvia Plath, Anne Sexton, and Robert Lowell advocated the lyric subject's autonomy. However, their adoption of a conventional lyricism did not reproduce a dominant liberalism; instead, it multiplied available forms and understandings of privacy and thus generated resistant differences. Nelson insightfully recasts the liberalist dynamic of identity politics as *contesting*, rather than merely reinforcing, reified constructs of liberalism and private citizenship. Confessional lyric supplied a paradoxically visible privacy for disenfranchised subjects, especially women, gays, and lesbians. A bid for privacy could be made by those who were proscribed, both ideologically and legally, from an exclusive and exceptional sense of "patriarchal privacy" that guaranteed rights and citizenship only to particular sorts of individuals (i.e., white, middle-class males) (ibid., xiii). Deemed inappropriate and too revealing, poetic disclosure draws attention to the fullness of citizens' otherwise censored interior lives. Excluded, improper citizens turned to lyric to represent the paradoxes underlying a Cold War sense of "a private self that is perpetually monitored by others"; thus, they exposed the extent to which "privacy" is itself a fiction (ibid., 30).

But our senses of what privacy is, or what it could become, are not proliferated only by confessional lyric modes. Much modernist and experimental lyric produced during and since the Cold War draws our attention to how language mediates and redefines our "public" lives by bringing it ever closer to our "private" selves. It does so by bringing the foreign and the external, what is im-proper to our selves, home through our bodies. That is, these other examples of lyric foreground the embodied production and reception of poetry to generate the contact and folding, the joyful similarity, I described earlier. Opposing Jacques Derrida's early claims about the problematically metaphysical nature of speech, Adriana Cavarero argues that vocality, one aspect of speech, actually counters Western metaphysical logic. Originating in the cavity of the singular body, the voice is "the musical way in which the speaker cannot help but communicate him- or herself by invoking and convoking the other" (*For More Than One Voice*, 180). Such a calling-to-presence need not be understood as granting the individual primacy; thus, it need not be read as reinforcing the foundation for liberalism and its humanistic faith in integral, inviolable personhood. Voice, working together with the body in the public space of democratic life, draws others close and so *opens* one's self to new vulnerabilities. A different ethic originates in this solicitation, seduction, contact.[32] But Cavarero falls shy of developing what I am about to suggest: *The voiced word—the lyric verse that exists somewhere between writing and song—is especially suited for opening one's self to others. Modern lyric introduces difference into our identities, rather than allows hegemonic and containing mechanisms of identity-based understandings of difference to domesticate what is most strange about our selves.* Poetry constitutes a fold between two otherwise intrinsic selves. It does not simply signal the existence of singularities (*I am here, you are there, and we are independently changing*); instead, it uses a tertiary body, a textual one, to signify different parties' co-relation (*we are and are becoming, together*).[33]

Modern and contemporary lyricists continually contest the boundaries between public and private by publicizing sentiment, publishing affect, rendering privacies both visible and audible. And they do so by foregrounding how we are vulnerable not only because of the embodied conditions of our lives, but also because of a similar set of linguistic conditions. Whether characterized as political liberalism, communicative rationality, or a more decorous civil moralism, our tendency to depict our civic lives as limited to a sphere of civility erects exclusivist boundaries and thus circumscribes possibilities for reimagining citizenship. Our encounters with poetry loosen us from any claims to absolute privacy or linguistic mastery. Thus, they qualify our steadfast democratic faith in individualist sovereignty. Consequently, our reading experiences instruct us in how to live in a critical relationship with our selves and our communities. Lyricism provides ethical lessons that *ulti-*

*mately* bear a political importance, even if the political narratives expressly communicated by the poems themselves are dated, incomprehensible, or unheard. It dispossesses us of our claims to any absolutely proprietary relationship to our selves.

~

*Queering Cold War Poetry* explores the writings of Wallace Stevens, José Lezama Lima, Robert Duncan, and Severo Sarduy, four poets who reflect on how lyric helps individuals discover new relations to their respective nations and the world. Even if some of them explicitly reference it as a key concept informing their poetics, implicitly they imagine poetry as helping us imagine a more vulnerable mode of relation. If queer theorists let themselves be seized by these writers' ideas about ethics and similarity, perhaps we, too, can expand our critical vocabulary and reappraise vulnerability's worth to our own intellectual and political pursuits. Oddly enough, my thinking about queer vulnerability began with my encounters with Stevens, a canonical straight writer. In his own day, he had become enamored with the queer literature of a nation that disrupted his own sense of selfhood. As the most metaphorical of American modernists, Stevens had a formidable direct and indirect influence on a transnational poetic line interested in elaborating ethics of vulnerability. That exposure could come in any of a number of aspects of one's day-to-day life, but Stevens's work emphasizes that vulnerability begins in our reading practices wherein we open ourselves to others' imaginaries and imaginations. Lyric, he believed, points to those resemblances that cause us to find likeness-in-difference. This condition of similarity disrupts normative and binding forms of group identification.

Stevens himself may not have been homosexual, but the degree to which his poetic rethinking of identity and difference garnered responses from later generations of queer writers warrants his place in this study of vulnerability as a kind of critical queerness. Indeed, it was his correspondence with the gay Cuban editor José Rodríguez Feo that prompted him to articulate the eroticized pleasures of reading as a resistance to the ready-made categories of identity and nation. Rodríguez Feo brought Stevens's reflections about resemblance and vulnerability home with him, and he shared them with José Lezama Lima, his co-editor at the vanguardist little magazine *Orígenes*. The two had published Stevens in their magazine's pages, and his influence on the group brings into relief the *origenistas'* postcolonial resistance to the imperialistic spread of *norteamericano* ideas about the invulnerable and private citizen-subject. Often misread as apolitical, in all actuality these Cuban vanguardists developed an intensely politicized ethos through their art. Lezama, in particular, was instrumental in this effort. Drawing on Stevens's lessons about the potential of metaphor to pleasurably unsettle established identificatory logics, the great Cuban lyricist developed a complex poetic system that doubles as a queer ethical philosophy. Coding queer desire as a "secret," Lezama's poetics unsettle the liberalist consensus defining the national culture of the Cuban Republic prior to the 1959 Revolution.

The later homosexual poets Robert Duncan and Severo Sarduy were avid readers of Stevens and Lezama, respectively. Their work engages, implicitly (in Duncan's case) or explicitly (in Sarduy's), their predecessors' poetic ethics of vulnerability. Each moves vulnerability away from a too close association with the particular lyric device of metaphor and instead associates it more closely with that condition which metaphor produces: a field of resemblance. Similarity and resemblance are postulated not only as necessary for furthering the ability of lyric to generally shake up the foundations of identification, but also to specifically link that disruption to the production of a collective climate more amicable to queer desires and subjects. That hopeful look toward a queer-friendly future is not synonymous with a liberal desire for a democratic safe space within the national civil sphere. Rather, it calls for a dynamic remapping of public spaces as simultaneously private ones. Such reconfigurations allow for a proliferation of intimacies and desires that insist we continually recognize, rather than try to deny, our continual vulnerabilities. We must take advantage of that condition in order to transform integral, commonplace understandings of nationhood and citizenry. In this way, we might find a new faith for individualism not based on the liberalist imperative that we care for ourselves and the people by shoring up our boundaries, our borders, our skins through a hard-and-fast identitarian logic that is more afraid of difference than accepting of it.

Read together, these four writers give us a glimpse into what past lyricists have imagined about the possibilities of vulnerability and similarity. Their work can school contemporary queer theory in the joys of rediscovering commonality, of learning what it means to live metaphorically, so that we might move beyond liberalism's constraints and exclusions. We begin our hopeful examination by considering the case of Wallace Stevens, a heterosexual North American poet who discovered the rather queer pleasures of his similarity to, and an unlikely poetic alliance with, a Cuban vanguard.

CHAPTER 1

# Intrinsic Coupling

## Wallace Stevens and the Pleasures of Correspondence

As modernism's foremost celebrant of the imagination, Wallace Stevens might be mistaken for an aesthete dilettante, a steadfast metaphysician, or an escapist. Yet, after the publication of his first book, *Harmonium* (1923), he moved away from a symbolist "pure" poetry and was less remiss about openly referencing political and social actualities.[1] Mindful of reports of the Spanish Civil War's atrocities, in the 1930s he consciously began to negotiate the realism preferred by the radical literary Left. He assumed a more socially critical position, which Alan Filreis has described as that of a "representative 'middle-ground' writer teaching himself to read the radical cultural position from right to left" (*Modernism from Right to Left,* 30).[2] It would be misguided to equate this "middle ground" position with any sort of progressive agenda, though. Politically speaking, Stevens remains very much in the middle, in what I would identify as a liberal space. But his later work attempts to arrive at a different sort of *ethical* relationship with liberalism, evident in how his poetry and poetics rearticulate individualism and agency.

Generally, interwar and postwar life in the United States was characterized by a conflicted relationship to the shifting nature of democratic ideals. Liberalist attitudes were openly attacked by the era's political radicals, and were redefined by the New Deal and other policies that attempted to dissociate democracy from laissez-faire capitalism. Joseph Harrington has argued that Stevens's lyric extends his professional duties at the Hartford Insurance and Indemnity Company into the realm of poetic discourse so as to erect poetry as a bulwark protecting the writer's economically liberalist interests from the welfare state's more collectivist realities. In this way, Harrington believes, Stevens used his writing to "privatize not just government functions but the rest of life as well" (*Poetry and the Public,* 84). "Insecure" in light of the Depression, unconvinced of socialist democracy's strength in light of the Spanish Civil War, threatened by Social Security's impingement on his own legal career, he offers poetic insurance against those "public events [which] threaten the privacy, individuality, and safety of the reader" (ibid., 95). I share Harrington's assessment that liberalist ideals favoring the private subject were the truths of Stevens's day, even of his professional life; thus, they do register recognizable effects on his poetry. I do not believe, however, that Stevens was poetically invested in a conservative notion of privacy or privatization. His is a case (not unknown to many of us in academia, I might add) where professional and intellectual interests conflict. Without endorsing either radical or New Deal platforms, Stevens's lyric still struggles to critically and ethically evaluate the U.S. citizen-subject's relationship to liberalism and its tenets of private individualism, coherent identity, and, most especially, nationalism. He saw his work as staging what he terms an *intervention* in ideas about, and experiences of, the world as he and his fellow Americans knew it.

In "The Noble Rider and the Sound of Words" (1942), Stevens observes that "the social obligation so strongly urged [by writers and critics] is a phase of the pressure of reality which a poet . . . is bound to resist or evade today" (*NA* 28). The high premium his contemporaries placed on socialist or empirical realism in literature propagates a "state of violence" akin to that executed by militaristic nation-states during the Second World War (*NA* 26). As Stevens's familiar adage runs in "Notes Toward a Supreme Fiction" (also published in 1942), poetry "must be abstract" (*CP* 380). Despite that abstraction, though, he would maintain that "the imagination and society are inseparable" (*NA* 28). Clearly, in their avoidance of realism's violence, his imaginative figures are intended as ethical responses to social particulars.[3] J. Hillis Miller even characterizes Stevens as charging poets with the responsibility for discovering a new "democratic and American" possibility (*Topographies,* 281). Due to our poet's own emphasis on the contextualized nature of that discovery, though, we should not see his democratic ethics merely as a rhetorical "act of place taking" (ibid., 277), through which "the performative power of language" works to "bring about the magical appearance of a 'world' with all of its topographical attributes" (ibid., 276). Rather than performatively conjuring a new world *ex nihilo,* Stevens might be better imagined as changing the contours of the existing republic. Like John Dewey, he is interested in imagining reform so as to produce the Great Community, "a society in which the ever-expanding and intricately ramifying consequences of associated activities shall be known in the full sense of that word, so that an organized, articulate Public comes into being" (Dewey, *The Public and Its Problems,* 184). For both the philosopher and the poet, this artful and visionary project of building new publics is explicitly critical of certain contemporary forms of liberalism.[4] Stevens's emphasis, though, is on the process of discovery rather than the end product itself. The final nature of his Great Community remains unknown, yet its mere promise helps reshape understandings of democratic individualism. Instead of place taking or even place making, then, he explores *how* "the imagining of community takes place," as one critic puts it (Quinn, *Gathered beneath the Storm,* 4).

"Every image is an intervention on the part of the image-maker," Stevens remarks in "Imagination as Value" (1948, *NA* 128). The imagination's capacity to intervene in daily life owes to its being "the irrepressible revolutionist"; every poem is testimony to "the power of the mind over the possibilities of things" (*NA* 152, 136). It would seem that his ethic is rooted in *thinking* about social codes and discourses. However, I want to distinguish this from a meditative, neo-Kantian reflection. The power of Stevens's poetic thinking owes less to a metaphysical capacity for rational, categorical judgment at a remove from things as they are; instead, it owes more to the fact that thinking occurs in social contexts. That is to say, *thinking is an embodied experience of one's material conditions.* As "Notes Toward a Supreme Fiction" qualifies poetry's abstract nature, lyric is actually "[a]n abstraction blooded" (*CP* 385). The imagination's ability to stage social interventions develops from the poet's "congenital" perspective (*NA* 136). In "Effects of Analogy" (1948), Stevens elaborates on this idea by noting that "poets are born not made"; that is, a poetic sensibility is a "problem of his [i.e., the poet's] mind and nerves" (*NA* 122). In a strange turn, though, he undercuts poets' seemingly fixed, aristocratic privilege by also linking them bodily to the very populace from which they are supposedly distinct, by nature. "It may be that the poet's congenital subject is precisely the community and other people" since, in the end, the writer is "inseparable" from what she writes about (*NA* 123).

Such a congenital bond does not mean that lyric must reproduce a community's values. If it does, it isn't really poetry; it then would be mere "propaganda on behalf of the community and other people" (*NA* 122). The imagination compels true poets to look through, and then beyond, the social immediacies into which they are born. The national culture, the population, the community as it is known all pose significant and inevitable limits to that imaginative enterprise; but instead of foreclosing the possibility of change, those limits spur a writer to take advantage of her singular perspective in order to find, imaginatively, difference in what's on hand. Writing of the local and commonplace, modern poets introduce new realities. Their perspectives let others find "satisfaction" with such simple things as "a man skating, a woman dancing, a woman / Combing" ("Of Modern Poetry," 1939; *CP* 239–40). This turn to common pleasures does not signal Stevens's abandonment of the *polis;* rather, it indicates his desire to use pleasure and the familiar to change the larger order of things. To redress the wartime and postwar crises posed by nationalism, though, "the speech of the place" ("Of Modern Poetry")—even "the place" itself—had to be redefined and rendered unfamiliar. The people to whom the poet congenitally belongs, as a matter of body and birthright, are not to be understood as merely a nationally circumscribed population. Rather, he belongs to, and works on the behalf of, a more global imaginary.

Foreign, potentially estranging elements were already a part of North American cultural life in the 1930s and 1940s. In political discourse, the word "American" was beginning to be used to denote a hemispheric, not just a national, locale separate from the Second World War's European theater. Early on, though, Stevens moved rather hesitantly toward establishing a poetic commonality with the South. When faced with the task of selecting one of his poems to appear in translation in the Argentinean magazine *Sur,* Stevens confessed to his friend Henry Church that "I cannot say that I have the slightest understanding of anything in South America. In a general way, I have a feeling that the people down there are not yet themselves" (*LWS* 418). When he finished composing "Notes Toward a Supreme Fiction," he sent it off to *Sur* to help his neighbors construct their selves, as well as to allay his own insecurities about "the difficulty of writing a poem definitely addressed to South Americans" (*LWS* 418). Despite his initial doubts, however, "Notes" does find a way to relate to Latin American audiences. Significantly, Stevens describes the hemispheric relation between North and South as an "intrinsic couple." As is the case with the other mentioned couples of "sun and rain" and "two lovers," the geopolitical entities are related in a disjunctive synthesis, not a dialectical one. That is to say, they are paired in an aporetic dependence resulting from, and maintaining, their fundamental differences: "Two things of opposite nature seem to depend / On one another" (*CP* 392).

Eventually, Stevens would reassess his idea that the South lacked an identity against which the North contrapuntally defined itself. On occasion, it is true, he still pined nostalgically for the comforts and securities only national fraternity can supply; but, increasingly, his poetry and poetics would demonstrate his conviction that his and his countrymen's own secure, liberalist sense of identity was itself a problematic fiction.[5] That shift in attitude owed much to the correspondence he conducted between December 1944 and February 1955 with José Rodríguez Feo, one of the founders of the Cuban little magazine *Orígenes.* The story of this unlikely epistolary exchange, first brought to light over twenty years ago by Beverly Coyle and Alan Filreis, founds a neglected North-South genealogy in modernist poetry.[6] Stevens's contact with the *origenistas* would influence, directly and indirectly, later writers' queer resistances to liberalist notions of autonomous selfhood, sovereign nationalism, and security.[7] Over the course of that decade-long exchange, Stevens recognized the North's similarities to its southern neighbors as unsettling the commonalities of his day-to-day life in Connecticut; for that reason, Cuba and the relations it inspired gave him pleasure. Thus, his hypothetical poet's congenital nature was not fated but instead was subject to change, as his perceptions of his circumstances shifted. This mutability enabled poets to help quell the Cold War's increasingly nationalistic zeal, by intervening in the North American public's understandings of their individual freedoms and collective possibilities.

## The Cuba of the Self

Stevens's southward turn in the 1940s marked a new phase of his longtime fascination with the Spanish Caribbean and the Hispanic borderlands of Florida and the Keys.[8] Initially, that private thrall had been enabled by imperialist policies which founded some of the Caribbean islands as independent republics and commonwealths while, at the same time, discursively and institutionally folding them into the North American political and economic fabric. Appended to the Cuban Republic's constitution, the Platt Amendment (passed 1903; abrogated 1934) established the United States' right to intervene in local politics, to determine the supposedly sovereign nation's boundaries, to regularize Cuba's trade with other countries, and even to manage its infrastructure for waste disposal so as to hamper the spread of disease to the Northern mainland. Another critical piece of legislation was the Jones-Shafroth Act (1917), which granted the residents of Puerto Rico qualified status as U.S. citizens with only limited representation in Congress and no Electoral College votes.[9]

In retrospect, it is apparent that a nascent biopolitical logic structured the political, economic, and even cultural management of Cuba's and Puerto Rico's respective populations as dependencies. This governmental strategy constructed semi-permeable, rather than fully permeable, boundaries that safeguarded the Northern population while allowing for a freer transnational movement of capital. It also permitted greater imperialistic control over the mobility of the Caribbean territories' residents, products, even waste. These acts and amendments did not really cordon off the South, then; instead, they produced new political imaginaries and infrastructures that affected Northern trade, tourism, and business, and that encouraged *norteamericanos*' residential colonization of the Caribbean. Consequently, new forms of contact—one could say new intimacies—emerged between the populations of the mainland and the islands. Until the late 1920s, *norteamericanos* found their Caribbean neighbors to be familiar *and* foreign, and, for the most part, that was deemed to be a manageable difference. With the onset of the Great Depression in 1929, those familiarities were popularly perceived as unbearable similarities. White, middle-class U.S. citizens found themselves on the socioeconomic margins previously imagined to be occupied only by racial and ethnic minorities at home and by citizens of the so-called "banana republics" and territories in the global south. Capitalism was revealed to be a faulty system, and meritocracy was exposed as a myth.[10]

Narratives and domestic policies suggesting the general populace's reactionary xenophobia and nationalistic nativism threatened the pluralized sense of American nationhood that had begun to emerge prior to the Depression. International initiatives and progressive politics that demonstrated quite the opposite attitude were reassessed.[11] Spurred by anxieties that the European war would spread to the Americas, the earlier administrative rhetoric of economic reciprocity between North and South—a "reciprocity" ultimately benefiting the United States—fell into disuse. It was replaced with an "idea of continental solidarity" that forged a united front in the Americas against the external threats of fascism and totalitarianism (Wood, *The Making of the Good Neighbor Policy*, 314).[12] It was the age of the Good Neighbor Policy, a hemispheric vision first introduced at the 1933 Montevideo Pan American Conference by U.S. Secretary of State Cordell Hull. Swearing not to intervene militarily in Latin America's external or internal affairs, and adopting noninterference strategies forbidding the use of sanctions, loans, or even verbal disapproval to influence foreign nations' domestic politics, the northern giant adopted a multilateral approach that sought to resuscitate the Monroe Doctrine's original spirit.[13] As the federal government reassessed its international role as an administrative and imperialist nation-state, unlikely progressive alliances were forged at home, too. During the Second World War, the U.S. Communist Party's anti-fascist commitment forced it to evolve into a "considerably larger and ideologically looser Popular Front left that shaded into mainstream liberalism" (Gosse, *Where the Boys Are*, 20). Rhetorical ambivalences, "with highly ambiguous connotations," resulted across the political spectrum as popular political movements adopted the language of "inter-American solidarity" deployed by the FDR administration (ibid., 21).

This moment of political commonality across party or ideological lines and geopolitical boundaries was short-lived. Beginning with the CIA-sponsored coup of Guatemala's communist government in 1948, the Good Neighbor Policy would be misrepresented as including, rather than outlawing, interference measures such as covert operations, economic support, and trade sanctions. It would be treated as an extension of the 1947 Truman Doctrine's official inauguration of containment policies to stop the spread of Soviet influence. To that end, it was cited as a premise for the suppression of all "revolutionary nationalism," whether or not particular Southern revolutions had communist aims (Green, *The Containment of Latin America,* 292).[14] Similarly, the United States' heterogeneous Popular Front would meet its own end as civil struggles for group identity rights were attached increasingly to politically progressive (though ontologically liberalist) agendas, beginning as early as the mid-1950s. Earlier forms of political liberalism would inform a much more conservative Cold War ideology espousing an American exceptionalism and a strong individualism based on capitalistic democratic ideals.[15]

Despite the conservatism that resurfaced during the Cold War, Wallace Stevens demonstrated his continuing commitment to the previous decades' political conviction that North and South do, indeed, constitute an intrinsic couple. This first principle was a product of his general belief that all boundaries—whether national or subjective—are not absolute. As he reminds us in the famous formula from "Connoisseur of Chaos" (1938, *CP* 215–16): "A. A violent order is disorder; and / B. A great disorder is an order. These / Two things are one." Analogously, Stevens would promote the necessity of reading the life of a national community through what is supposedly alien to it. He preserves the hemispheric ideal underlying FDR's Good Neighbor Policy, then; but his work demonstrates a way of thinking at odds with how it was implemented, even before the war. In international relations, power asymmetries had become reified because the government acted according to static ideas about participant nations' cultural and political identities.[16] In contrast, Stevens's work evinces his attempts to read self and nation more completely and dynamically *through* difference, rather than just defined against it. He struggled to read foreign texts not just as sources of another national or regional culture's authentic expressions. As we shall see, he did run into the pitfalls of cultural comparison because he could not wholly extricate his thinking from a liberalist predisposition; ultimately, though, Stevens was more interested in using his contacts with representations of foreign life from the South to catalyze changes of his own self and national culture.

In short, he perceived a need to disrupt prevailing identificatory logics. Stevens would tell Rodríguez Feo that "there are very few living individuals because we are all compelled to live in clusters: unions, classes, the West, etc. Only in such pious breasts as yours and mine does freedom still dwell" (*SM* 137). If new connections are foreclosed by static identity groups, or "clusters," individuals will not be truly "living." For Stevens, communism was especially "specious." Its "damned nonsense" propagated a language evacuated of meaning, and its insistence on the party line offered only a formalism that actually inhibited individuals' independence by imposing containing identity structures (*SM* 137). His disdain for communism is not proof that he was swayed by American Cold War propaganda, however, for he was critical of his own country's "democratic" ideals, too. In the postwar U.S. mainstream, a resurgent nationalism urged citizens' identification with their country and people, with "the West." Although this was different from radicals' preferred category of class, Stevens rankled at any compulsory group identification.

He initially turns to the South, then, not to find new alliances but to disrupt the supposedly inviolable integrity of the easily identifiable American individual. Only in this way could he challenge liberalist corollary of a "we" that, according to Alain Badiou, merely pluralizes the individualistic "I." Where the coherent subject is lauded, collectivity is imagined as militaristic, imperialist, and nationalist: in short, as one where individual freedoms are impaired by biopolitically collective forces' domination.[17] If language practices ideologically perpetuate group mentalities, other kinds of linguistic praxes might enlighten one about different possibilities of experience. Stevens believed that true freedom and a fuller, redefined sense of the individual necessitate exposure to a discourse that openly reveals, rather than dissimulates, its mediated and artificial nature. In this way, the individual—and, by extension, the nation—might be read as corresponding to, and in contact with, others from whom one is usually cut off by the Cold War's identitarian linguistic mediations. Poetry is a perfect vehicle for such liberation since in its foregrounding of a metaphorically metamorphic language it actually encourages readers to look beyond familiar and legible forms of community. In the more unfamiliar and defamiliarizing terrain of modern lyric, where what's close at home is perceived to extend into a larger world, one can discover echoes and traces of likeness that frustrate easy or a priori sympathies. In this way, poetic resemblance spurs one to recognize hitherto invisible commonalities. It generates a productive and ethical crisis disruptive of dear liberalist precepts.

Stevens's correspondence with Rodríguez Feo provided him an opportunity to think through how lyric's semi-public, semi-private form can realize such an ethical project. Through his personal contact with the Cuban editor, he could rediscover the difference at the heart of his *norteamericano* self. The first two poems that he wrote specifically for his correspondent, "A Word with José Rodríguez-Feo" (1945, *CP* 333–34) and "Paisant Chronicle" (1945, *CP* 334–35), are relatively minor pieces. Stevens himself dismissed them as "two scraps" he rushed off, and he asked Rodríguez Feo not to publish them (*SM* 46). Nonetheless, we can conclude that Stevens eventually did judge them to have some value since he included both in *Transport to Summer* (1947). More tellingly, he reprinted them in *The Collected Poems* (1954), from which he had omitted several other previously published texts. Whatever he saw in them, their value for us owes to their theorization, albeit rather clumsy and ineloquent, of how poetry teaches us to live intimately with difference and less dependently on identitarian boundaries.

"Paisant Chronicle" begins by repeating a question Rodríguez Feo had posed in an earlier letter: "What are the major men?" (*SM* 38) In setting out to answer this inquiry, from its opening line this poem perpetuates the same sort of pedagogical relation characterizing that between the ephebe and the narrator in the earlier "Notes Toward a Supreme Fiction." Three years after writing that other poem for an anonymous Argentine audience, Stevens finally had come into personal contact with a Southerner to whom he has learned to address himself, as both an acquaintance and a poet. Originally, Rodríguez Feo was curious about the meaning of the enigmatic phrase "major men," which had recurred in "Notes" as well as in "Repetitions of a Young Captain." Stevens regarded this inquiry as a chance to think about the phrase's significance *now*, rather than an opportunity to explain past poems.[18] The lesson that unfolds in "Paisant Chronicle" is not so much about fixing the identity of Stevens's good neighbor as it is about unfixing his own.

Stevens works through the significance of the phrase Rodríguez Feo had asked about by way of the new one introduced in the poem's title. His term "paisant" is a neologism, mixing the French *paysan* and the English *peasant* to produce a bastard word that also calls to mind a mutilated version of the word *pleasant*. In the poem's narrative, paisant chronicles are defined as the tales of "a multitude of individual pomps," or the "funeral pomps of the race." These historical narratives foreclose pleasure because they keep the people separate from one another, a mournful fate that produces only a funereal and dour literature. Problematically, individuals are encouraged by such poetry not to experience their own historical agency, but to become heroic *objects* who only "live to be / Admired" by others. This desubjectifying desire is highly esteemed, even to a point bordering on worship or envy. Worse still, it is doubled at the level of the nation-state: "Nations live / To be admired by nations." The predicament shared by the nation and the individual is symptomatic of a general devaluation of life's vitality and pleasure. One maintains one's ego by upholding and meeting others' expectations. The heroic stories created by such circles of admiration reduce "humanity" to a mere "sum" of such objectifying "chronicles."

In contrast, there is the major man. "That is different." Stevens's emphasis on *difference* here is not incidental. This figure is "The fictive man created out of men." These poetic fictions do not constitute a chronicle, but instead are "artificial" *images* of men that encourage the "easy projection long prohibited." Imaginary rather than individual, mediated images rather than supposedly transparent representations, the major men allow one to move beyond the limiting and ideologically motivated narratives, or chronicles, of group identification that foreclose change and compel individuals to live for the approval of others. Acting as a pedagogue, Stevens proceeds to offer Rodríguez Feo, and later his general reader, an antidote for paisant chronicles' pleasure-killing banalities. He urges his reader to find his own examples of major men: "see him for yourself." He tailors this advice to what he imagines his Cuban correspondent would see in Havana. The major man "may" be found sitting at a café, before cheese and a pineapple. "It must be so." His imperative ("must") interestingly offers a jarring contrast to the preceding line's more conjectural tone ("There may be . . . "). It also echoes the directives in the cantos' titles from "Notes Toward a Supreme Fiction" ("It Must Be Abstract," "It Must Change," "It Must Give Pleasure"). The resultant continuity with the long poem suggests that in "Paisant Chronicle" Stevens is rethinking the nature of intrinsic couples, as introduced in "Notes." Here, the American reader who encounters the poem upon its publication is asked not just to look to the South for a quantifiable and identifiable difference, a lack of identity, or even a quaint image that will reproduce objectifying nationalist narratives. Instead, the South is a proximate setting where Stevens and his countrymen can find differences that will affect understandings about their selves and, ultimately, humanity.

If we limit our reading to Rodríguez Feo's perspective, Stevens appears to be making a merely empirical move: look at what is there, in your actual social setting. What begins as a private lyric in a private correspondence, though, would be made more public upon the poem's inclusion in later volumes intended for North American audiences, most of whom at that time lacked a café culture or easy access to exotic fruit such as pineapples. Stevens really expands the domain of what counts as "reality" through the poem, then. Rodríguez Feo may be explicitly asked to find his own major men in a café with a pineapple on the table; however, the general reader is *also* implicitly asked to do the same. In her case, though, that meaning-giving object is an image; it is found in the language of the poem itself, rather than happened upon as a physical referent outside the text. For someone holding Stevens's book, perhaps even reading it at a restaurant or lunch counter, what is most proximate is the page itself. The poet's artful mediations of a Havana Rodríguez Feo had described for him will be the general reader's resource for solving the problem of paisant chronicles. Through such successive mediations (the writer poetically mediating his correspondent's descriptive mediations of Cuban actualities), readers are presented with ample opportunities for finding new connections to reality and, in the process, new modes of linguistic agency. With the help of a poet who imaginatively reflects on others' perceptions, we might become truly living individuals once more.

The lesson of "Paisant Chronicle" is continued in the second poem Stevens sent to his Cuban friend in 1945. "A Word with José Rodríguez-Feo" was written specifically as a response to his correspondent's passing question in an earlier letter about why Ernest Hemingway and other foreign writers have "not exploited the grotesque in our [i.e., the Spanish-speaking world's] lives" (*SM* 42). Rodríguez Feo closely associates the term "grotesque" with a baroque or mannerist aesthetic, and his question points to his group's ambition to extend that aesthetic sensibility to characterize an ethic and lifestyle of the Americas, generally (see chapter 2). In the process of answering this inquiry, "A Word with José Rodríguez-Feo," like "Paisant Chronicle," echoes some of the attributes of "Notes Toward a Supreme Fiction." Namely, both "Notes" and "Word" problematize lyric's supposedly private nature. The earlier poem had included an uncharacteristic personal dedication to Stevens's friend Henry Church, in which Stevens imagines them as sitting together "in the central of our being." Both the public poem and the private correspondence it grows out of are actually overlapping, semi-public spaces much like a train station, such as New York City's Grand *Central* Station; through those textual fields, they connect to one another's private lives (*CP* 380). What is more, the three movements of "Notes" consist of "630 lines—excluding the 21-line epilogue and 8-line prologue—commemorating his [i.e., Stevens's] sixty-three years" (Richardson, *Wallace Stevens,* 196). The long poem's body, in other words, contains a life: Stevens's life. Similarly, the very title of "A Word with José Rodríguez-Feo" marks a connection between lived fact and poetic fiction. Through his *personal* appeal to the young editor, Stevens makes a disciplinary argument about poetry's *public* value. He pulls his correspondent aside to have a "word" with him, to set him straight about what is really at issue with the aesthetic category of the "grotesque." Despite the fact that the poem originally accompanied a letter, Stevens's decision to answer Rodríguez Feo's questions in this form suggests that the poet was consciously deploying a public mode intended for a general readership. That publicity would be fulfilled when he collected it a few years later in *Transport to Summer.* As public as a theatrical aside, Stevens's admonition in this addendum to "Notes" really is meant for everyone, not just his original Cuban reader.

Identifying his addressee as "one of the secretaries of the moon," Stevens affiliates Rodríguez Feo with a lunar and nocturnal imagination that "Makes everything grotesque." Is that grotesque limited to the tropical setting inhabited by the Cuban and his countrymen, however? Do they have a particular aesthetic sensibility because they experience the moon and the night in a particular way? Stevens preferred to see the moon's transformative power as owing to a more universal set of conditions with which his public readership might identify, no matter where they were. After all, the moon makes *everything* grotesque. But he questions whether that aestheticizing result owes to the fact that evening itself reflects "man's interior world." Did *norteamericanos,* out of habit or custom, not make use of this interior? Is that why they lacked a literary grotesque tradition? Stevens doubted the worth of equating darkness with interiority, the supposed seat of an authentic private identity. Such possibilities introduced a problematic egoism or a fixed idea of an appropriate cultural attitude wherein artists are congenitally alienated from, rather than connected to, their world. Posing a second question immediately after the first one, Stevens awkwardly tries to reframe the discussion. "Is lunar Habana the Cuba of the self?" Here private or personal interiority is abstracted to the level of a general ontology (*the self*). The actual nighttime city of *la Habana,* at that time the national capital in which and of which Rodríguez Feo writes as its "secretary," now metonymically represents the metaphorical nighttime "world" hidden in *every* individual. With this second question, Stevens begins to speculate about the value of folding interior and exterior into one another. This route more desirably averts a psychologism he later dismisses, when he rejects understandings of the grotesque as "a visitation" of "another consciousness" or as "the spent, unconscious shapes of night." Unlike those gothic fantasmagoria, Stevens's lunar imagination does not exist inside the self, as is popularly believed; rather, it is an extension of the outside, where one naturally finds the moon.

That he asks a Cuban to see Cuba in this way is quite important. The poem's occasional origin, of which the title continues to remind us, forces us to think of lunar Habana as an actuality experienced anew by a living addressee familiar with that setting. Even a Cuban will see the Caribbean city differently or grotesquely in a poetic light. Stevens works through the logic of this reorientation to the outside world through a hypothetical ("For example . . . ") selected from the imagined Cuban landscape. He instructs Rodríguez Feo to notice "this old man selling oranges." The indexical modifier "this" points to a specific entity at hand, who is then realistically described: he "Sleeps by his basket. He snores. His bloated breath / Bursts back." This description paints a vivid picture for which Rodríguez Feo can find actual or easily imagined correspondences. More importantly, the rather generic description also draws Stevens's North American readers closer to the man at whom he is pointing. In that proximity, this "Cuban" example is rendered less like an object; he is less likely to be fodder for some paisant chronicle. Indeed, the figure becomes exemplary of what "Paisant Chronicle" defines as a major man.

The tropics do not provide a key to the unknown, the unconscious core of any reader's being. This image of an unremarkable, quite ordinary old man is conveyed in undecorated language that only reinforces its realistic objectivity for both the original audience and the larger, more general one of the published poem. This is not to suggest that there is no poetic quality mediating that quotidian image, though. Stevens's diction linguistically reinforces the intimacy one might feel with such a familiar figure. What is more, it does so in such a way that the poem compels the reader to share the figure's bodily rhythms, which destabilize and complicate the easier mode of sympathetic identification encouraged by the surface narrative. The descriptive alliteration of labial "b" sounds, occurring in staccato monosyllables or trochaic two-syllable words, causes the reader, when voicing these lines, to mimic the old man's breathy expulsions as he snores ("*b*asket," "*b*loated," "*b*reath," "*b*ursts"). Propelled outward, her bursting breath synchronically commingles with that of the slumbering figure. Yet, we know from Stevens's line that this man's idiosyncratic exhalative bursts move "back." So, if the reader breathes like the vendor, then her outward projection paradoxically carries her backward, too. If this is the prime example of what Stevens means by using imagistic major men to discover "the Cuba of the self," then his North American readers are encouraged to do something other than imperialistically seize a foreign object, colonize another people, or territorialize an exotic landscape. They are offered a space for living, quite literally for *breathing* differently. Through poetry, readers come into a closer and estranging contact with the quotidian by bringing themselves bodily into synch with the major men about whom they read. Since readers are sent back into themselves, this is not an appropriative identification; rather, it is a mode of *disidentification.* We must move outward to "boldly" venture inward, toward that terrain known as "the Cuba of the self" where we can "pick up relaxations of the known." Categories framing our knowledge are not wholly cast off in this process of disidentification. They are merely *relaxed.* Despite the apparent heroism of this embarkation, these experiences are casually "pick[ed] up" like objects (or even erotic trysts) gathered in the course of poetically rereading our selves in light of others' self-conscious and imaginative renderings of the world.

In the last half of the poem, Stevens returns to the original question that prompted his excursus on Cuba, interiors, and fruit vendors. He definitively concludes that if the grotesque is not a psychological attribute, then there is an "absolute" form of it found "within / The boulevards of the generals." That is, the material spaces readers inhabit provide access to a wholly imaginary view of the world. Stevens asks us not to travel *upon* the monumentalizing boulevard whose names evoke the paisant chronicles of a people's history. Instead, we must search the space cordoned off between the streets, into the neighborhoods *within* the official infrastructure's planned and pragmatic grids. Straying off the boulevards, we can approach those interior areas where we build our homes, live our lives, conduct commerce, communicate with one another, and, most importantly, read. If we take notice and learn to live and breathe with often overlooked actual objects or representations of commonalities like fruit vendors, we will find that they can introduce those "relaxations of the known" with an intriguing, and transformative, unfamiliarity.

Stevens's lesson ends with a description of this outward-bound journey to the interior as producing a "simplified geography" seen in the light of a newly arisen "sun." Described as "news from Africa," the remapping heralded by this new day's dawning introduces a defamiliarizing distance that expands, yet "simplifie[s]," interior spaces and common realities. Ultimately individual psychologies are not altered, but the "geography"—the cartographical schema upon which we map and make sense of our experience—is. Here, Stevens is clearly playing with a racialist, if not racist, trope. But he doesn't associate Cuba, or even the alterity of an experience of "the Cuba of the self," with an Africanist primitivism. The dark heart of the world is not an unconscious discovered in the colonies, as we have been trained to believe by Joseph Conrad. Indeed, in this moment at the end of the Second World War, as global decolonization begins, it does seem that a change in the world's geography is imminent. Stevens wanted to ensure that his poetry complemented people's shifting political understandings of their relation to place. When we breathe more easily and relax in the company of its major men, we experience a transformation that Stevens deemed necessary for warding off the perpetuation of nationalistic objectifying narratives. Rather than shepherd us onto the appropriate path so as to maintain our proper selves and secure an admirable homeland, poetry can teach us how to find a bit of pleasure while preserving our individual freedom to find our own ways in this remapped, evolving world.

## On the Pleasures of Resemblance

I cannot overemphasize Stevens's aversion to psychologism. "A Word with José Rodríguez-Feo"'s depiction of the grotesque as beginning in external factors, rather than in an individual's personal taste or proclivity for phantasmagoria, is but one facet of his conviction about this matter. As I discussed earlier, Stevens posited the imagination as a congenital affair; its limits are posed by the body (as he specifically notes in "Effects of Analogy," by one's "mind and nerves"), for it is the body that connects one to a people and to a place. Contrary to a liberalist ethos, then, the individual is always somewhat public, and her lyric endeavors always function as public commitments even if they originate in personal circumstances and contexts. If the poet's function is to intervene in the social imaginary, a portion of that project resides in seeing how the interior actually is an extension of the external world. In the years following his renunciation of psychology and nationalism in "Paisant Chronicle" and "A Word with José Rodríguez-Feo" for their similar bolstering of the ego in chains of admiration, Stevens counterintuitively began to articulate an individualistic basis for his critique of liberalism. How might he rescue the individual, yet be critical of egoism? This contradictory urge, this ambivalence about the individual's priority in ontological and social relations, exposes the degree to which he was unable to extricate himself wholly from his ideological climate. On the one hand, existing as part of an intrinsic couple with the South redefines his sense of self and national belonging as a U.S. citizen. On the other hand, his later work exhibits Stevens's belief that Cuban residents should do the neighborly thing and provide him with the material—that is, the images—he needed to ensure his *own* imaginative freedom. Thus implicitly hierarchizing populations, he imagines his poetry as developing out of private and largely intellectual encounters with others who estrange him from himself. Privileging the mind, and troublingly occluding the embodied nature of relations to which he usually paid more attention, his work is limited to recasting predominant ideas about public living for North American readers. His ethic's resultant problematic core can be phrased as an extrapolation of one of the tenets from "Notes Toward a Supreme Fiction": *Poetic composition must give pleasure.* This element of Stevens's thinking supplies a corollary to queer theory's cherished concept of desire. If not carefully addressed, both pleasure and desire actually can reintroduce subjective, individualized dimensions that impede ethical disengagements of liberalism and its nationalism and identity politics.

We can find Stevens's most sustained theorization of pleasure in a pivotal, yet often overlooked, essay crucially connected to his correspondence with Rodríguez Feo. Originally delivered at Harvard University in February 1947, and published in June of the same year by *The Partisan Review* and then separately as a pamphlet by Cummington Press, "Three Academic Pieces" is composed of a short lecture and two new poems ("Someone Puts a Pineapple Together" and "Of Ideal Time and Choice"). Stevens begins the prose section with his then decades-old insistence that reality is the basis for the imagination, that "the accuracy of accurate letters" is determined by how imaginative literature relates to "the structure of reality" (*NA* 71). Immediately, though, he qualifies that such "accuracy" cannot be measured according to mimetically realistic standards. Instead poetry discovers "the resemblance between things"; he adds that this resemblance "constitutes a relation between them since, in some sense, all things resemble each other" (*NA* 71). Stevens supplies an example from nature. Traces of a common color produce relations between objects on a distant seascape: "There is enough green in the sea to relate it to the palms. There is enough of the sky reflected in the water to create a resemblance, in some sense, between them" (*NA* 71). This visual principle is extrapolated into a universalistic one: "So, too, sufficiently generalized, each man resembles all other men, each woman resembles all other women, this year resembles last year" (*NA* 71–72). Such a relation based on similarity "binds together" things that otherwise would exist in unrelated difference if one concentrated only on their particularities (*NA* 72).

"The proliferation of resemblances extends an object": this production of likeness is "[t]he point at which process begins" (*NA* 78). Such a sense of processual extensiveness brings Stevens's thought closely in line with Leibniz's monadology, Spinoza's ethics, and Alfred North Whitehead's philosophy of organism. Elsewhere I have described this phase of his work as evincing a "baroque poiesis" based on intersubjective monadic relations.[19] Here I wish to refine my earlier conclusions. What Stevens's poet-subject discovers outside her self is not at all a Romantically sublime otherness. Such an idea of radical difference would reproduce and secure his self-enclosed identity, much like the Good Neighbor Policy and its model of dependence and national hierarchies from which he struggled to differentiate his ideas. Instead the discovered resemblance extends the poet *beyond* her proper self. In such similarity, she recognizes that her boundaries do not really contain her. This ecstasy spurs a crisis, or an ethical self-reflexivity. She is not the person she thought she was. She may be *like* that ego-ideal, but she *does not fully embody* that identity. Coming to terms with that difference is part of a *process* of learning about one's self. Writing is an invaluable contributor to the process of subjective composition. Through its publication, poetry ties the private experience of discovery to a public revelation of what has been discovered. As readers rediscover the poet's experience in their encounters with her written mediations, and as they find themselves involved in and extended by those discoveries, these transformative resemblances continue to proliferate.

Stevens had long believed that metaphor is poetry's primary rhetorical trope. By definition, it creates a similitude between "unlike" things. But with his rethinking of relationality in "Three Academic Pieces" comes a subtle qualification of his understanding of metaphor's centrality to lyric's social intervention. Metaphor, he suggests, is synonymous with the "better word" of "metamorphosis." For the antithesis to this term he proposes "identity," which he defines as "the vanishing-point of resemblance" (*NA* 72). Metaphorical resemblance is more than mere substitution, then; it is a metamorphic transformation of two previously independent entities.[20] This metamorphosis rewrites the world as we know it by disrupting the discrete identities through which we make sense of it. Those transformative resemblances are not created by the artist, though; rather, they are garnered from a preexisting "text." "What the eye beholds may be the text of life. It is, nevertheless, a text that we do not write" (*NA* 76). The perceptions themselves remain "private resemblances," insofar as they unfold from the poet-subject's private and congenital experience. Nonetheless, they do become quite public because "one's meditations on the text and the disclosures of these meditations are no less a part of the structure of reality" (*NA* 76). "[T]he mind begets in resemblance," particularly through the aesthetic texts which permit one's imaginings to be shared with others. In other words, the poetic communication of those simultaneously figurative and disfiguring compositions returns privately observed and conceived resemblances to a public forum.[21] As these newly discovered relations circulate in a public imaginary, "the text of life" is clarified a bit for everyone because the poet's metaphorical language "heighten[s] our sense of reality" (*NA* 77).

Although metaphor undoes the securities of a self-same identity, the extensive resemblances engendered by the trope make the resultant state of exposure to the outside world surprisingly delightful. Stevens remarks that "[t]he relation between the ego and reality must be left largely on the margin" (*NA* 79). Relegating psychoanalysis and its ego to the sidelines, he clears the way to move beyond misreadings of lyric as the product of what he calls elsewhere the poet's "direct egotism"; instead he moves toward an account of poetry's pleasures (*NA* 46). Curiously, his refusal to address the ego opens a discussion of Narcissus, that mythic figure who inspired a central Freudian concept. As he "sought out his image everywhere," Narcissus seems to have overlooked those objects he "did not expect" to see where his reflection and nature overlapped: a water snake nesting in his hair, a "look of hate" in his own eyes, the generally "inexplicable ugliness" of bare life (*NA* 79). What Stevens resolves from the lesson of this mythic major man is quite unlike the theory psychoanalysis developed out of the tale of Narcissus. Neither the ego nor its misrecognized objects provide the content discovered in one's search for resemblances. In Stevens's thinking, the substance of a resemblance is almost secondary. *Pleasure*—both the effect of and desire motivating resemblances—is what matters most: "as we seek out our resemblances, *we expect to find pleasure* in doing so; that is to say, in what we find. So strong is our expectation that we find nothing else" (*NA* 80; emphasis added). Narcissus, the paradigmatic poet, finds and delights in the desire which precedes the relation. That desire itself inflects the discovered relation. Stevens's ideal poet finds the desire his heart desires, a self-fulfilling mode of production.

We might invoke Gilles Deleuze to revaluate this as something other than merely an affirmation of the poet's a priori self. Rather than just actualizing a preexistent desire to secure his self, Stevens's poet actualizes a virtual potential. He lives for the "middle," the virtual experience of the similar relation itself rather than the constituent elements and part-objects out of which resemblance is produced. Actualizing that potential ends up disrupting the identity of the subject who originally imagined it.[22] If identity is the "vanishing-point" of resemblance, as Stevens maintains in "Three Academic Pieces," then identity is the *limit* at either end of that experience, that middle, which gives our bodies and minds pleasure. When the poet encounters an image, a process begins whereby she finds a relation that pleasurably extends her beyond her own personal boundaries. This extension is "some extraordinary transfiguration," a passionate discovery of a potential to become part of the world and to be connected differently to others in some new, enlivening way (*NA* 80). Although such discoveries affect the person and her sense of self, and although the poet already lives longing not to be restricted to the sense of her self she already knows, ultimately these estranging discoveries are impersonal because they are gifted. One may seek one's pleasures, but one doesn't know where they will come from. Even a reflection of one's self will contain surprising elements; thus, it will supply "one of those amiable revelations," a gift of awakening "vouchsafe[d]" by nature and reality as if they were divinities aiding the poet in his own epic process of becoming and self-refashioning (*NA* 80). Disrupting identity conventions determined by clear-cut distinctions between self and other need not be painful, then. In fact, for Stevens, they are joyful metamorphoses because they relieve modern life's pain and doldrums.

Ontologically, this principle does critically revaluate the foundations of liberalism; however, problems ensue when we consider the power dynamics underlying those reflections wherein Stevens saw himself anew. As mentioned earlier, his correspondence with Rodríguez Feo helped produce this strange idea that narcissism is actually a pleasurable disidentification. Two months before he delivered "Three Academic Pieces" at Harvard, Stevens wrote the Cuban editor that he was "[t]aking a new and rather quackish subject and developing it without the support of others" (*SM* 93). This solitary and academic enterprise, though, does not really occur without others' "support," for his correspondent (unbeknownst to himself) actually aids Stevens in his poetic endeavor. In the same letter, a few sentences after a rough summary of his upcoming lecture, he suddenly and perhaps inappropriately confesses, "I love the little vistas of Cuba that you put in your letters" (*SM* 93). Below, in the next section, I consider what those "vistas" comprised and how they interfered with Stevens's rethinking of national difference, thus limiting the efficacy of his project. For now, though, I merely want to point to how those Cuban images sent by or through Rodríguez Feo supplied Stevens with a gift of resemblance through which he was able to pleasurably rediscover himself and disidentify with his *norteamericano* ego. Indeed, literal gifts supported and encouraged Stevens in this transformative, narcissistic process. I am referring especially to two watercolors that the *Orígenes* painter Mariano Rodríguez (known in the art world simply as "Mariano") had sent to Stevens through Rodríguez Feo in January 1945. The North American poet would write that the paintings were "both a good deal more Cuban than you are likely to realize" (*SM* 39). He was particularly smitten with the picture of a pineapple, which he chose to hang in the most intimate and private of spaces: his bedroom. Oddly, he declared to Rodríguez Feo that it "is now quite the master of that scene" (*SM* 38). Refiguring his inner sanctum as a theatrical space (a "scene"), Stevens qualifies how we're to understand his private and supposedly authentic self. That once interior but now rather public space is newly inflected by Mariano's pineapple. The painting's representational embodiment of Cuba's botanical exoticism introduces into Stevens's Connecticut home "the sense of an unfamiliar place" (*SM* 39). The result: the poet abdicates sovereign control, and surrenders his own claims not only to mastery but also to the master bedroom! Boundaries of propriety and proprietorship, two hallmark conditions of liberalism, queerly break down because he discovers pleasure in sharing this intimate setting with an idea, or paper image, of foreignness.

Mariano's painting finds its way into "Three Academic Pieces" two years later, via Stevens's inclusion of the poem "Someone Puts a Pineapple Together" (*NA* 83–89) in his lecture. An unnamed narrator reflects on "A wholly artificial nature" while observing a picture of a pineapple, "This husk of Cuba." The image provides the narrator-poet with a "tangent of himself," a relation produced by "Chance" and noted to be a kind of "ephemera." Only through aleatory discoveries of such oblique relationships to one's self can one "Divest reality / Of its propriety," or challenge the liberalist and moralistic codes fixing one way of being a proper self. Though tangential, it is reality, "the irreducible X," all the same. What is more, his newfound and estranging sense of self literally *resides* in the image. As the "Inhabitant and elect expositor" of this condition, it is his responsibility to reveal that he, like all of us, is a citizen of an artificial world. That is to say, this lived condition and freeing of oneself from the strictures of identity owe to the mediations of art and representation. The word *elect* signifies a governmental representative chosen by the people, as well as those chosen by God to receive His grace and to experience the rapture. Given that dual connotation, the poet's duty is presented as politicized *and* salvific. He helps construct major men by intervening and putting a pineapple together *again*, by discovering, via this image, the relation between himself and that "X" of reality. That account of resemblance is the pleasurable medium for his messianic mission of saving the rest of us from liberalism, egoism, and nationalism. Who knew that such narcissistic pleasures could prove to be the remedy for the ills of the Cold War's paisant chronicles?

## Reading from the Exterior

Stevens's theorization of resemblance in "Three Academic Pieces" lays bare the ontological foundations of his ethic; however, his letters and poems to Rodríguez Feo redirect us to that ethic's social stakes. As "Paisant Chronicle" and "A Word with José Rodríguez-Feo" make clear, his late career's poetic is oriented specifically toward a revision of nationalistic attitudes. That desired intervention highlights embodiment in such a way that it frustrates the cerebral and narcissistic pleasures of composition. Interestingly enough, when Stevens tries to accommodate those social ambitions, he cannot fixate on writing and pleasure as much as he would like. Contrary to what one might expect from letters exchanged between a poet and an editor, Stevens's ideas about reading—not his theories of writing—are at the heart of their correspondence. In reading, pleasure is resignified: a dynamic that we shall see again and again in the chapters that follow. Approached from the angle of the reader, rather than from that of the writer, textual pleasures are less capable of being misconstrued as private affairs, for the writer is compelled to acknowledge how lyric encounters' persistently public dimensions render the stakes of any kind of personal transformation shared with her audience. Stevens's implicit emphasis on, and figures of, reading throughout his oeuvre would lead later writers such as Robert Duncan and Rodríguez Feo's *origenista* colleague José Lezama Lima to regard him as a valuable poetic precursor.[23] Yet, his emphasis on readership cannot be flatly celebrated. It also got him into trouble, and was the lever others used to force him to recognize the incompatibility of his one principle of narcissistic pleasure and his desire to produce a critique of liberalist nationalism.

Early on, Stevens portrayed himself as the target audience for his friend's magazine. "[F]or the reader of the exterior," he would write in 1945, "what is of particular interest [in *Orígenes*] is the Cubans themselves" (*SM* 35). Much like in "A Word with José Rodríguez-Feo," he remarks on the importance of Cuban realities making their way into literary texts. His characterization of that importance here—as a "particular" appeal or an "interest" for the ideal reader outside Cuba—can help us address the ambivalences of that peculiar phrase I noted earlier, "the Cuba of the self." Stevens strategically situates himself in Cuba's "exterior." The folding between subject and object, interior and exterior, gleaned in "A Word with José Rodríguez-Feo" must begin from a fixed spot, a knowable location. That is to say, even if he is interested in ultimately deconstructing identitarian divides, Stevens still depends on an initial assertion of an identity-based difference, a clear geopolitical division, between North and South. Despite his desire to use his pleasurable poetic pursuits to disrupt conventions of identity generally and to pose a meaningful intervention that might transform his social context, he is still involved in—or, literally, folded into—his American liberalist setting. Only in such a self-recognizable site can he really *know* and *recognize* his pleasure as such. From "Mariano's happy little drawings" to "the philosophical and cultural work" of its poetry and critical essays, everything in *Orígenes* was valuable to Stevens because, as he put it, "Nothing quite so unconcerned has come my way for a long time" (*SM* 35). "Unconcerned" is a troubling choice of words, especially when read in light of his 1946 confession to Rodríguez Feo that "I love the little vistas of Cuba that you put in your letters" (*SM* 93). Stevens openly prefers renditions of bucolic scenes of *güajiros* and farm animals to reflections on literature and philosophy. "True, the desire to read is an insatiable desire and you must read," he admits. "Nevertheless, you must also think. Intellectual isolation loses value in an existence of books" (*SM* 73). Pay less attention to books, he urges Rodríguez Feo; instead, physically and intellectually attend to Pompilio the mule and Lucera the cow in Villa Olgas, "just to show your interest in reality" (*SM* 74). The *norteamericano* freely reads southern authors' literature to cull from it images that will serve as realities suitable for his pleasurable discovery of self-extensive resemblances; yet, in his mind, Cubans don't have that luxury. They must read and think about the text of life through actual immediacies, rather than learn of themselves through others' textual mediations. Stevens's advice seems even more strange, if not more hypocritical, in light of the fact that quaint countryside scenes like the ones he recommends were uncharacteristic of much of Rodríguez Feo's experience as an urban, bourgeois world-traveler.

We can interpret Stevens's advice two ways. On the one hand, it suggests the North American poet's own provincialism, his inability to shake off the congenital limits of an imperialistically nationalist mindset. Of course, there is a power asymmetry here; but it would be an injustice to dismiss his comments out of hand as imperialist.[24] After all, Stevens does know full well the realities of Rodríguez Feo's experience. So, his advice might be more generously interpreted as an encouragement of the editor to engage a lunar imaginary. That is to say, Stevens asks his correspondent to engage a *particular hermeneutic strategy* that would let Rodríguez Feo *read* Cuban actualities *like a poet.* Instead of attributing the most cultural capital to European and North American writing, he first ought to read the book of life in an interested fashion. Stevens was well aware that he had made a faux pas in his letter. In no small part, that error in judgment owed to the ways his own pleasures of composition blinded him to his correspondent's need for similar pleasures. He struggled to rectify his misstep in a later letter, where he cautions Rodríguez Feo against misinterpreting his earlier warning that "Cuba should be full of Cuban things and not essays on Chaucer." He clarifies himself by noting that his aversion to such essays in *Orígenes* "is not a question of nationalism" (*SM* 57). That is, he does not endorse an essentialist aesthetics insisting that Cuban authors read only Cuban or Spanish-language literatures. Nor is he acting as the gatekeeper of his own English-language heritage. Instead, his advice originates in a dual idea. Trying to transcend one's nation or period by including *everything* in a magazine is irresponsible; however, a too strict fidelity to time and place—to be provincially nationalistic and to cling to the securities of readymade identities—is equally undesirable. For fear of being read as provincial, Rodríguez Feo placed too much stock in foreign writing and was inclined to err on the side of transcendence. Exegeses of medieval English poetry were too academic in Stevens's opinion; they were not sufficiently *imaginative* engagements with affective and living cultural texts, so they didn't warrant attention. If *Orígenes* continued on such a path, Rodríguez Feo actually risked recapitulating a tendency in poetry (and in this instance literary criticism, as well) to produce paisant chronicles that objectified individuals and perpetuated nationalistic mindsets.

To facilitate the ability of *Orígenes* to meet readers' pleasurable expectations both on and off the island, Stevens gives a last bit of advice: "The job of the editor of *Orígenes* is to *disengage* the identity of Cuba" (*SM* 56; emphasis added). "Disengage" is an odd, but crucial, choice of words. It's not exactly clear how his earlier recommended provincial scenes would "disengage" a provincial colonial mindset if we read them as narcissistically pleasurable images. What they could do, though, is stymie a growing Cuban nationalism echoing modernity's precepts of liberal individualism and clear-cut national differences. In the letter where he mentions his interest in Cuban things, Stevens subtly qualifies what appeals to an "exterior" audience about *Orígenes:* "Man's fever is not present here" (*SM* 35). His concern with "fever" is an indirect reference to the Second World War, which the vanguard refused to explicitly address. The poetic and visual images originating in Cuba offered readers respite from the grips of media and artwork that focused on the international conflict, then. Looking beyond the militaristic events that seemed to testify to the "fever" of a humanity defined by the state, the magazine seemed favorably "unconcerned" with nationalistic matters and thus was freer to explore other forms of connection and life.[25] From Stevens's position in "the exterior," *Orígenes* and the letters and gifts he received from the vanguard valuably influenced his revision of his own country's liberalist articulations of nationalism. In their emphasis on the artificial nature of images, these texts presented Cuba (or at least its artists) as adequately "disengaged" from the paisant chronicles of the modern world. Through them, Stevens became a better reader not of the Cuban Republic but of *life* itself. It would be reductive to say that the reader of the exterior is outside Cuba, then. She is actually on the *margins* of life, looking at its *center.* Certainly this disengagement would satisfy the narcissistic interests of Stevens as a poet, but it also could help fulfill the ethically inspired pleasures of a general audience on and off the island.

Stevens's belief that art should prioritize its vitalist commitments to help us move beyond nationhood and toward the forgotten center of experience is dramatized by the title of "Attempt to Discover Life" (1946, *CP* 370). Inspiration for the piece came from a letter written by Rodríguez Feo in March 1946 while recuperating at San Miguel de los Baños, a resort in Matanzas (*SM* 82). The Cuban remarks upon his racial and class difference from others: "the town's capitans (that's how we call here the Chinese)," as well as "the modest citizens (really very poor)" who stroll around selling lottery tickets or ride on "their sad-looking horses." The atmosphere is conveyed as one typified by impoverishment, where residents struggle to get a "few pesos" from "some rich sick-visitor" such as himself. Rodríguez Feo also notes that he has been reading James Joyce's *Ulysses* "again." (The repetition of the experience of reading this particular text is very important. It indicates that he saw reading, and even modernism itself, as a luxury that reaffirmed his difference from the poor locals in Matanzas.) The poem Stevens produces out of his reading of that letter actually bears no resemblance to Rodríguez Feo's account. This difference is significant, for Rodríguez Feo had purposefully included provincial details to entertain the *norteamericano,* who had complained earlier that the Cuban editor didn't pay enough attention to Cuban things. Instead of the wandering peasants one might expect from an exoticizing or imperialist text, Stevens's poem focuses on the moneyed invalids. At a café where a waitress makes table settings by arranging colorful roses around a volcano made of "black Hermosas," "a cadaverous person" and his "brilliant and pallid-skinned" woman appear. She mysteriously seems to materialize out of thin air when the man "bowed, and bowing, brought" her. The two do not speak; the accompanying woman merely smiles and moistens her lips as she "stood with him at the table." Just as suddenly as they appear, they're gone. On the table by where they stood are "dos centavos," the few pesos mentioned in Rodríguez Feo's letter.

If this narrative indicates where Stevens found pleasure in the images supplied by Rodríguez Feo's letter, it may seem surprising—yet it's incredibly telling—that he does not mention the horses, Sino-Cubans, peasants, and other quaint or exotic details. Instead of a titillating adventure set in a far-off place, he realistically conveys small happenings in a quite ordinary, though foreign, setting. The opening line establishes that the drama is set in a café "At San Miguel de los Baños," and the flowers adorning the tables are specifically noted to be "Of the place." Rather than actors in an intriguing story-driven drama, the wan man and woman function merely as indexical figures that point us to the coins left in their stead. This economic detail is "the irreducible X" of reality, as Stevens calls it in "Three Academic Pieces." These coins are traded merely for a waitress's services, something far more commonplace than a picturesque pony ride in the Cuban countryside. Despite the poem's quotidian contents, however, the situation becomes quite interesting if we consider that these bare realities lack narrative support. Consequently, the reader must rely on her imagination to make sense of them. We don't witness the waitress actually *serving* these customers. They don't sit down at the table, much less eat or drink. As far as we know, the patrons don't even exchange words with her. So exactly what service does she provide? Her actual work is like that of Stevens's ideal poet: in her floral arrangements, she takes the things of the place and re-composes them, imaginatively. Not incidentally, the waitress's work goes up "In smoke" after the sickly couple arrives. Stevens curiously describes the arrangements as dissolving into the air in "fomentations of effulgence." Clearly, this dissolution is radiant; but, the word *fomentation* has two distinct connotations: the floral compositions are spectacular either because they incite rebellion or because they offer a medicinal therapy. The circumstances of the couple's departure help clarify the meaning. When the flowers dissipate, the man and woman do not just disappear from the café but are "*dispelled.*" Flower arranging—that is, composition—has the force to ward off sickly and even "cadaverous persons," then. It is strange that the couple *pays* to be driven away, but this detail suggests that art's "fomentations" are not at all revolutionary. Rather, composition's ability to transform reality owes to its healing power. It is an ethical, rather than a properly political, intervention.

If the waitress's art is curative, it makes a bit more sense that the morbidly vampyric pair left a tip for her services. But that gratuity would bother Stevens. "The question that is prompted by the poem," he would gloss later in a letter to Rodríguez Feo, "is whether the experience of life is in the end worth more than tuppence: dos centavos" (*SM* 91). If in reading from the exterior one can encounter the realities of life outside the political framework of nation and economy, can the health supplied by compositions' resplendent images really receive sufficient compensation? Does monetary retribution bind art's curative powers to a national economy, and thus diminish the life-value, the pleasures, of poetry? That more common life-value is at odds with the individualized narcissism Stevens also esteems. His anxiety here throws into relief that his project's ethical and curative dimensions depend on reclaiming the individual from modernity's liberalist and nationalistic logics. Unfortunately, he hadn't quite worked out the kinks of his own counter-logic. Reading images from the exterior, rather than writing before them as if facing a distorting mirror, caused Stevens to take only solitary pleasure in his narcissistic compositional pursuits.

When one acts primarily as a reader who engages images located elsewhere, rather than as a writer using images to perpetuate one's own ideas and to pursue one's own pleasures, one stands a greater chance of discovering a new commonality. Because it is not properly political but is instead ethical, such a collective is substantially different from the imagined communities thought to consolidate nations through literary and print cultures that produce group identities in contradistinction to others' differences.[26] As Stevens puts it in one of his last poems, "Artificial Populations" (1955, *Collected Poetry and Prose,* 474): "The centre that he sought was a state of mind." By disengaging the nation, the poet is brought to a new state, a psychological one that foregrounds consciousness ("mind"). Once this "state of the mind" is achieved, politically motivated sociocultural divisions disappear. "[T]he Orient and the Occident embrace / To form the weather's appropriate people." Such an embrace evokes a physicality that qualifies the otherwise cerebral pleasures of this state. Indeed, it is an intrinsic coupling that imaginatively repopulates the world not in the poet's own image, not as a means of securing his own predetermined pleasures, but in the terms of poetically discovered resemblances. This population does not belong to the nation or even the world. It belongs to the *weather.* That may seem ethereal or intangible, but weather is actually quite physical. It supplies the conditions and context through which we are most conscious of our bodies and their physical location in the world. And as we know (often to our dismay), we cannot control or govern or administrate the weather. It goes to follow, then, that we cannot control or even determine the shape this atmospheric commonality-to-come will take. In keeping with his aversion to psychologism and the unconscious's fantasias, Stevens affirms the link between pleasure and consciousness; yet, he notes that this relation cannot be administered and controlled. In short, it can't be forethought, as he once deemed it in "Three Academic Pieces." Pleasure can affect the individual, much like the weather can; thus, it corporeally affects the starting point of an identity one knows, an identity that necessarily begins in a consciousness of one's distinction—in body *and* mind—from others' recognizable differences. A person thus can be led—willingly and consciously—by the imagination to a horizon where identity itself matters less, where outcomes cannot be predicted. In some ways, then, Stevens instructs us that we should be less wary about the boundaries that identity and community provide. They supply useful ways for knowing our bodies; it is only from the groundwork they establish that we can imagine extending or even articulating the possibilities of their pleasures. We must know the body as it is, we must read it as a positive quantity, in order to deconstruct it by rereading it in light of other texts, other images.

Such a mode of imaginatively yet consciously reading one's self and one's environment, in the hopes of augmenting pleasure and of producing a new state of mind, bears important consequences for changing how we perceive the realities of the nation-state. Much like the rose's sanative "fomentations of effulgence" in "Attempt to Discover Life," the later poem's titular "artificial population" is a means of healing the modern subject: "A healing-point in the sickness of the mind." Stevens's description is reminiscent of Deleuze's claim that "[h]ealth as literature, as writing, consists in inventing a people who are missing" (*Essays Critical and Clinical,* 4). Indeed, poetry is a means of restoring collective health by discovering the new terms for community. When identity is the vanishing-point of resemblance, as Stevens believed, the irony of that condition is that when one fully inhabits one's self, one disappears. If poetry addresses the ailments of the individual, the patient can be brought back, refreshed, to reality. As she imaginatively rediscovers her body and finds new health, though, she does not return to the original vanishing-point. Instead, she emerges at a different place, the "healing-point" where she connects differently with a new commonality. Everyone just has to look beyond her ego to find those points of reconnection or, if I may, *cor-*

*respondence.* The cosmopolitanism Stevens gestures toward at the very end of his life is a lot like lyric, then. It is a semi-public reiteration of individualism that disengages the subject from a nationalistic liberalism; but it does so in the name of preserving the individual's power, pleasure, and freedoms. Our readerly correspondences help us see beyond the state's biopolitical horizon.

As Stevens's lessons were translated into queerer registers, later writers from both Cuba and the United States would put less emphasis on pleasure's narcissistic nature. José Lezama Lima, Robert Duncan, and Severo Sarduy understood full well that any pleasure found in extending their selves owed to how they willingly exposed their selves to language and to others. No matter how idiosyncratic or unorthodox Stevens's understanding of it is, narcissism ultimately runs contrary to his desire to free himself and his countrymen from a liberalist idealization of the ego. Whom does such a pleasure benefit? Doesn't it actually instantiate other inequities? If one party serves as a supplier of necessary images to those in the exterior, isn't she excluded from the pleasures of dynamically participating in a process of social transformation? Where his narcissism introduced incommensurable problems, the dynamic Stevens termed resemblance—like that extensive relation I call similarity or metaphorical living—is key to later queer writers' work. Through it, they could refigure lyric pleasure in such a way that it becomes less egoistic, more vulnerable, and thus much more effective as a tool in their own resistances to liberalist identitarian and nationalist attitudes. If we heed the connections they draw between similarity and vulnerability, and if we respect and analyze the limits attending these writers' resistant projects, we can learn much about what we need to articulate our own less revolutionary, yet nonetheless resistant and transformative, theorizations of desire and queerness.

CHAPTER 2

# A Nation's Secrets

## Resistance and Reform in José Lezama Lima's Poetic System

José Lezama Lima, the co-editor of *Orígenes* during its twelve-year run from 1944 to 1956, regarded Wallace Stevens as an important ally and friend. The North American's work contributed to his own ideas about queerly resisting the liberalist logics of imperialism and postcolonial nationalism. In "Alrededor de una antología" ("About an Anthology"), Lezama credits such foreign-language poets as T. S. Eliot, St. John Perse, and Stephen Spender for contributing a sense of "the new" (*lo nuevo*), "a knowledge [*un conocimiento*] approximating a dialogue and creative community [*comunidad creadora*]" (*IP* 176).[1] Above all, though, he deemed "the great poet Wallace Stevens" responsible for "the fundamental acquisition of *Orígenes*": "the concept of the *imago*," according to which "the image [*imagen*] functions in history with a force just as creative as semen in the domains of creatures' resurgence" (*IP* 176). Lezama mentions how Stevens's poems "Attempt to Discover Life" (discussed in chapter 1) and "The Novel" bibliographically originated in letters from his co-editor, José Rodríguez Feo. About the second poem he writes that from the young Cuban's letter Stevens drew "the detail, the situation, the unthought-of groupings, touching, like creators that scratch and awaken [*como arañazo y despertar creadores*], the distant poetic imagination; an unequivocal sign of universalization, appearing in the transmutations and imaginative mysteries of other creators far removed from our latitude and landscape. The *imago* in the faith of its incarnation in history and the mysterious successions of novelty [*lo novelable*]" (*IP* 176–77). For Lezama and his colleagues, this *imago*—feisty and scratching to awaken distant readers and to turn them on—demonstrates art's attractive ability to create new beginnings (*orígenes*) and to rediscover life by telling it anew. Local particulars thus enter into an appealing tension with a universal poetic imagination. Lezama's playful neologism *novelable*—which suggests both a *novel quality* (*novedad* or *novel*) and *the novel* (*novela*)—links that aesthetic reconstitution of the world to an imaginative retelling of history. Like the literary genre to which he alludes, poetry can remake the nation. Because it lacks transparency, though, it can also gesture toward difficult-to-pinpoint similarities that link Cuba to other countries.

It is not so strange that Lezama singles out Stevens as the *origenistas'* "fundamental" influence. Indeed, that is how Rodríguez Feo envisioned the U.S. poet. In his very first letter to Stevens in 1944, Rodríguez Feo also wrote of the "similarities" and "affinities" he found between his own ideas and the older writer's work (*SM* 33). He describes his first translations of Stevens's poems as having "the Spanish polish" and as demonstrating "the perfect recognition of similar images, combinations, and affinities which make it so difficult to keep the poem from turning into something quite foreign" (*SM* 33). His translations were too domesticating, though, for they hid what he most valued in Stevens's poetry. Rodríguez Feo wanted to be more faithful to Stevens's struggle against a culturally colonizing imperative, a struggle one can witness in the poet's language (see chapter 1). This is precisely what was so "novel"—in Lezama's doubled sense—about Stevens's work for postcolonial Cuban writers and editors. Rodríguez Feo's early translations possessed a "Spanish polish" that was "foreign" not only to the American poems but also to their Cuban translator. If they had been retranslated back into English, their new tone would have rendered them a bit too "anglicized" (*SM* 33). Rodríguez Feo wanted to rectify that and believed he now could better present the North American poet in *Orígenes* as a modernist who escapes provincialism and colonial gentility. In short, as a writer who usefully models for Cuban audiences what it is that the *origenistas* themselves also hoped to do.

The fact that the editors of *Orígenes* assembled an international roster of contributors, including North American writers such as Stevens, to cultivate their anticolonialist agenda was no small matter. Following Cuba's late-won independence from Spain, the United States exercised a strong formal influence over the island's politics and economy until 1934. The effects would be felt well into the 1940s. Cuba only began to shake off the North's economic and political sway when the corrupt military leader Fulgencio Batista, who presided over several puppet administrations only to become *de jure* president for four years, was voted out of office in 1944. (He resumed dictatorial power with a military coup in 1952, four years before *Orígenes* terminated publication.) At that time, a new constitution was passed to ensure public education, land reform, and a minimum wage. This is not to say that U.S.

influence disappeared. Often legislators still were in the pockets of Northern businesses and barred the implementation of progressive measures. Less menacingly, a wide range of Northern cultural objects—from baseball to Protestantism—were also valued by Cubans. Rather than being symptomatic of the islanders' caving to a *norteamericano* cultural imperialism, the appropriation of North American media and goods popularly signified Cubans' resistance to a Spanish colonial heritage. Nonetheless, such cultural appropriations also imported American values of democratic nationhood that were attached to prized institutions and objects. As a result, a "new moral order" emerged that "implied acceptance of the idea of personal transformation and social change, a means of self-invention and self-actualization" (Louis A. Pérez, Jr., *On Becoming Cuban*, 343). Northern liberalism, reflecting ideals of personal autonomy and national sovereignty, thus found its way into a postcolonial Cuban imaginary.

This liberalism inflected how social differences were perceived on the island. Those members of *Orígenes* who may have felt especially marginalized by their minority status had particular interest in their culture's democratic fate. Numbered among the magazine's collaborators were three women (Bella and Fina García Marruz and Cleva Solís), a Catholic priest (Angel Gaztelu), a gay Afro-Cuban (Gastón Baquero), and several gay *criollo* men (including Lezama, Rodríguez Feo, and Virgilio Piñera).[2] But the kind of resistances that their little magazine proffered to liberalist attitudes about identity, difference, and nationhood was unlike other Cuban vanguards' resistances to U.S. imperialism. In the 1940s, the Havana literary scene was dominated by what Jesús Barquet calls "the combative attitude" of *Gaceta de Caribe* and *Viernes*, which continued the tradition of the *minoristas* who published the seminal *Revista de Avance* (1927–30) (*Consagración de la Habana*, 24). These publications exemplified the tendency of Latin American vanguards to stage "a reenactment between art and experience" by expressly promoting postcolonial nationalism and by directly protesting colonial rule and imperialist influence (Vicky Unruh, *Latin American Vanguards*, 26).[3] Like Jean-Paul Sartre's existentialist artist, they espoused aesthetic transparency to politically redress the dehumanization of art and the alienation of society. In contrast with such artistic militancy exacted through self-evident sociopolitical referents, the *origenistas* endorsed "a resistant ethic" (Barquet, *Consagración*, 79). As Lezama famously articulates this ethic in the opening of his lecture series *La expresión americana* (*The American Expression*, 1957): "Only the difficult is stimulating; only resistance that challenges us is capable of uplifting, sustaining, and maintaining our potential for understanding" (*EA* 279). The aesthetically difficult texts appearing in *Orígenes* equipped readers to come to critical terms with Cuba's enigmatic cultural ties to Europe and the United

States. Rearticulating, rather than summarily rejecting, those connections was key to a resistance premised on neither the nation's nor the citizen's liberalist sovereignty.

Like Stevens, Lezama believed metaphor was the best tool for his ethic. In "La dignidad de poesía" ("The Dignity of Poetry"), which appeared in the final issue of *Orígenes*, he complains that ethics is erroneously thought of as a codification of social conventions; thus, it "has been made an enemy of creation and life." Instead, ethics are found "in creation, a direction [*conducta*] inside poetry, that sometimes is interpreted and at other times passes by our side like a mass of bumblebees, icicles of light, a cluster of golden rhythms in two-four time, upon which our hands do not take hold" (*TH* 305). Poetry is a lesson in "an oblique experience" (*una vivencia oblicua*) (*TH* 308). Lyric offers readers a sense of conduct intuited from, rather than prescriptively communicated by, the very device Lezama uses to describe it: a proliferation of elusive and unrelated metaphors (bees, light made of ice, golden rhythms). As Emilio Bejel explains, such buzzing and luminescent metaphors construct "a new reality" out of "new combinations" of linguistic materials ("Lezama Lima," 21). Presented by such figural texts with more uncertainties than answers, Lezama's readers find themselves "always in the borderland of reality," specifically "outside the social and linguistic order of consumer society" as it existed in liberalist, pre-Revolutionary Cuba (ibid., 22).[4] Each enigmatic metaphor provokes an "interminable reading" in which "we put ourselves at risk" (*nos arriesgamos*) by willfully accepting a "tentative and dynamic" hermeneutic that unsettles *a priori* identifications (ibid., 30). If approached historically within his cultural moment, Lezama's writing can be seen to have posed particular risks for his Cuban readers. Exposing the little commented-on similarity between North and South, the mysterious and elusive nature of Lezama's metaphorical verse estranges his Cuban readers from an easy rejection of Northern culture.[5] U.S. and Cuban cultures are shown to be similarly invested in a liberalist imaginary, and those resemblances (as Stevens would call them) refigured the Cuban citizen-subject as particularly vulnerable. Lezama's exposure of those vulnerabilities pushes lyric and the resistances to liberalism prefigured by metaphor into a queer and postcolonial register.

## Early Twentieth Century Cuban Nationalism and Appropriations of Northern Liberalism

In 1898, at the conclusion of the War of Independence, Cuba was en route to securing its status as an independent state. For over three decades, though, it had political sovereignty in name only. The Platt Amendment, originally passed by the U.S. Congress as a rider to the Army Appropriations Act in 1901, was incorporated into Cuba's 1903 constitution. Until it was abrogated in the spirit of FDR's Good Neighbor policy in 1934, this piece of legislation set the terms of U.S. political and economic influence over the Caribbean republic. In addition to forbidding Cuba from ceding or selling land to any other nation, it gave the United States power to place tariffs on Cuban goods; to regulate the island's trade, foreign policy, and negotiation of treaties with other countries; to launch military interventions in Cuba as it saw fit; and even to oversee the management of the new republic's infrastructure and sanitation systems. Understandings of national sovereignty were further confounded by the blurring of geopolitical boundaries. Due to the provisions of Article VI, the Isle of Pines, a sizeable territory off the main island's southwest coast, was "omitted from the proposed constitutional boundaries of Cuba."[6] Proprietorship of this small territory was subject to future negotiation. Article VII stipulated that the Cuban government was required "to sell or lease . . . certain specified points to be agreed upon by the President of the United States." The Permanent Treaty of Relations, substituted for the Platt Amendment in 1934, specified that space as Guantánamo Bay. It granted the United States exclusive rights to a naval station there until both parties cancel the lease, a condition that, to this day, has not been met.

The Platt Amendment, as the historian Louis A. Pérez, Jr., characterizes it, offered "an adequate if imperfect substitute for annexation" that "served to transform the substance of Cuban sovereignty into an extension of the U.S. national system" (*Cuba under the Platt Amendment*, 109).[7] The Reciprocity Treaty of 1903, which was passed on the heels of the Platt Amendment's passage, "accelerated the integration of the Cuban economy into the North American system" by eliminating tariffs (ibid., 122). U.S. goods flooded the Cuban market, and land speculation by Northern industries grew as did "large-scale colonization schemes" that resulted in the establishment of "agricultural colonies" throughout the archipelago (ibid., 123, 124). With stunning transparency, the very name of the Cleveland-based Cuban Colonization Company, one of the principal land brokerage firms that settled Camagüey province, attests to the imperialist drive underlying the North's relationship to Cuba at the turn of the century.[8] More than the lines between the two nations' political systems and consumer markets were blurred in this blatant recolonization. Cultural distinctions were affected, too. Pérez deems "social realignments" in Cuba between 1903 and 1934 as ultimately having a "larger significance" to shaping U.S.–Cuban relations than any diplomatic, political, or economic shifts in either nation since. Several military interventions and over three decades of democratic and capitalist stewardship were exacerbated by the continuing presence of U.S. settlers, laborers, tycoons, and tourists. The combination led to an "Americanization" of Cuban industry through "the introduction of North America's accumulated technical knowledge, advanced industrial systems, new machinery, capital flows, new business organizations, and modern building innovations, all of which came loaded with meaning and metaphors as well as models of identity and self-representation" (Pérez, *On Becoming Cuban*, 115). The transformation of the island's economy reinforced how other forms of contact with the North, both within and outside Cuba, had shaped the islanders' imaginary about citizenship since the nineteenth century. *Criollos*, or colonists of Spanish descent born on the island, had made it a tradition to vacation in the United States. They also sent their children to school there, to be educated outside the Spanish colonial system. Prior to independence, exiles settled in the Florida Keys and in major metropolitan areas on the Eastern seaboard, and these areas became hubs for Cuban political dissidents and revolutionary presses. The United States had long offered Cubans what Pérez provocatively describes as "a world that they could *enter and dwell in*, a place where they could size up their own [colonial] situation and explore new means of self-fulfillment and self-representation" (*On Becoming Cuban*, 64; emphasis added). The North's more recent colonialism and penetrative market metamorphosed Cuba's home terrain. One did not need to literally go into exile to cultivate intimacies with *norteamericano* culture. Now even living in the homeland was a kind of exile existence, an inhabitation of a foreign and potentially estranging space.

Cubans sought to define themselves through that alterity. A wide range of Northern cultural objects and institutions "were appropriated to affirm the ways Cubans differed from Spaniards to demonstrate that who they were and what they wanted to become were not of Spanish origin" (ibid., 69). Democratic values and concepts, with which those objects were associated and through which the United States' own pluralistic nationhood was articulated, were also adopted and inflected as Cubans appropriated Northern cultural iconography. The popular embrace of narratives about a modernity aligned with transnational consumer capitalism led to the close association of a sense of Cuban national sovereignty with a cultural ideal of personal autonomy. Lacking a corporatist tradition for expressing utopic resistances to modernity, a tradition available in other former Spanish colonies, Cubans from the political Right were drawn to Northern liberal ideals of personal autonomy; and those on the Left also "inscribed themselves in the liberal spectrum" (Rafael Rojas, "*Orígenes* and the Poetics of History," 156).[9] An appropriative cultural imaginary fueled a consciousness of political autonomy. Thus, it helped form a Cuban liberalist ideoscape, which Arjun Appadurai defines as an assemblage of images that "are often directly political and have to do with the ideologies of states and the counterideologies of movements explicitly oriented to capturing state power or a piece of it" (*Modernity at Large*, 36).

Fraught with contradictions about who counts as a citizen and what qualifies as freedom, however, the U.S. cultural texts, institutions, and practices with which Cubans identified presented ambivalences about the democratic nature of sovereignty, historical agency, and privacy. Consequently, opportunities were opened for appropriating liberalist tenets to transform a sense of Cuban nationhood and freedom, but to do so by imagining the limits of subjectivity and identity *differently* without recapitulating problematic, divisive rhetoric about personal and state autonomy. This form of appropriation, exemplified by Lezama and the *origenistas*, cultivated an idiosyncratic understanding of nationhood much like what Iván de la Nuez theorizes as the unconventional national identities that recently emerged in Cuba's post-Soviet and protocapitalist *periodo especial.* Neither a rejection of one's similarity with Northern or European ideals nor an adoption of an exotic or primitivist idea of one's otherness (what Nuez terms *confrontation* and *reproduction,* respectively), *appropriation* develops a new sense of self and nation out of the very tools linking one culture to another. In the 1990s, members of the diaspora, as well as Cubans who never entered exile but participated in the island's newly opened limited markets, became conscious of a cultural continuity between the island and the rest of the world. These experiences established "zones of otherness" (*zonas de la otredad*) individuals could inhabit. Such appropriative praxes let one enter "that space where the other is one's own self" (*ese espacio donde el otro es él mismo*), an extranational borderland that allows enough room to recognize intimacies with others that render one more of a stranger, a foreigner to one's self and one's community insofar as one embodies a connection between the local national culture and other global sites (de la Nuez, *La balsa perpetua*, 40).[10] The resultant sense of nationhood is disconnected from an identification with the state (*cubanidad*) or even with a given community (*cubaneo*). Instead, it founds a sense of belonging to a diverse and dispersed population, what Gustavo Pérez Firmat calls *cubanía.*

In the pre-Revolutionary appropriative milieu described earlier, Lezama imagined these cultural practices as producing a sense of national belonging that is diversified insofar as it leads readers into *the distance* (*la lejanía*). This cosmopolitan space of difference would not only reconnect exiles and islanders in the Cuban diaspora, but also all Cubans to the rest of the world. Finding oneself in this difficultly articulated global identification is a product of the passionate nature of appropriation. As Pérez Firmat characterizes it, appropriative *cubanía* is both self-reflexively agentic (it is "an act of the will") and beyond one's absolute control (it is "a vocation, a calling" to an identification) (*My Own Private Cuba*, 233). A sense of self can be constituted only through cultural resources provided by others, the cultural landscape, and language. One is lured to a new sense of self and commonality by some irrevocably alien, yet nonetheless seductive, quality. In Lezama's contributions to *Orígenes*, this passionate nature of cultural appropriation specifically exposes the continuing prevalence of *norteamericano* liberalist ideals in a national culture that declaims all imperialist and colonialist influences. Attempting to articulate the influence of transplanted *norteamericano* liberalism, he exposes the impossibility of Cubans' absolute independence. He also runs up against the fact that the passionate cultural appropriations performed by both his own poetic and Cuban popular culture contradict liberalism's fundamental tenets about the citizen's autonomy and the nation's absolute sovereignty. By accepting that surrender, poetry might model a different kind of resistance and a different understanding of agency, one that would not reductively perpetuate a facile nationalism or blindly reproduce idealizations of absolute liberty and independence. His lyric does not merely describe or represent social and cultural realities; instead, it strives to *embody* them—in the fullness of what one can and cannot know about them. The secret has its place in that fullness, and Lezama gravitated toward what *cannot* be known about liberalism to reformulate a Cuban imaginary. The results elucidate a queerer form of connection and freedom than did the period's prevalent nationalist discourses.

## A Poetic System of Oblique Experience

One of the phrases most associated with Lezama's work is "para llegar a," which may be translated as "to get to" or "to reach."[11] His poetry attempts the impossible: to approach the fullness of Being that cannot be fully known or disclosed because life itself is too fleeting and too multifaceted to be captured by words. Lezama calls this ungraspable *telos* the *image*, and metaphor is the device one uses to approximate it.[12] Because a metaphor invokes a resemblance to only one facet of life's multidimensional and shifting visionary image, one strives to represent the desired totality by proliferating descriptions. As Lezama writes in "Las imágenes posibles" ("Possible Images"; *Orígenes* 17, 1948), "In all metaphor there is something like the supreme intention of making [*lograr*] an analogy, of spreading a net of similes, in order to precisely account for each one of its instants with a resemblance [*un parecido*]" (*RI* 221–22). Such a descriptive augmentation does not definitively capture an overarching image of life, though; it only results in a baroque text that makes the whole seem all the more enigmatic and secretive. "Metaphor carries its dark letter, not knowing the message's secrets, recognizable only in its veil in the momentary light of the image's candle-flicker" (*RI* 221). Since each description only catches some fleeting glimpse or fragment of what one wishes to convey, as if it is illuminated by a flickering candle, obfuscation rather than clarity results. One cannot fully know one's own existence, then. Thus, Sartre's classic formulation is mistaken: existence cannot precede essence. But if essence is unknowable as well, all we are left with are representations that approximate both the essence of Being and the particularities of our shifting experiences of it. Furthermore, these representations produce new mysteries, blind spots that interfere with our vision. *Lo profundo* or *lo oscuro*—terms signifying depth and darkness, as well as profundity and obscurity—frequently recur in Lezama's writings. All creation begins by bringing the blind spot to the surface, by letting metaphor do its work of generating resemblances so that we may approach—but never truly arrive at—what is, by its nature, unknown. Implicitly, then, metaphor has the ability to denaturalize the equation of Being with identity. An inescapable feature of language, metaphor makes entities less knowable and thus instantiates an epistemological crisis that Paul de Man once noted as especially troubling for the father of liberalism, John Locke.[13] Lezama self-consciously deploys this device to purposefully disrupt liberalist tenets.

Although he appreciated how metaphor disrupts epistemological and identificatory conventions, Lezama sometimes still invokes sovereign figures to elaborate the secretive nature of metaphor. Subjectivity is achieved through what he calls *oblique experience* (*la vivencia oblicua*), which occurs "between the dark letter [*carta oscura*] delivered by metaphor—precise unto itself and mysterious in its associative ends [*decisios*]—and the recognition of the image" (*RI* 222). Oddly, Lezama compares the subject who recognizes the image to Louis XI and unnamed "medieval kings" (*RI* 222). Such allusions suggest that, despite the secret's disruptions of liberalist certitudes, the poetic subject is still a sovereign one. But the sort of sovereignty poetry discovers is popular or commonal; it is not an individualized privilege or volition that imbues one figure with absolute power and autonomy. Instead, *everyone* becomes a king. Metaphor's enigmas point readers to the "pauses, the suspensions where the force [*fuerza*] of the noncausal design, which constitutes the kingdom of absolute freedom and where the person incarnates metaphor, are half-opened. Man and the people can achieve their living in metaphor and the image, maintained by oblique experience; they can trace the charm [*encantamiento*] that assumes unanimity" (*RI* 222). The task of constructing a new "man" is thus not the aristocratic privilege of the poet alone. The people also play a role in oblique experience. Like the poet, they, too, can encounter, through language, a magically transformative secret. When the population pursues this common freer "kingdom," the circumstances amount to a cultural discovery of collective impersonality. Such "unanimity" is a condition of the popular incarnation of life's mysteries.

To have such an oblique experience, the people must inhabit the gaps, the suspensions, and the uncertainties that surface as they metaphorically convey their individual experiences. Lezama describes this peculiar state as a matter of occupying a structure situated between "the woods and the cities" (*RI* 222). This "penultimate wall" is not a defensive border but a "suspension, from whence the new cavalcade springs, the interminable army in different uniforms" (*RI* 222). Here an offensive is launched; however, the spectator cannot clearly discern, much less claim an allegiance to, one identity from among the motley assortment. Standing together on this parapet is an act of coalition that complicates any idea of a self-same population. The offensive witnessed below, between the cities, never ends; its "interminable" nature suggests that individuals are *always* trying to reach or defend some city's border, to breach or secure the limit defining an identity for their selves and their people. Located on this wall, suspended by the secret of oblique living, we, the people, do not wear uniforms. Instead of identity, we find "unanimity." We are removed from any secure way of life that is allegorically associated with a city, a nation, or a domain. Unanimity is a loss of individualism, a precondition for that *anonymity* which, ironically, permits self-discovery and freedom. Because this collectivity is gathered in the face of metaphor's darkness and before an ongoing struggle, unanimity never resolves into a popular consensus. Instead, it is an opportune condition that lets one know one's self differently. Without uniforms, we must ask: Who stands here beside me? Why are we here together? Even though one ceases to know which way of life distinguishes one culture from others, civic cohesion continues. The univocal parameters of identification disappear. One exists in a precarious state of resemblance and looks on with interest at—but is curiously removed from—the identity-based struggles occurring within sight of where one stands.

The relatively static text of the poem (*el poema*) is the space of suspension from whence civilization's identity-driven struggles are observed and questioned. (This stasis is opposed to the dynamic process of poetry [*la poesía*], the movement of metaphor causing the subject's displacement.) This is not just a space one slips into while reading, though; rather, it is a space of incorporation, where the critical and enigmatic experience of suspension is given "a body" (*un cuerpo*). Because Lezama's poet doesn't understand or know the full significances of the relation manifested by any given poem, he is unlike Stevens's narcissistic writer who seeks out resemblances because they give him pleasure (chapter 1 above). As a space of incorporation, the poem is the product of an uncontrollable and unknowable passion that brings together poet and reader. Reading is like standing on that bulwark's penultimate wall, between cities and woods. In that suspended space of relation, one belongs to some political commonality but is also aware of a world close by, just beyond those definitive borders. One's attention is directed not only to the skirmish below, where uniformed soldiers invade or stave off invasion, but also out of a sphere of familiarity and into a hitherto unnoticed *distance.* "The distance between persons and things creates an other dimension, a species of entity that is not being: the image, what locates the vision or unity of those interpositions. . . . So that distance, that absence of things, is not its [poetry's] enemy; rather, it's a fullness of immediacy, where we slide the mirror that sweats a dew of enigmas and the slow transpiration or vapor of images" (*RI* 235, 236). The page and its metaphors are like a mirror we hold up to reality to catch a glimpse of the ungraspable truth about the relationship between identity and life. Unlike Stevens's narcissistic reflection, wherein one's own image is mixed with other objects, however, Lezama's mirror never reflects the reader back to herself. Instead, the play of condensation and evaporation—that is, the representative play of metaphor—*refracts* and *distorts.* One sees life, and oneself, obliquely. Poetry's distortions and fragments supply "one of the most powerful nets man possesses for trapping the fugitive and for animating the inert" (*RI* 235). The glimpse afforded by such a strange mirror is a form of power, a way to freedom. Extrapolating from "Possible Images," we can conclude that poetry enables the people, as a whole, to realize a potential freedom and self-actualization once reserved only for monarchs. However, that sovereignty is unlike anything previously known in monarchical ages. It also differs dramatically from liberalist individualism *because* it can be discovered only in a moment of sharing. That common experience makes it impossible for anyone to claim that she knows hereself fully or autonomously, and it makes it impossible for them to claim allegiance to only one national collective. All that one can claim is the space of suspension.

In his last prose contribution to *Orígenes,* "La dignidad de la poesía" ("The Dignity of Poetry"; *Orígenes* 40, 1956), Lezama equates modernity with "the dialectical period" that emerged with the teachings of Socrates. Since antiquity, "modern" man has been plagued by "the individual *daimon* [that] replaces the hereditary enchanter, [and thus] surrenders the Delphic to the fate of the liberated individual of the *polis.*" With modernity's emphasis on individualism over mystery, "poetry is extinguished" (*TH* 317).

Dialectics are associated with causality; that is, motive and autonomy are figured as the only true means of agency. Consequently, our sense of what constitutes history has been diminished to a progressive, linear narrative wherein individuals are presumed to have the natural right to act with uninhibited freedom. Contrary to that sense of history and the subject, Lezama envisions the distance we are drawn into by poetry's secret as introducing what he elsewhere calls "poematic time [*tiempo poemático*], a subtle form of resistance without making history" (*RI* 227). One does not seek to make history; rather, one lives creatively within time. Rather than causing disenchantment or alienation, this different kind of historical experience *enables* a new form of resistance and sovereignty better suited for the reality of our not fully knowing our selves, much less the friends who stand beside us.

When Lezama explicitly writes of poetry as an ethos in "The Dignity of Poetry," he notes that it does not constitute a revolutionary gesture ("in its dimensions as liberator"). Instead, poetic ethics emerge if texts let one act as an "interpreter of two polar opposite foci: the original act [*el acto primigenio*] and the configuration of kindness [*bondad*]" (*TH* 307). The poet (and, we might presume, the reader brought with the poet into the poem's suspended space) moves dynamically between these two foci, as if tracing an ellipse. That movement constitutes a new sort of dialectic. Surprisingly, the focus Lezama describes as most "elevating" is not the one associated with creation. The "laws of the imagination" are "weighting," not as free and individualistic as too often is presumed. But poetry escapes that gravity by approaching the focus associated with kindness and its "laws of customs" (*TH* 323). Kindness is not something one shows others. Instead, it is a consciousness of how a desire to befriend others—to found unanimous communities via poetry that looks toward the distance—imposes limits that, in the end, disrupt senses of self. Even the most common companion thus seems like a Delphic oracle or a recipient of religious grace. A sense of self, as well as the language for expressing that sense, are dictated or compelled by those companions. This cosmopolitanism causes "a breakdown [*rompimiento*] of all causality in conduct" (*TH* 317). Obliging the kindness of such personages' inscrutable natures does "detain" our "action," as Lezama writes earlier; but they only hold us briefly (*TH* 308). When one pauses to wonder how to address a companion and share a vision, liberating commonalities are discovered. That suspension, that retarding of agency, is necessary, for it gives one time to stare into the distance and to describe anew the puzzling struggles between identity and difference that surface behind a city's gates or a country's borders.

Living where the laws of cause and effect are suspended, we experience time in what Lezama famously called *imaginary eras* (*eras imaginarias*).

Rather than starting with our selves, we start with an imagined relation to another subject, even another historical moment. Our attention should always be trained outward, away from our selves and our cities or nations. Each of us will strive to interpret what transpires there, to bring it close. Although that effort is doomed to occur perpetually, to fail to produce a consensual and definitive interpretation of what we observe, it allows us to become unanimous in our resolve to continue to stand, and to live, together. Lezama offers a strange ethic, then, which lands us squarely *between* self and other, identity and difference. Concentrating on the relation itself, he attempts to occupy an insecure and risky zone. He asks us to realize that *we live metaphorically.* Never existing in complete identification with others or images, we live only in forms of likeness, proximate to one another and in liminal spaces. In such a world of similarity and difference, there are no proper selves.

## "A State Organized before Time"

By locating poetry's struggles outside history proper in so-called "poematic time," Lezama seems to consign his poetic ethics to the realm of metaphysics. Indeed, many readers have presumed as much ever since Julio Cortázar's essay "To Reach Lezama Lima," which introduced many in the Spanish-speaking world to Lezama's poetic novel *Paradiso* (1966). He portrays Lezama as the exemplary "primitive" who "wakes up on his island with a preadamite happiness, without a fig leaf, innocent of any direct tradition. . . . He is Cuban with only a handful of his own culture behind him and the rest is knowledge, pure and free, not a career responsibility" ("To Reach Lezama Lima," 146, 147). Reminiscent of Wallace Stevens's characterization of *Orígenes* as idyllically uncorrupted by concerns with the state (see chapter 1), Cortázar's description of Lezama's poetic as prelapsarian and outside a national culture or tradition seems to render it utterly apolitical and metaphysical.[14] His idea of poematic time does seek to effect an immediate social intervention, though; and that objective is clarified in an earlier piece suspiciously recalled by Cortázar's depiction of Lezama's innocently awakening poetic subject. The Spanish philosopher María Zambrano's essay "La Cuba secreta" ("Secret Cuba") appeared in *Orígenes* 19 (1948), two issues after Lezama's "Possible Images."[15] Having lived in Cuba for thirteen years while exiled from Franco's Spain, Zambrano refers to her new home as her "pre-natal country" (*mi patria pre-natal*) (*La Cuba secreta y otros ensayos*, 107). Cuba is a sleeping land that has only recently begun to wake up to modernity, and thus it preserves a dreamlike "secret and silent life" (ibid., 109). Zambrano's vision of a sleepy Caribbean island republic is not as colonialist as it appears. In her philosophy, innocence and secrecy are not idyllic states preceding rational consciousness, nor are they indicators of an individualistic prelapsarian nostalgia like what Cortázar reads into Lezama. Instead, they are tools that *transform* understandings of rationality and *refigure* modernity.

Distrustful of how passions were excluded from theorizations of action, Zambrano condemned revolutionary rhetoric for overly idealizing clarity, rationality, and singleness of purpose. In *Persona y democracia: La historia sacrificial* (*Personhood and Democracy: Sacrificial History*) (1958), she writes that the long road (*camino*) to realizing one's own sense of personhood begins with "waking up from a nightmare" (14). One does not suddenly assume a new consciousness, though; this awakening is "the opposite of a Revolution" (ibid., 13). Instead of finding absolute certitude, one wakes with an "instantaneous clarity like a lightning flash [*relámpago*] that makes visible a situation, the situation of someone who, by wandering off the beaten path [*andar en lo erróneo*] also walks about errantly [*anda también errante*]" (ibid., 31–32). By going astray, one finds a path. Ironically, however, staying on that path necessitates proceeding without a plan. Lightning throws light on a subject for only an instant; moreover, it has a way of doing so by putting the shadows and darkness into relief, not by removing them. So, as we walk along, we are always stumbling, as through a darkened wood. Neither revolutionary nor paradisiacal, this momentary enlightenment is actually an "instant of perplexity that precedes consciousness and, indeed, forces [*obliga*] it to be born" (ibid., 13). Zambrano's subject never experiences a full revelation of that new consciousness, however. The possibility which she continually glimpses remains on the "horizon," like the skirmish witnessed from the penultimate wall in Lezama's "Possible Images." It is observed only as a "distant reality" and "a living focus" that "magnetically" (*como un imán*) draws one toward a promise of "things-to-come" (*porvenir*) (ibid., 32). Because each rise to consciousness is shadowed by perplexity and confusion, not knowing is part of the human condition. As Zambrano figures it, this mysteriousness and incertitude enables action and is the precondition for freedom. Only through such a project can humanity realize its personhood (*la persona*) and transcend a scenario that reduces mankind to a mere cast of masked characters (*personajes*) in a scripted historical tragedy.[16] Once the individual is redirected from particular contexts' dramas, she can face the possibility of universality because she realizes that "all nationalism has its end . . . it is condemned to cease to be one day" (ibid., 153). Such a view of passion-driven agency thus ultimately promotes cosmopolitanism.

Despite its transcendental dimensions, Zambrano's philosophy is very much concerned with redressing modern society's valorization of only certain kinds of individualized historical agency. When she wrote of Lezama's concept of the secret in 1948, she was not opposing *norteamericano* liberalism per se but was taking an implicit stance against Jean-Paul Sartre's idea of engagement in "Existentialism Is a Humanism" (1946), a philosophy that later influenced nationalistic articulations of postcolonial resistance in Cuba. Sartre's famous dictum that "existence precedes essence" would have been especially problematic for Zambrano. That existentialist formulation depends on a fully revelatory consciousness embodied by a human subject "who hurls himself toward a future" and even imaginatively visualizes himself there, "at the start of a plan which is aware of itself" (Sartre, *Existentialism and Human Emotions*, 13, 16). In their shared notions of distant horizons, of the necessity of disorienting passions, and of darkened glimpses luring subjects toward future possibilities, Zambrano and Lezama obviously differ from Sartre.[17]

The differences of their ideas about action and responsibility are even more pronounced when art is the primary subject of consideration. In "What Is Literature?" (1947), Sartre argues that poetry precludes engagement. Only prose, which trades in a transparent realism, can realize a desirable "action by disclosure." He continues: "The 'engaged' writer knows that words are action. He knows that to reveal is to change and that one can reveal only by planning to change" (*Essays in Existentialism*, 320). Poetry, in contrast, heightens the individual poet's isolation. Engaging the word as if one were confronting "his own image, like a mirror," Sartre's poet is a narcissist who exists only in a private relation with the rest of the world (ibid., 311). Reminiscent of Roland Barthes's opposition to Sartre in his ironically titled essay "What Is Writing?" (1947, later the first chapter of *Writing Degree Zero*), Zambrano's response lauds the poetic subject as exemplifying a different sort of agency.[18] "Secret Cuba" narrates that understanding through the lens of Lezama's secretive and difficult metaphorical writing, which, Zambrano argues, models an alternative form of engagement in its refusal of disclosure. "The poetic word is *action* that frees the pairing of forms enclosed in the dream of materiality and the sleeping blast [*soplo*] in the heart of man," she notes. "Man does not awaken into solitude; rather, when the word awakens it also parcels off, as a country [*patria*], the reality that has been granted to his soul." That is to say, the lightning flash of consciousness embodied by a poem helps the subject overcome alienation in an unexpected way: through the secrecy of the poetic word. The surfacing of this secret engenders a suspension wherein one rediscovers one's self and one's affiliations with a commonality. Unlike existentialism's favored mode of revelation, the force of the secret's irruption and the strengths of the commonality it promotes owe to the fact that poetry "is *not* transparency" (Zambrano, *Cuba secreta*, 111; emphasis added).

Even the title of "Secret Cuba" highlights how she recognizes that the ethical force of Lezama's work owes not to its metaphysical abstraction but to its grounding in a particular geography. Reflecting on his poetic in "José Lezama Lima en la Habana" (1948), Zambrano writes that "the poet's universality seems to rest . . . in ascribing him to a certain place" (*Cuba secreta*, 171). In universality's eventual transcendence of place, one's home is a point of origin rather than an immobilizing anchor. In moving from locality to globality, the poet brings with him the secret, the uncertainties characterizing a culture once believed to be fully known. If Cuba is the Spaniard Zambrano's own "pre-natal country," its social reality is the fantasy preceding her (re)birth as a worldlier subject, one who is "without identity" (ibid., 111). If Cuban culture in the 1940s and 1950s was characterized by a mysterious connection to the North, if appropriation rather than authenticity was at the heart of its nationhood, the "place" Lezama inhabited was, by its very nature, foreign. His poetry's acknowledgment of the northern shadows thrown on Cuban architecture permits a new country to emerge, via secretive and fragmentary glimpses of future cosmopolitan possibilities.

The political dimensions of such an ethic are thrown into relief when considered in light of Lezama's response to public attacks by Jorge Mañach, a chief member of the *Minorista* vanguard whose work modeled a combative postcolonial ethic and a proto-existentialist aesthetic for later Cuban poets. In an open letter published in the magazine *Bohemia* ("El arcano de cierta poesía nueva," September 1949) as a reaction to Lezama's collection *La fijeza* (*Fixity*), Mañach denounced the *origenistas*. He judged their thematic concerns with religion and a literary absolute as generating a hermetic attitude symptomatic of the decadence and provincialism that isolated Cuba from the modern world. He also felt that their metaphysics caused them to endorse the bourgeois norms responsible for political corruption and the republic's Americanization. Lezama replied the next month. *Orígenes* endeavored to form what he provocatively calls "a little republic of letters" (*IP* 20). Unlike the Minoristas' magazine *Avance* or even the *origenistas'* previous short-lived publishing ventures, their magazine skirted provincialism by securing contributions from many of the world's most famous modernists.[19] The most biting part of Lezama's letter, though, is his reply to Mañach's accusation that difficulty is uncritical.

> Almost all art and a great deal of contemporary philosophy raise their inquiries [*problemas*] further from the edge [*contorno*], the wall, or the limitations of causal logic. . . . Dostoevsky, Claudel, Proust, Joyce, all those who have felt

> pressed to raise language to unheard of possibilities: Is it not from beyond the limit where they have situated their barbs and insinuations? And is it not precisely in their fury against the limit—against language and situations so encysted [*enquistada*] by a bourgeois treatment—where we encounter the best enjoyment of a voluptuous intellect, on first glance? Perhaps all this turns out to be a little too obvious, given the malice of his [i.e., Mañach's] *I don't understand.* (*IP* 189)

Mañach, the self-proclaimed aesthetic revolutionary, was the real victim of an "encysted" bourgeois malignancy and provincial worldview. His expectation of literary clarity testifies to his uncritical acceptance of convention and his being out of step with Euro-American modernisms. Esotericism, hermeticism, difficulty: for Lezama, these qualities disrupt social norms by pushing language practices beyond habitude. Oriented toward founding a "small republic of letters" tied to the rest of the literary world, the success of Lezama's poetic rests upon how its secretive metaphorical nature, the root of its difficulty, provides glimpses of an otherwise indefinable cosmopolitan promise.

His cyst metaphor is quite revealing about his opposition to the popular encouragement of Cubans' unquestioned optimism about their country's independence. Ultimately, such ill-founded high spirits caused blindness about the realities of Cuba's continuing connection to other cultures. Political and aesthetic utopianism was often coupled with a nationalism that fostered a sense of insularity and a backward glance toward Cuba's illusory glory days. In "La otra desintegración" ("The Other Disintegration"), an opinion piece appearing in *Orígenes* 21 (1949), Lezama inveighs against such unwarranted optimistic political rhetoric. Beliefs that the republic was on the cusp of reclaiming its lost past grandeur, he felt, actually belied a "current, almost untouchable, in the depths of negativity" (*IP* 196). He diagnoses any "projection or drive to more splendid zones" through supposed past glories as a "critical symptom that signals the failure of the state imagination" (*IP* 194).[20] Recuperating a mythic past so as to suture the present's uncertainties or to legitimate a corrupt status quo is the political version of T. S. Eliot's mythic method. Lezama expressly opposed contemporary poetry adopting such models because it deployed "critical" or "synthetic" forms that have "no great passion" (Lezama, *Diarios 1939–40/1956–58*, 39).[21]

Instead of narrating a predetermined and persuasive idea of hope in a rhetorically fabricated optimism that belied an actual negative or pessimistic worldview, he himself preferred to be *lured* by poetic images toward more hopeful possibilities. As legacies of a Cartesian Enlightenment mentality, state politics—like typical Cuban vanguardism and Eliotic modernism—problematically endorses clarity and seeks security. Such utopic nationalism and totalizing poetics lacks the sort of "erotic understanding" (*el conocimiento erótico*) he and Zambrano appreciate, "an understanding of the other and of multiplicity, simultaneously tempting and obscure [*oscuro*]" (*IP* 195). In contrast, the enticing darkness and inscrutability of metaphorical images resist full disclosure, and so passionately engender an "ethical attitude" (*la actitud ética*) (*IP* 196). Artists are compelled to "creat[e] tradition for futurity, an image that searches for its incarnation, its realization in historical time, in the metaphor that participates" (*IP* 196–97). Such resistance hinges on letting oneself be drawn into circumstances that perpetually unsettle one's expectations and introduce hitherto unrecognized connections and possibilities. In an untitled opinion piece from around the same time (*Orígenes* 15, 1947), Lezama asserts that artists who refuse exile and remain on the island—implicitly meaning himself and the *origenistas*—supply "another kind [*suerte*] of politics, another way [*suerte*] of ruling the city in a profound and secret manner" (*IP* 193). Playing with the doubled meaning of *suerte* (both "fortune"/"luck" and "sort"/"type"), he suggests that the politics of poetry offers a future orientation, born of chance. Unlike nationalists' revolutionary promise, it cannot be perceived teleologically, in its scientific totality. Instead, this aleatory politicized future prospect emerges in an unplanned way, with the help of the impassioned labor of those who "desire succession and work in secret, amorously" (*IP* 193). As Lezama writes a few years later in "About an Anthology" (1952), the same essay where he mentions Stevens's influence, *Orígenes* saw itself as "something more than a literary or artistic generation, it is a *state* organized before time [*un estado organizado frente al tiempo*]" (*IP* 173; emphasis added). His choice of words could not be more deliberate. *Orígenes* is not a generational style, not even an organization. Instead, it is an *ethicopolitical strategy* confronting time itself. As such, it is a state (*un estado*) that doubles for the *polis*. By strategically facilitating dialogues between geopolitically and chronologically distant texts, the group's magazine exists out of dialectical history in order to realize a "secret history" (*la historia secreta*) that reveals alternate forms of historical and political experience (*IP* 173).

Lezama's poetic reimagining of history draws readers toward the unspoken, secret connections between people, arts, and cultures to which the state and popular Cuban culture are blind. The resultant uncertainty cultivates a kind of vulnerability conducive to moving away from rigidly nationalist attitudes. "Our Island commenced its history within poetry" (*CH* 83). So begins "Prólogo a poesía cubana" ("Foreword to Cuban Poetry"), Lezama's introduction for a three-volume edition of Cuban poetry published in 1965. Christopher Columbus's record of the isle's discovery, he argues, supplies the original link between poetic writing and Cuban nationhood. Since poetry and history come from the outside, originating with the colonizer, a poetic conception of the nation is incompatible with the political one of an authentic, absolutely independent state. Although the famous image of a burning branch falling into the sea originally lured Columbus to the island and attracted Lezama to these journals, the poet admits an even greater fascination with the voyager's metaphorical description of the Taínos' skin. "It is necessary to emphasize the accent of that expression—*a horse's silkiness*—, with which the allusion [by Columbus] is made not only to a beautiful presence, but also to the burden [*carga*] of an ethicality buried deep, like a silky and fine resistance that was to be characteristic of all *lo cubano*'s noble purposes" (*CH* 83–84). Not only do poetry and language come from elsewhere, but that outsider's perspective is the seed of Cuban writers' enduring obligation to the past. It also marks the origin of an idea of belonging to the landscape that is fully embodied only by an absence, the enticing skin of the exterminated indigenous peoples. That absent presence—the metaphorical preservation of, and continuing connection to, a violently erased past—is a forceful reminder that the colony from which the nation would spring was founded on genocide. Consequently, Lezama implies that other Cuban writers who carefully read Columbus's journals are compelled to look at their land and their history from the very position of the colonizer from which they wish to extricate themselves.[22] Like him, they too desire contact with some pure and noble ideal of nativist authenticity.

That authenticity is forever inaccessible, though. By focusing on Columbus's bestial metaphor, Lezama draws attention to the significance of the natives' skin, not their interiors wherein, according to liberalist logics, one's authentic identity is found. The epidermis here does not just signify racially. It also is the limit of others' bodies, what makes these subjects vulnerable in their exposure to the rest of the world. It is an indicator of a bare life at odds with the privileges of sovereignty and right enjoyed by Columbus and his modern Euro-American world; as such, it is a reminder in need of extinguishing. Since the Taínos' skin is imagined specifically in equine terms, their difference assumes ambivalent connotations. Superficially, Columbus's metaphor dehumanizes them. Yet it also brings the natives metaphorically closer to European culture since horses are not indigenous to Cuba. Ultimately, their difference makes them susceptible to harm and a racist dehumanizing impulse; yet its familiarity also associates the Taíno with a cultural element—not just a natural beast—imagined as embodying resistance, endurance, and nobility. Their skin presents an *attractive* and *erotic* limit, strong in its vulnerability and thus alluring to both Columbus and Lezama. Despite that attraction, however, both the journals' figurative portrayal and

Lezama's recounting of it keep readers at a distance. The essence and the interior of the indigenous subject's singular mystery are left undisclosed. To responsibly produce a national character for Cuba, poetry must contend with that alterity which simultaneously embodies vulnerability, erotic magnetism, and resistance. Rather than restore a mythic heroic past, one historical duty writers have is to resurrect the missing native body. Such re-membering—both a historical mnemonic and a reconstitution of the past's dismembered, victimized bodies—does not ground a nativist ideology. Instead, it fosters a repeated contact with an otherness that resists a totalizing knowledge and possession. It reminds Cubans of their own cultural and erotic investments in modernity's genocidal and imperialistic nightmare, not the idyllic dream Cortázar believed to inform Lezama's poetic. It encourages an appreciation of stumbling upon and being drawn to images that elicit vulnerability and loving attachment, rather than an engagement of a self-glorifying autonomy and agentic violence.

## Reforming Liberalism

In February 1954, Lezama wrote Zambrano that he was frustrated with how Batista's new regime corrupted language to render meaning utterly indecipherable, for its own political ends. "The word is corrupted; through a process of oozing moistness, words are corrupted scarcely before they throw their voice into the half-open space [*al espacio entreabierto*]." Consequently, politicians seem to avoid "the right interpretation," as well as "truthfulness" (*la veracidad*). Instead, "everything's the fruit of scandal, of substitutions" (*Cartas a Elóisa*, 291). If substitution and obscurantism were typical of Cuban political corruption, a poetics based on a secret that emerged from metaphorical substitutions and prevented direct access to the truth would seem circumspect. Indeed, as direct action to resistances heated up, even some *origenistas* felt that the magazine's mission was misguided. Rodríguez Feo and Virgilio Piñera left *Orígenes* to found the rival magazine *Ciclón*, which served as "a laboratory for experimentation and necessary risk-taking" not provided by the other magazine's poetics of difficulty or its resistant ethics (Roberto Pérez Leon, *Tiempo de Ciclón*, 28). Hard-pressed to distinguish his concept of the secret from the nation-state's more malign, corruptive praxis, Lezama used the forum of his 1957 lectures for the National Institute of Culture's Center for Higher Education to directly relate the ethical program of his poetics to Latin American histories of postcolonial resistance. The result, *The American Expression*, implicitly argues for an ethical appreciation, rather than hasty dismissal, of *reform* as a viable alternative to revolutionary upheaval.[23] Lezama felt too connected to other periods and cultures to suppose that he, or anyone else, could easily cut those ties and proclaim absolute autonomy. One had to work through, rather than reject, liberalism. In that process, one would uncover secret histories—much like the aforementioned one between Columbus and the Taíno—that would promote new understandings of Cuban citizens' connections to the rest of the world.

In his lectures, Lezama characterizes aesthetic texts as historical actors. Pointing to similarities in images supplied by *The Book of Hours* and paintings by Brueghel, van der Weyden, van Eyck, and others, he argues that these texts introduce "natural presences and cultural artifacts that act like characters [*personajes*], which participate [in history] as metaphors" (*EA* 282). The topical resemblances in these compositions enact a historical drama staged through the texts' figurative correspondences with one another. These engagements occur outside dialectical time. The past speaks to the future, and the future and present speak back to the past. In this manner, dialogues conducted through art produce a dramatic intervention in the order of things (*EA* 283). In Cuba's changing social and political climate, though, Lezama would have been unlikely to win over an audience solely with a theory of the aesthetic agency of texts. So, he also characterizes the artist—not just texts—as what he terms a "metaphorical subject." Each text's dramatic intervention in the current order of things is a production overseen, even "driven" (*impulsado*), by the artist, "who through his counterirritant [*revulsiva*] force, puts the whole line into motion" (*EA* 282). Acting as a director, the artist coordinates the resemblances surfacing between her own and others' texts. The resultant dialogue moves the aesthetic assemblage "toward [a] new vision," so as to produce a "metamorphosis" (*EA* 283). Both textual actors and artistic directors have agency; however—and this is a crucial qualification—they *limit* one another. The representations' dramatic performance is coordinated by the artist (thus limiting the texts' agency), but the artist cannot always anticipate the full ramifications of textual correspondences and as a result is prohibited from using art didactically, as a vehicle for self-expression. The artist's efforts to realize an aesthetic and ethical vision are further limited by "cultural" resources (the imagination rooted in, and limited by, a cultural imaginary) as well as "natural" materials (the geographical context where the artist works).

Lezama was not interested in turning writers and other artists into a separate, noble class. As was evident in his imagining in "Possible Images" of the people standing together on the city's penultimate wall, he long believed that everyone can discover new forms of agency by witnessing the adventures of metaphor that occur in poetry. *The American Expression* clarifies that the agency of the artist, like that of the audience, actually originates in *surprise* at discovering unexpected correspondences between texts. Reflecting on post-Carolingian art, Lezama rhapsodizes about how "the elect" imaginatively approach reality through the lens of the marvelous and miraculous, rather than through narratives of "simplistic causality" (*EA* 287). Contemporary audiences and artists who are similarly open to the surprises revealed by textual correspondences have an analogous experience. "That surprise over those intersections establishes something like the luck [*suerte*] of retrospective causality" (*EA* 287). Instead of narrating progress, texts thus produce a historical intervention. "Our point of view parts ways from [one that upholds] the impossibility of similar styles, of the lack of identity of two apparently concluded forms, of the creativity of a new concept of historical causality; it destroys the pseudo-temporal concept that everything is directed toward the contemporary, [and, instead, moves us] toward a fragmentary time" (*EA* 290). The high estimation modernity places on historical progress and state-inscribed aesthetic movements must be abandoned; only then can art produce new commonalities by linking actors and texts that otherwise would remain unrelated because of instilled notions about the propriety of one's place and time. Agency originates in this so-called retrospective glance, which lets one re-narrate connections to other places, times, and peoples based on the lessons one has had the luck, or good fortune (*suerte*), to learn from aesthetic texts' correspondences (*EA* 370). When historical convention stops making sense, available narratives about coherent, self-contained identity are disrupted because the connections between past and present are revealed to have "a secret continuity" (*EA* 371). Lezama's secret, then, does not merely obfuscate meaning like Batista's corrupt political rhetoric. Rather, it embodies the unconscious process of cultural appropriation responsible for the Cuban *landscape* or *countryside* (*paisaje*), as Lezama differentiates the cultural country from the political one (*país*). Facets of a secret relation between Cuba and the rest of the world stand to be discovered through the imaginary eras established by the correspondences of artworks, in their drama outside the dialectical history associated with revolution and modernity. In the remainder of *The American Expression*, Lezama himself acts as a metaphorical subject who directs the dramatic interplay of otherwise unrelated aesthetic and historical texts from the North and the South. Figures ranging from José Martí to Ralph Waldo Emerson and Walt Whitman, from the Mexican *corredigedores* to the Gershwin brothers, supply glimpses of the Americas' secret continuities so as to begin the process of ethical reform.

Appropriation facilitates this cultural interplay, and that aesthetic embodying Lezama's ideal of appropriation is the baroque. In his oft-cited second lecture "La curiosidad barroca" ("The Baroque Curiosity"), he calls the baroque "the art of counterconquest [*contraconquista*]" (*EA* 303). Indeed, the heart of his secret history is that *contraconquista* art is not merely an aesthetic relic from the mannerism of Spain's Counter-Reformation; rather, the baroque is an *ethos*, an artful way of life, still very much a part of his Cuban audience's experience.

> It is not a degenerate form, but a fullness, that in Spain and Hispanic America represents acquisitions of language, perhaps unique in the world, furniture for experience, forms of life and of curiosity, mysticism that signals new modes of prayer, ways of flavoring and treating delicacies, that exhale a complete, refined, and mysterious life, theocratic and lost in thought, errant in form and deeply rooted in its essences. (*EA* 303)

Although he likens this baroque to a "Platonism, whose origin was the breaking and uniting of fragments," he undercuts its metaphysical dimension by describing it as a material *lifestyle*, replete with furnishings, recipes, and a spiritual program. This style structures Latin American architecture and the American subject alike, both of which are "established" in the landscape "with delight [*fruición*] and a normal style of life and death" (*EA* 303). The great architects of the first American baroque age, which Lezama dates from the end of the seventeenth century through the eighteenth, were not Europeans. Instead, they included the Quecha artist Kondori, whose work creates a continuum between the natural environment and human habitats, and the manumitted Brazilian leper slave Aleijadihno, whose stone architecture puts Hispanic colonialism into conversation with African traditions (*EA* 324). By providing structures for dwelling, by influencing the cuisine that provides sustenance, and by producing linguistic idiosyncrasies, the baroque's cultural appropriations and the resultant cultural contacts between colonizer and colonized generate a desirable ethos for the Americas.

Because this resistant style is predicated on secret histories and unconscious connections, though, it is no surprise that, in the New World, it is connected to the philosophical principles informing the same Reformation tradition opposed by the original Spanish baroque. As Lezama oddly depicts this relation, the American baroque is "firmly friendly [*firmemente amistosa*] with the Enlightenment" (*EA* 305). The nature of that amicable connection is not at all transparent or conventional, though. "Before resting in its idleness, the gift of its harsh Episcopalian paternity, it was incorporated with Cartesian cautions, in order to avoid the drop [*gota*] of coarse [*tosca*] amethyst" (*EA* 303). With prophylactic wariness, baroque subjects deploy a retrospective rationality, an inductive Cartesianism, in order to emerge dry and unscathed from their encounters with the Reformation's liberalist ideal of autonomous individualism. Tellingly, that ideal is described as a "drop" of stone, the baroque's sterile inheritance from the Enlightenment.

The next lecture, "El romanticismo y el hecho americano" ("Romanticism and American Fact"), explains how the earlier American baroque informs a later epoch's adaptation of a liberalist individualism and nationalism. In the wake of the French Revolution, many Latin American priests who had "abjured" the Church either "converted back" or "opted for English liberalism." These developments reprised Catholics' obsession with "the constant question about the exercise of freedom"; despite these resurgent debates, however, the Church made "no qualification of its dogma" (*EA* 328). The peregrinating Jesuit priest Servando Teresa de Mier supplies Lezama with a middle-ground position, where the passion of the Catholic elect and the willful autonomy of a reformative Protestantism (and, he adds, of British Romantics) intersect. Often misunderstood as a rebel, Fray Servando is reimagined by Lezama as "reforming from within the previous order, not breaking [it] but taking up the thread again" (*EA* 330). In other words, he freely reforms liberalism to adapt it to seemingly incompatible Catholic tenets: mystery, passion, lack of autonomy. Refusing to submit to Enlightenment ideals, Fray Servando learns to live differently in relation to them.

This reformative spirit permits Fray Servando to enter freely into relations with those others from whom he would be discouraged, if not forbidden, to have contact if he abided by the Church's conventions. Lezama focuses on the Jesuit's encounter in the Bayona synagogue with Jews who speak "a meticulous Spanish." Mediated by a common language, that encounter allowed both Jesuit and Jew to discover resemblances to one another. "Like a good American, he is gifted in *sympathos*," Lezama comments (*EA* 330). Sympathy is that quality that an appropriative or reformative practice cultivates, and it is what Lezama later characterizes as endemic to the Americas' creative and transformative "gnostic space" (*EA* 387). He pushes his Cuban audience to recognize themselves in this Spanish Jesuit: "Another American sign: he enters the foreign [*aleja*] temple out of curiosity, in order to win sympathy and to bring them [i.e., the Jews] afterward to a taste of our omniscient freedom." It is a conversion scene, but one in which the believer foregoes proselytizing. Fray Servando engages the other with "the refinement of asking with mystery, [ . . . ] with a dream that [the Jews'] alien, fine attention is going to be obliged to decipher" (*EA* 331). In other words, he interacts with the Jews through a *mysterious* and *poetic* language. Since they share his tongue, he could have transparently communicated his beliefs. Yet, the wandering priest tries to draw his others into a deeper commonality by presenting a communiqué they are "obliged to decipher" for themselves.

Through Fray Servando, Lezama presents a metaphorical subject that complements his previous discussion of the baroque and thus creates an oblique link between cultural appropriation and a reformist approach to liberalism. By retrospectively situating themselves in relation to that lesson in *The American Expression*'s surprising secret history, Lezama's listeners are encouraged, in a gently seductive fashion, to free themselves from the stranglehold of identity. He reads the Jesuits' reformism alongside the fierce individualism of Simón Rodríguez who, driven by "a very agitated demon to be a citizen of the world," lived among Native Americans and enjoyed their culture's celebration of Eros (*EA* 341). To this secret history of great Americans is added General Francisco de Miranda, a military figure renowned in pre-Revolutionary Russia, France, Britain, and England for "assum[ing] the risk" of petitioning William Pitt for the independence of the Americas. Miranda's efforts would inspire the pan-European vision of a young Napoleon (*EA* 343). Lezama traces a lineage for Cuban nationhood—or, *cubanía*—through idiosyncratic figures and historical moments rather than through official histories' celebrated romantic and nationalist figures, such as Simón Bolívar. In this way, he *forcibly interrupts* the causal history narrating the rise of a liberalist *independista* spirit in Cuba. Although none of his figures illustrates a revolutionary rupture with tradition, Fray Servando and the rest demonstrate a curious form of freedom through their aspirations for new commonalities and cultural orders and their explorations of sympathetic resemblances. Through their examples, Lezama appeals to his audience to reformatively temper liberalist rationality and individualism with a passion that lets others' embodiment of mystery, of singular differences, draw them outside dogmatic politics and institutional positions.

The force of these surprises owes to the erotic, passionate dimensions of the secret inducing that experience. As María Zambrano writes in "Secret Cuba," "True secrets do not consist in being unveiled; what constitutes their maximum generosity, or what lets them remain being secrets, would keep empty that place in our soul destined for them. Our life would be seen as vulnerable to their loving presence. Because a secret is always a secret of love" (*La Cuba secreta y otros ensayos*, 106–7). The secret is not what is withheld. Rather, it is the very *substance* of friendship; it is the *experience of connection* arising upon the discovery of unexpected sympathies. It is the essence of what one still has to learn about oneself, spurring an ever outward movement and preventing the promotion of self-interest. One is free only insofar as one acts, amicably and amorously, within the mysterious limits of kindness imposed by others. Lezama explicitly addresses this erotic element of his reformist ethic in his brief discussion of the long poem *Primero sueño* (*First, I Dream*) by the Mexican nun, Sor Juana Inés de la Cruz. The text documents "the secret journey of our communications with the external world through subterranean dwellings [*moradas*]." It is an erotic lesson that can seduce anyone. Earlier Scholastic traditions mark a "spirit subdivided on its exterior and melted [*fundido*] by Eros"; however, Sor Juana's verse demonstrates a "scholasticism of the body, which passes whole through her poem" (*EA* 314). Instead of a false unity forcing together a subject cut up by various epistemological categories, she poetically re-presents an integral body that traverses the space of the page. Eros itself, then, is defined as a textual encounter with another's body, present yet mediated through a highly metaphorical language. With each line of *First, I Dream*, readers glimpse Sor Juana's sleeping and dreaming body. Yet, she still remains obscured, semi-clothed, in the shadow of her words. It is a strange sort of fan-dance, by a nun who wants to convert us to the object of her ecstatic vision.

Lezama sensuously describes the effect of reading this metaphorical tease: "Its darkness descends to our depths, in order to merge [*fundirse*] with the unexpressed, so as to block the light, inviting the unexpressed, warding it off, and to favor its emission through the descent to the depths that always give darkness" (*EA* 315). Rather than gilding her verse with an erotic content that reproduces distracting and divisive categories, Sor Juana's lyric "invites" comprehensible interpretations of these desires. In the end, though, her invitation is impossible to act on since her poem continues to evade and even "block" the figurative light one might throw on it. In an echo of the Spanish modifier for "molten" (*fundido*), Sor Juana's text—wherein her body floats—thus "merges" (*se funde*) with an unknowable part of readers' selves. That is to say, the poem's erotic charge owes to how it plumbs readers' depths, rather than what it reveals about Sor Juana's private desires. Sympathetic with and desirous of the poem's body, her readers are seduced into a state of *ek-stasis*, standing beside their selves. They are then free to leave behind what is known so that they can move toward an altogether different life, a possibility, glimpsed in the poem's seductively mysterious gestures.

As Lezama specifies, the experience of reading Sor Juana is quite distinct from encounters with the erotic literature of French Surrealism or German Romanticism. Whereas those traditions look for "another reality, another causal magic"—what we would call an unconscious—Sor Juana's desire is, oddly enough, quite a conscious affair. Lezama describes it as "visibly reminiscent of Cartesianism; the dream [conveyed by Sor Juana's poem] appears as a form of control by the superconscience. There is a knowledge [*sabiduría*]:

it seems detached by the poem, in the dream, but is worked over the material of immediate reality." Lezama points to the fact that this eroticism is *crafted*, that Sor Juana's proliferation of metaphors is "a work in which is continued the world of *conscience* [*conciencia*] and of *consciousness* [*conocimiento*; or, *understanding*]" (*EA* 315; emphasis added). Generally, such poetry is "reminiscent of Cartesianism." Although it seems like an Enlightenment ideal of knowledge based on scopic distinctions between self and other, it is actually more like baroque art that had been described earlier as "firmly friendly" with the Enlightenment. That is to say, it bears a resemblance to an Enlightenment paradigm yet somewhat "detaches" itself from it. This queer sympathy with what we might extrapolate to call liberalist rationality moves toward a more physical and intimate knowledge. This "understanding," conveyed through an obfuscating and difficult metaphorical language, attaches the subject to material conditions. The text—and, through it, the author—are put bodily into contact with readers.[24] The resultant conscientiousness and consciousness, morality and understanding, supplies "a living form" (*una forma viviente*) that confronts the unknown, head-on (*EA* 316). This engagement with secret matters is "not that dilettantism of old cultures, a form of domestic ornamentation, but a healthy passion of the enthusiast, a curiosity indulgent of terror" (*EA* 316). A "healthy passion," but not at all domesticated. Unsettling, yet encouraging readers to live, even if it be in "terror," with difference. Such eroticism schools us in how to hold difference in reserve, as part of the medium and substance of our lives. This reserve is the essence of reform: of *re-formation* and *re-formulation*. Living with difference, seduced by its many forms, we move closer to the image of Lezama's own dream: his queer, cosmopolitan vision of a Cuban life connected to others beyond his country's borders.

## Closets and Sympathy

Lezama obtusely and allusively addresses eroticism, that trope where his poetic system's queerness is located by various ciphers: *love*, *friendship*, *seduction*, and, not least of all, *the secret*. When critics or other authors read his work for its sexual content or only in light of biographical narratives about the author, they deploy the same logic of straightforward liberalist identification contested by Lezama himself.[25] Secrecy is his strategy for resisting liberalism, as it is tied to both imperialism and heteronormativity. As a resistance to the latter, though, it is seriously limited because his critical ethic's queer dimensions are even less explicit than its subtle postcolonial elements. Secrets suggest a privacy upholding, rather than transforming, liberalist tenets. Such privacy reinforces liberalism's historical exclusions and injurious heteronormativity. Indeed, Lezama has been read in precisely this way. In an embittered memoir, former *origenista* Lorenzo García Vega accuses him of having embodied the conservatism of Batista's dictatorship. He portrays Lezama as: a closeted homophobe and misogynist disengaged from Cuba's early homosexual and women's rights movements of the 1940s and 1950s; a fallen *petit bourgeois* nostalgic for his family's lost status; a tyrant who masters a vanguard that refuses confrontational avant-garde engagement. Because he and the other gay *origenistas* adopted a "prudish and hermetic attitude," because they "wanted to present themselves as incarnating the values of a foreign, petit bourgeois aristocracy," they hid "the demoniac [*lo demoníaco*] and the sickly that could have stuck out." Both their homosexuality and discontent with Batista's regime were closeted by tropes of hiding or darkness (*formas del ocultamiento*) (García Vega, *Los años de Origenes*, 124). We cannot argue against the reality that, evacuated of all sexual content, Lezama's trope of the secret is an empty form susceptible to cooption. In contemporary Cuba, the liberalism of the intersection of strong individualism with the existentialist ideal of the revolutionary subject is exacerbated by the state's adoption of limited private enterprise. In this climate, Lezama's poetic hermeticism, once denounced as counterrevolutionary, is now ideologically valued. The state-sponsored academy treats him as "a symbol of power," as reinforcing the elite status of those few who are privy to governmental secrets. Moreover, "his idea of the secret of Cuban culture, astonishingly, has been incorporated into official rhetoric" and is regarded as affirming the value of less, rather than more, truly public spaces (Rojas, *El arte de la espera*, 190–91).

Given these strong criticisms and undeniable appropriations of his ideas, it is true that we should exercise caution when turning to Lezama's poetic for an ethical model. Nonetheless, it would be fallacious to dismiss his work as having little or no value for contemporary queer theory. As Eve Kosofsky Sedgwick reminded us long ago in her extension of Michel Foucault's work against the repressive hypothesis, the closet and the binaries it instantiates—public/private, self/other, gay/straight—are predicated on knowledges governed by the imperative that *the subject must have no secrets.* This epistemology of the closet is most effectively countered if attention is focused on "how certain categorizations work . . . rather than what they essentially *mean*" (*Epistemology of the Closet*, 27; emphasis in original). Rather than assign an identity-based sexual significance to every secret, it would serve us better to investigate *how a specific occurrence of a secret functions.* The value of Lezama's secret is thus not in the homosexual content it supposedly occludes but in the dynamic whereby his secret's very refusal of disclosure functions to disrupt how liberalist frameworks control difference by circulating and governing conventions and knowledge about identity. His secret exposes what Gayatri Gopinath calls "a different economy of desire that escapes legibility" (*Impossible Desires*, 13). In her analysis, this illegibility proves crucial for resistances by queer postcolonial subjects. Often they are codes borrowed from elsewhere, translated into their own cultural vocabularies in such a way that they are visible but not entirely decipherable. In Lezama's case, Northern liberalist individualism provides such a code, and he isolates it as the substance of that mysterious relation continuing to connect his newly "independent" Cuba to an imperialistic United States. But when he appropriates that individualism, Lezama inflects the liberalist values of *freedom* and *privacy* with Cuban Catholic resonances of *mystery, passion, ecstasy*, and *incarnation*. The result is not just evidence of a queer subject's resistant ethics. It also demonstrates the queerness that emerges when one opts for postcolonial resistances based on passions that leave one vulnerable to others. Thus, one is better able to explore similarities than if one pursued a kind of resistance based on a revolutionary agency and the assertion of autonomy and divisive, identity-based differences.

Given that he develops this idea of the secret through cultural appropriation, by re-forming (in the sense of reconstituting) the liberalism governing Cubans and other postcolonial subjects, Lezama's poetic usefully extends Sedgwick's idea that part of what the epistemology of the closet occludes are the differences existing between people who inhabit the same identity rubric.[26] Identity is not merely an affair of identifying "as"; it also entails identifying "with" and "against." That is to say, difference always attends identification; when it surfaces, it can render insecure those liberalist forms of knowledge that leave no room for vulnerability, change, or future uncertainties. Lezama's secret promotes a paradigm of *similarity*—both within identity categories and between them. Like the metaphorical images of his poetic system, they are only partially disclosed resemblances to a transcendent unity, what we might call a universalized vision of humanity. Though mere glimpses of a humanistic promise, they still function to foster an understanding and a sympathy whose premises disrupt prevailing humanistic narratives based on easily categorized and contained differences.

Lezama rejects homosexuality only insofar as he rejects all *a priori* forms of identity. His secret lays bare the unacknowledged difference residing at the heart of liberalism's celebration of individualism and individuation. Secrets call attention to themselves. As José Quiroga argues, a "homosexual text does not necessarily proclaim its own identity in words but in acts—in the coded secrets that it tells, and in the decoding that it wants" (*Tropics of*

*Desire*, 100).[27] We do not need to read these acts as indicative of the author's desire for the reader to decode the text by throwing open the closet door. Instead, we would do better to accept the text's secrets as a queer sort of come-on, a seduction of all readers into a different way of thinking. This lure consists of what Leo Bersani and Ulysse Dutoit call a "double movement," or a "soliciting move toward the viewer, and [a] self-concealing move away from the viewer" (*Caravaggio's Secrets*, 5). This "noninterpretable address" through "the enigmatic body" is a playful come-on that cannot be acted on, a mystery that cannot be solved (ibid., 8, 9). The advance leaves us to contemplate the relations between our bodies, and the eroticism traversing those relations. Thus, art constitutes "an ontological laboratory" that points to "pure relationality, of being *as* relationality" (ibid., 59, 58; emphasis in original). Lezama's secret exposes the nature of relationality, too; however, he is not interested just in revealing ontological states of Being. He specifically makes liberalist democracy's autonomous citizen-subject appear differently, more seductively. His poetics thus suggestively hint that we are always connected to others. Impassioned, we entice others to draw them close; yet we turn away to continue to freely proliferate new connections and contacts. Such an identity that exists in ever-multiplying resemblances, which draw readers ever onward, is more befitting Lezama's Cuban postcolonial condition wherein citizens were intimately bound to outside spaces. In turning his back on historical fictions of security and nationalist rhetoric about independence, in favoring reform over revolutionary rupture, Lezama is vulnerable to critics' accusations of conservatism. Yet, that risk of others' misunderstanding is necessary—and one that queer theory should pay attention to—for it is what imbues his work with the optimism of looking outward in search of a queer cosmopolitanism's evasive promise.

CHAPTER 3

# Vulnerable Households

## Containment and Robert Duncan's Queered Nation

Thom Gunn once remarked that Robert Duncan was a "chief originator" of "a way of speaking about homosexuality"; however, he also believed but that his friend was "a homosexual poet only secondarily" ("Homosexuality in Robert Duncan's Poetry," 159). Instead of representing the gay community or expressing a gay male perspective, Gunn provocatively suggests, the homosexual content of his lyric promotes "inclusiveness" by supplying "evidence of the many ways in which people live their lives, of the many available ways in which people love or fail to love" (ibid., 159–60). Indeed, Duncan maintained throughout his career a steadfast resistance to identifying with a sexual minority. In 1976, following the heyday of gay liberation, he would announce, "Well, come to think of it, I don't see myself as gay at all" ("A Conversation with Robert Duncan," 2: 95). Such statements should not be read at absolute face value, however. Duncan was quite public about his sexual attractions to, and relationships with, other men; and, unlike José Lezama Lima's writing (chapter 2 above), the queerness of his poetics does not result from an eroticized secret. Rather, his aversion to identifying as gay owes to a fierce antinomianism that rendered homosexuality, like any other identity, a merely secondary concern.

Decades before gay liberation, and even several years before the founding of the Mattachine Society, the first U.S. homophile organization, Duncan made his initial sizeable contribution to an American way of speaking about sexuality with "The Homosexual in Society" (1944). This seminal essay, which appeared in the little magazine *Politics*, argues for detaching homosexuality from the liberal advocacy of minority rights, subcultural identification, and the classification by American psychoanalytic institutions of same-sex desire as deviancy. Instead, Duncan links homosexuality to an aesthetically rendered ethic whereby the individual engages an anarchic pursuit of freedom.[1] He condemns most postwar gay artists for forming a "homosexual cult" that promotes a campy "group language" (*SP* 48, 47). Such "gaiety" is nothing but a codified "self-ridicule" that demonstrates their uncritical acceptance of normative classifications of their desire and that sets their writings apart from other American letters (*SP* 47). Duncan's judgments were not well received by Parker Tyler, Charles Henri Ford, and others whom he implicitly attacked.[2] Perhaps most upsetting was his assertion that their divisiveness and cliquishness evince a kind of "inhumanity," on par with "patriotism" and "bigotry" (*SP* 48). The true artist, Duncan maintains, has "only one devotion": "a devotion to human freedom, toward the liberation of human love, human conflicts, human aspirations. To do this one must disown *all* the special interest groups (nations, churches, sexes, races) that would claim allegiance" (*SP* 47; emphasis in original). Since this "is a battle that cannot be won in the immediate scene," the writer must demonstrate a "continued opposition" to the so-called "inhumanity" reinforced by group identity in order to perpetually strive after an ever-elusive promise of freedom and, yes, humanness (*SP* 48). An unwavering skepticism about group identification set Duncan apart from later avant-gardes. Michael Davidson notes that straight *and* gay poets associated with Black Mountain, the New York School, and the Beats tended "to perform and engage social alliances, not represent them separate from the poem" because they "addressed specific constituencies without consideration of a larger public" (*Guys like Us*, 17–18). Such closed aesthetic communities, he argues, were founded on an entrenched masculinism. Duncan opposed such gendered attitudes because they, like the campy code of earlier gay coteries, minimized the very freedom he felt poetry could discover.

Premised on undoing the liberalist logic of identification and difference that excluded gays, women, and others from a supposedly all-inclusive democratic field, Duncan's work anticipates Judith Butler's own considerations of universalism by half a century. "Universalism belongs to an open-ended hegemonic struggle," she argues, yet we must understand that the object of that struggle does not exist, in any positivistic sense ("Restaging the Universal," 38). "To claim that the universal has not yet been articulated is to insist that the 'not yet' is proper to an understanding of the universal itself: that which remains 'unrealized' by the universal constitutes it essentially" (ibid., 39). Like Butler, Duncan saw universality as a process of liberation and contestation. Unlike Butler, though, he tended to see such liberation occurring in an anarchic fashion, rather than through a group with which one is identified. Such individualism does not wholly do away with collectivity. Like other anarchists in the American tradition—including Alexander Berkman and the feminist and sexual advocate Emma Goldman—Duncan tied his idealized individual to collective life.[3] Indeed, he believed that the individual artist's charge for producing a new universality made her responsible for generating a new *commonality*. This term signified something much different from a "community" or "communitarianism" based on *a priori* identities. Duncan's idea of anarchic commonality is a belief that writing discovers modes of public living that challenge liberalism's normatively gendered and sexualized constructions of private individualism. Art helps individuals realize their own possibility so they can adapt—or, what we might term after Lezama, *re-form*—existing identity categories.

In the additional commentary included for the 1959 republication of "The Homosexual in Society," Duncan posits that the poet is responsible for generating a "public trust."[4] Such a trust would relieve individuals from "the dominant competitive ethos which gives rise to the struggle of interests to gain recognition or control and discourages the recognition of the needs and interests we all know we have in common" (*SP* 49). Overcoming laissez-faire liberalism mandated rethinking liberalist ideals of identity and individualism, especially as they were embodied by what William H. Whyte described as the "organization man." To this end, Duncan sought to *link* gender, sexuality, and nation so that they are no longer treated as discrete categories dividing the population and encouraging inter- and intragroup competition. Instead, his lyric imagines them as interrelated, similar entities. Rather than rubrics that function as containers, they form a field of identificatory possibilities, the space of commonality itself, through which individuals are free to move. To facilitate such movement, Duncan opposed gendered and heteronormative presuppositions about authorial and social agency. Rather than beginning with the individual's volition to express her difference, agency actually grows out of an eroticized openness to foreignness, an initial *receptivity* or *vulnerability* to differences embodied by others. Just as poststructuralist thought appealed to American intellectuals in the 1960s because of its self-reflexive engagements with "the problems with the logic of containment[,] its blindness, its contradictions, its duplicities," Duncan found lyric capable of staging disruptions of those same logics (Alan Nadel, *Containment Culture*, 3). Poetry that models such a deconstructive dynamic might help make a queer*ed* nation, even a queerer humanity, imaginable.

Butler cautions, though, that the only recourse available to someone excluded from liberal democracy's supposedly universalistic parameters is to "agree to falsify" one's self (*Undoing Gender*, 91). That is, even the socially marginalized must represent their selves in terms of the very discourse excluding them: "A discourse that effaces you in the act of representing you, a discourse that denies the language you might want to use to describe who you are, how you got here, and what you want from life" (ibid., 91). To deconstructively transform a discourse and a social field requires the disenfranchised to first repeat hegemonic representations. Although Butler holds out for the possibility that the "performative contradiction" of such reiterations ultimately leads to a reimagining of universality, Duncan's attempts to articulate an excluding principle—rather than just liberally redress his own gay exclusion—evinces more skepticism about the possibility that deconstruction of one identity can affect all of society (ibid., 191). Consequently, his project attempts to deconstruct an entire social field rather than just one identity-bound portion of it. However, this ambitious effort is ultimately limited by two factors. First, Duncan's anarchist disposition leads to a consequential blindness to the norms that foreclose (as Butler terms it) resistant introductions of difference, especially as those norms are introduced through identificatory codes that contain and are written on his body. Second, his emphasis on poetry's ability to heighten readers' sense of vulnerability only foregrounds the body's role as a deconstructive vehicle. Although Duncan's queerly universalizing project does encounter formidable limits, those blind spots still open possibilities for queer theory's reconsideration of the importance of similarities shared between identities—in the plural—to any deconstruction of liberalist and nationalistic culture.

## Political and Cultural Containment and the Poetic Counterstrategy of Vulnerability

From the proposal of the Marshall Plan in 1947 to the withdrawal of American troops from Vietnam in 1973 (two years before the fall of Saigon), popular, political, and ideological discourses in the United States were overtly concerned with preserving boundaries. Whether one considers the Iron Curtain dividing Soviet-controlled Eastern Europe from the West or Korea's 38th parallel or Vietnam's Demilitarized Zone, imaginary lines figured prominently during the Cold War as impassable limits that could contain communist threats. At this time, one particular kind of boundary subjectivated individuals above all: that of the nation-state. Nationality is a "secondary identity that presupposes primary identities" such as race, ethnicity, gender, sexuality, and class, as Étienne Balibar theorizes it. Although it is secondary in nature, it ultimately permits a collective sense of national belonging to "distinguish itself from them [i.e., primary identities], stand above them, and legitimate them for its own ends" (*We, the People of Europe?* 25–26). The result is the construction of material and imaginary structures that establish a symbolic hegemony by determining which "primary" identities are included or excluded by the so-called "secondary" identity. "Primary identities, in order to be incorporated into national identity, must be worked on a long time and in some sense 'deconstructed,'" a process that is attended by an intense "structural violence (or 'symbolic violence')" (ibid., 28, 29). During the Cold War, it was imperative that U.S. citizens identify with their nation, no matter if it caused costly contradictions for those minorities who were excluded by their state and culture from a place at the American table.

Duncan was particularly sensitive to this situation. In 1969, he wrote to Denise Levertov: "Nationalism has often and still can appear to me as monstrous evil: but then I have in mind Viet Nam nationalism North and South as well as American, Israelis as well as Arabs—those who would use the actual suffering of a people in order to transform them into a Nation" (*LRD* 629). Rather than a *focus* or an *end* for representing the right to civil inclusion, primary identities offer, on the domestic front, structural analogies or identificatory metaphors through which one might stage a critique of the nationalist politics setting the parameters for universalism. To fold not only the homosexual but also the American into the human, the nation as a whole had to be queered. To achieve this end, Duncan had to simultaneously draw attention to the multiple exclusions of the logics of containment. The lecture "The Adventure of Whitman's Line" offers valuable insights about how he imagined the analogous relationship between the primary structures of gender and sexuality, as well as their similarity to the secondary one of nation. Walt Whitman's lyric models how poetry might disrupt the norms governing all three identity forms. Duncan connects Whitman's free verse to the "arousal of a strength in man's sexual love that is to be throughout 'tender' and 'boundless'"; moreover, "in each line this tenderness and boundlessness [is] deliberately renewing itself" (*FC* 194). The most valuable aspect of the nineteenth-century poet's precedent is not its frank treatment of homosexuality but its open form and expansive line. These elements evoke an ever-changing sense of masculinity and cast all forms of male sexual desire in an unusually open way. Idiosyncratically representing male sexuality as effeminately "tender" yet still "boundless" in its desire, Whitman's verse introduces a different sense of commonality at odds with nationalism. Readers are encouraged to follow his example, to "extend our common time and space, to open out, lead toward, a larger, an unknown global destination" (*FC* 201). This cosmopolitan impetus unsettles not only nationalism but also the cultural masculinism that accompanies jingoistic fervor:

> It is this [duality] that underlies the very line of Whitman—that it be at once bold, advancing, and also tender, seeking mutualities. It is this male tenderness, this manliness, the line is a vehicle of—nowhere of the *macho*, the seeking dominance and authority that we are today in crisis of—it is the determination to create a new male feeling that has made many men enemies of Whitman, for they feel threatened in their sexual needs if they have not the guarantee of being master and over-lord. (*FC* 195–96)

Even at the level of the line, Whitman's poetry is not bounded. And just as his line is free, he does not present the rubrics of gender and nation as fixed, closed forms. Instead, they are open processes readers are invited to explore.

This is a very imaginative misreading, or at least a very selective reading, of *Leaves of Grass*. Duncan glosses over evidence of Whitman's machismo in order to portray him as a poet of "male tenderness."[5] In his earlier "Changing Perspectives on Reading Walt Whitman" (1968, published 1970), he himself had criticized his predecessor's work precisely for such biases. There, Duncan takes Whitman to task for demonstrating "the deadly boast of the Chauvinist, the patriotic zeal of a spiritual imperialism," elements too close for his liking to the Vietnam era's "fearful" rhetoric of "presidents, congresses, armed forces, industrialists, governors, police forces" (*FC* 169). His misprision in "The Adventure of Whitman's Line" is no mere oversight or inconsistency, then; rather, he strategically links an ethical ideal of erotic "tenderness" to Whitman's poetically formal innovation. Thus Duncan draws readers' attention to the link between a decades-long "crisis" in American poetry and what he perceived as continuing crises in gender and national identities. Deviating from Whitman's example, many of Duncan's contemporaries insisted on a masculinist, authoritarian control over their material and thus redoubled the norm of containment even long after McCarthyism itself subsided. Returning to Whitman's example, then, would allow for a reimagining of commonality. As Duncan muses in an early installment of his decades-long project *The H.D. Book*: "To write at all is to dwell in the illusion of language, the rapture of communication that comes as we surrender our troubled individual isolated experiences to the communal consciousness" (*HD* 1.6: 131). Poetic manipulations of language can generate the "cosmopolitan man" and "an environment enhanced by his realization of the work and experience of others involved, into an increase that was not taken from things but taken in them" (ibid., 133). In short, language supplies poetry with the foundations for new forms through which we can reimagine social interaction and collectivity.

Duncan's ideas about commonality reframe sociality in a manner that challenges Cold War containment systems, a point nakedly exposed by the poem "Up Rising, *Passages* 25" (1966; *Bending the Bow*, 81–83). In an uncharacteristically polemical fashion, Duncan singles out Lyndon Baines Johnson as the perpetrator of a military aggression in Vietnam analogous to the genocides ordered by Hitler and Stalin. My interest in "Up Rising" here, however, is not in its explicitly antiwar stance; rather, I am interested in the poem's quieter suggestion that bellicose jingoism and imperialist ambitions of the United States targeted *more* than an external ideological threat.[6] The Johnson administration did not just wage war on the Viet Cong. As Duncan writes in "Up Rising," it was also responsible for "the burning of homes and the torture of mothers and fathers and children." As he judges it, the most elementary units of human community—home and family—had fallen victim to a brutal violence born of one politician's thirst for power. The war on communism thus threatened a cultural idea valued as much in America as abroad: an idealization of "all communal things, of communion, / of communism." To compensate for the insecurities of military and ideological conflicts overseas, the state believed it was culturally and even politically imperative that a sense of security be found for the nation at home. Gender and sexual issues opened a second front, and the American home was ideologically and rhetorically refigured by what Elaine Tyler May calls "the domestic version of containment." "Within its walls," she elaborates, "potentially dangerous social forces of the new age might be tamed, where they could contribute to the secure and fulfilling life to which postwar women and men aspired. . . . Domestic containment and its therapeutic corollary undermined the potential for political activism and reinforced the chilling effects of anticommunism and the cold war consensus" (*Homeward Bound*, 14). The everyday effects of domestic containment were reinforced by the ideological narratives underwriting international policy. As Jane Sherron de Hart notes, "The new gender and sexual politics of the long fifties provided Cold War liberals and conservatives alike a way to maintain the fiction of a stability in intimate matters that so eluded them in national and international affairs" ("Containment at Home," 129–30). Such desired "stability" produced "strenuous, systematic efforts to maintain traditional gender and sexual boundaries, ideologically as well as behaviorally, through cultural imperatives and social policy" (130). The maintenance of a nationalist fiction that projected U.S. political strength abroad necessitated the domestic policing of all, as well as the exclusion of some, primary identities.

Such ideological containment assumed a greater cultural priority in light of political, social, and medical developments following World War II. Middle-class homes and families, once imagined as sites of sexual and gender normalcy, were revealed to be riddled with perversions. The entomologist Alfred Kinsey published the reports of his behavioral studies of American male and female sexuality in 1948 and 1953, respectively. These studies revealed that it was statistically normal for the average American man and woman to masturbate, to engage in premarital intercourse, to experience same-sex encounters, to have extramarital affairs. In short, it was normal to be deviant; or, as contemporary critical parlance would put it, a queerness predicated on desire—rather than a categorically defined set of acceptable sexual mores—was discovered to be the norm.[7] As shifting attitudes about women's sexuality complicated the traditional equation of sex with reproduction, heterosexuality came to be identified conservatively as the evaluative norm, or the standard, for ensuring the stable boundaries of North American homes and families.[8]

If individuals posed a risk to the gender or sexual norms that made the family safe, they were imagined to threaten the very security of the nation. Beginning with the House Un-American Activities Committee's first investigative hearings of Hollywood figures in 1947, and extending through the McCarthyism and Red-baiting of the "long fifties," homosexuality and communism were virtually coterminous. A veritable homosexual panic linked homosexual men's and lesbians' supposed "psychological maladjustment" to the likelihood of their becoming "security risks" (David K. Johnson, *The Lavender Scare*, 16). The weakness of character associated with homosexuality led to the belief shared by the state and the general American population that the presence of gays and lesbians in governmental positions presented a vulnerability that might be exploited by Soviet forces. In the wake of ninety-one homosexual employees' termination from various federal agencies in 1950, even the number 91 became a popular cipher for "queer." Known and suspected queer citizens were increasingly subject to arrest, surveillance, and entrapment, often under the pretense of unearthing "pinko" traitors and spies.[9] Such conflations continued well into the 1960s, and gays' and lesbians' lack of access to government jobs was an object of activist criticism even after the 1969 Stonewall riots.

Duncan questioned the Cold War's ideological defense of both internal and external boundaries, especially since the security desired for home and nation reinforced rigid gender and sexual lines that limited individuals' freedoms. Although some may suppose he had a vested interest in ameliorating the ostracism he and other homosexuals suffered, much of Duncan's vision for a poetic reshaping of the national climate is actually oriented toward a larger goal: opening various Cold War containers in order to salvage a general, national spirit of *communitas* and democratic ideals of diversity, difference, and change. In the wake of the Lavender Scare, Duncan found lyric's capacity for promoting "male tenderness," such as that evident in Whitman's open form, a means of helping him make unconventional connections between gender constructs, same-sex desire, and an "un-American*ist*" (rather than "un-American") vision.[10] Such tenderness would threaten the Cold War order of things by modeling a desirable form of risk. Lyric manifests what he perceived as a much needed vulnerability that permits one to live more freely, no longer contained by the impenetrable boundaries of ego, home, or nation.

According to his above-noted diagnosis in "The Adventure of Whitman's Line," Duncan found it necessary for American poetry to move beyond an aggressive masculinism that reinforced a "patriotic zeal" and "spiritual imperialism." Such posturing originated in gendered ideas about language held by earlier modernists, such as William Carlos Williams and Ezra Pound. In an analysis of these predecessors in his *H.D. Book*, Duncan notes that in order to be perceived as "American" they were compelled to prove their work's virility in addition to its compatibility with other forms of national culture. Many male modernists assumed defensive and antagonistic attitudes more in line with "the competition and profiteering of the capitalist society," even though they were interested in challenging existing socioeconomic systems. Consequently, their rhetoric "presented a show of even brutality in defense against any hint of vulnerability" (*HD* 2.9: 79). Such "man-talk," like the colloquial tone and abusive misogyny often found in men's locker rooms or military barracks, creates "a divorce within the language itself, a hidden divorce between man and woman" (ibid., 79, 80). Thus, outward signs of femininity, such as expressiveness or sentiment, were consigned to the margins of literary culture because poets judged them to be "womanish things, a song Herakles sang while sewing for Omphale" (ibid., 80). Perhaps mythic heroes could pull off singing in drag, but Williams and Pound doubted their own abilities to do so. Instead of lyric expression, they developed a polemical poetic in order to connect the oppositely gendered spheres of literature and politics.[11] "He-man bravado or working-class lingo was their *affectation of the vernacular*," Duncan writes elsewhere in *The H.D. Book*; it was "meant to cut thru the genteel affectation of devotion or culture with which the middle-class poetry-lover read" (*HD* 2.5; 58; emphasis added). To trope Pound, "making it new" between the World Wars meant masculinizing poetry by replacing one kind of affectation (sentimental lyricism) with another (political directness). Duncan concludes, however, that modernists' pre-Cold War versions of the "organization man" were nothing but "a defensive strategy" (ibid.). Their machismo is the true drag, a rhetorical performance intended to hide their proclivities for "feminine" lyricism so as to strengthen their challenge of bourgeois poetasters.

During the 1950s and 1960s, poetical polemic assumed a new, liberalist guise whose gendered dimensions threatened the democratic principle of commonality. Duncan was particularly wary of Beat poetry. In principle, he might have appreciated how, in aspiring to produce a new communal spirit, it broke down the barriers between public and private. What he opposed, though, was its aggressive means of making the private public in the poets' pursuit of what Norman Mailer famously dubbed "the apocalyptic orgasm" ("The White Negro," 593). This sexualized masculinity challenged the domesticated masculinity embodied by the suburban-based family and "organization man," whose compliance with Fordist socioeconomic ideas interpolated him as a white collar laborer who worked to secure power only as a consumer. This marked him as an effeminate subject lacking volition and innovation.[12] Such willful resistances to cultural norms, however, merely produced a counterculture that separated the Beats from the rest of the country. Paradoxically, it also reproduced the majority's liberalist faith in a strong, patriarchal ego and perpetuated earlier modernists' "man-talk." For example, even though Allen Ginsberg's quintessential Beat poem *Howl* (1955) redefines masculinity and community by including such marginalized male figures as the homosexual and the insane, the text can also be read as an elegy for a lost virile potency. Ginsberg's narrator laments not only a sense of isolation felt as a "Cocksucker in Moloch" but also the fact that he is "Lacklove and manless in Moloch" (*Howl and Other Poems*, 22). He mourns his lack of both a male lover and a recognizable masculinity for himself.

Duncan was especially suspicious of *Howl*, and his lukewarm response to other Beat writing signals his awareness that queer or countercultural expression was not exempt from the problems of exclusionary masculinism.[13] His critique is most evident in his published response to Michael McClure's long poem "Dark Brown" (1961). Collapsing the distance between his writerly self and his poem's persona, McClure insists that the exterior "BREAK TO WHAT I AM" so that he can transform "The word [into] a sound made of the thing / felt" by the reader (*3 Poems*, 221). He likens this creative forcefulness to his own embodied maleness. His texts are "not hard as my cock," yet they bear some connection and resemblance to McClure's creative body because each word is "a motion of mine" (ibid., 220). Although this physicality is only metaphorical, he emphatically insists that it is absolutely "REAL!" (ibid., 220). Duncan wrote "Properties and Our REAL Estate," which appeared in the 1961 inaugural issue of McClure's short-lived *Journal for the Protection of All Beings*, as a subtle criticism of "Dark Brown." Simply by capitalizing the word "real" in his essay's title, just as it appears in McClure's poem, he draws a connection between the pieces. He specifically takes issue with his former student's declaration "I AM MAMMAL" (McClure, *3 Poems*, 217) and shifts our attention toward a less corporeal way of conceiving the human subject. "It is easier for me to see that we are all men, of one species," Duncan argues, "and that nation-thinking or race-thinking is damned-thinking; for I am surely of mixed race and have no pride there." This humanistic universalism is qualified, though: "And I believe that we are mammal before we are men; animal before we are mammal: that most truly we are light" ("Properties," 91). Duncan sets out to lighten the forcefulness of McClure's "mammal-body," or whatever other form male physicality takes in Beat poetry.

From the vantage of quantum physics, even light has a body, so Duncan's seemingly immaterial metaphor does not really disembody poetic production or ignore its material contingencies. McClure's emphasis on a particular *sort* of physicality, though, perpetuates a Cold War masculinist aggressiveness and defensiveness about the need to safeguard and contain all forms of property. Earlier in the essay, Duncan meditates on the original title of McClure's little magazine: *The Protective Association for All Beings.* As might be expected given his anarchist harangue against "old protective associations" almost two decades earlier in "The Homosexual in Society" (*SP* 47), Duncan positively rankles at McClure's title. "The whole density [of the journal] seemed to gather about those words of the title McClure has proposed: 'protective,' 'association,' 'beings.' All three words, if they were meaningful, kept, formed a picture of life and manhood or gave terms to life and manhood that called up in me a dissenting voice. Wasn't *vulnerability* the very quick of the light?" ("Properties," 85; emphasis added) Duncan does more than nitpick about the meanings of the words in an abandoned journal title; instead, he starts to formulate a less defensive and group-oriented poetic that does away with "protective associations" altogether to reimagine "life" and "manhood" as permitting more "vulnerability." For all his rhetoric of light, however, it would be egregious to believe that the "vulnerability" Duncan proposes is rooted in the ethereal sweetness and light of sentimental lyricism. Rather, it is the product of an erotic submission, which results in an amorous dispersal of personal boundaries. A politically and nationally inscribed body re-enters the moment of composition here but does so in such a way that it is better equipped to deconstruct the norms subjectivizing the poet. "Falling in love means losing my being," Duncan writes. "Love exposes us to the first body and to the light; we might even fall in love with what we hate or what hates us. Only a protective association of all beings will keep us from the threat of invasion" ("Properties," 87–88). To some extent, Duncan does not fear this vulnerability. He *desires* it. If poets assume a "protective" stance, then they prevent any number of kinds of invasion: an individual's loss of self-control to a "hated" other, a violation of geopolitical boundaries by an enemy, even a penetrative sexual encounter. All of these senses are in play throughout the piece, but his mention of "invasion" in 1961 is more than a figure of speech. In April of that year, the United States staged a military invasion at the Bay of Pigs, Cuba, where the Central Intelligence Agency had deployed Cuban exiles it had trained to remove the communist threat of Castro's government. Duncan, in fact, explicitly references mounting international tensions. "The United States in Eisenhower and then in Kennedy; and Cuba in Castro are what Hell is. They are drawn together" ("Properties," 86). Poetic vulnerability could rectify that political hell by making us think about "invasion" differently, as openness. Duncan's oblique criticism of McClure implies that he felt such an ethos could be achieved if the country's poets modeled a less defensive form of relationality and revised their attitudes toward what he calls "manhood."

By emphasizing passivity and vulnerability, Duncan breaks down bounded senses of *personhood.* When they are receptively passive, writers remain open to their passions and are worked on by external forces so that they no longer need to defend, or be defined by, national, gender, or sexual boundaries. Literature, Duncan posited throughout his career, is a *gift* freely given and shared among members of a community. The gift is received by the artist first: "The work of art appears as a gift for another but also as a means for another to be there. Self-expression may be an urgency of art, but the self has no expression except in this other" (*HD* 2.2: 29). This gift is then passed on to others. To accept it, readers must be open to the text, just as the writer is receptive to an inspiriting force. Expressed through the media of others, continually opening by receiving the gift of language, this community of readers is not recognizable as a "nation" per se. It is a new social order, which emerges from a *queered* Cold War United States.

Although Duncan often described himself as a Romantic poet, his work does not reinforce the misunderstanding of Romanticism as willful lyric self-expression; rather, he relies on a concept of passive or passionate genius, in which a poetic imaginary is produced from the surrender of a personality ("the artist") to the imagination ("another"). In this act of submission, writers do not channel a second party as in a theosophist séance (a practice with which he was familiar through his adoptive parents and grandmother), nor do they tap their own subconscious minds as in the automatic writing practices of the French Surrealists and some Beats. "A poet must follow his own ideas or feelings," Duncan asserts. He immediately qualifies the volitional nature of this pursuit, though. "In a way, instead of having ideas or feelings, the poet lets ideas or feelings 'have' him. Seized by an idea" (*HD* 1.1: 29). The poet is responsible only for inviting the foreignness, simultaneously a conceptual and a sentimental entity, the presence of which destabilizes language and linguistic praxis. Attracted since adolescence to the Imagists' personae and to the dramatic monologues of Robert Browning and W. B. Yeats, he elsewhere describes writing as "at once a dramatic projection and at the same time a magic ritual in which a poet was to come into being—only in this art, it seemd [*sic*] to me, could my inner nature unfold. I had no idea what that nature was, it was to be created in my work" (*The Years as Catches*, i).[14] Poetic personae allow writers to be seized by an idea that chooses them, not the other way round. Through vulnerable submission and dramatic portrayals of one's self-as-another, they discover their own singular identities. Thus the ethic underlying Duncan's project inheres in this dynamic: rather than mount an offensive against others' verse, poets must invite an invasion by those foreign elements. Only then can language—the radical alterity constitutive of human selves—help them discover an uncontained identity. The passivity modeled by Duncan's poetry aids readers in the imagining of a new, desirable form of subjectivity. By losing our selves while reading, by acting more receptively and less defensively or offensively, we find new bases for commonality.

## The Queer Foundations of a Vulnerable Household

As Michael Davidson rightly notes, Duncan's work produces a "feminization of tradition"; but it is misleading to read that gendering, as Davidson does, as a *consequence* of the poet's affiliation during the early to mid-1950s with the homosexual coterie of the "Berkeley Renaissance" (also including Robin Blaser and Jack Spicer) (*The San Francisco Renaissance*, 130). We should avoid equating "male homosexual" with "feminine"; instead, Duncan's feminization of lyric is an *ethical strategy* that directs readers' attention to the American home. Between the late 1950s and the mid-1970s, the *household* was the central trope in Duncan's general deconstruction of Cold War containment strategies. Unlike the paradigmatic home, his novel conceptualization of the household does not reinforce the nation-state's security but instead promotes a mid-century mode of queering by encouraging vulnerably receptive and passionate attitudes. There, the structural analogies between different identity markers—gender, sexuality, and nation—are localized in a public space that disrupts liberalist expectations of privacy and contained identification. In the process of refuting and responding to containment logics, though, Duncan's texts end up reproducing some of their ambivalences. Despite his valorization of the individual's anarchic singularity, he cannot escape the limits of group identity, since homosexuality is written upon his body and thus overwrites his household. The feminine acts as an allied second primary identity to aid in his attempt to deconstruct liberalist logics, but it is not enough to help his project escape all identificatory rubrics so as to move through a queered nation toward a cosmopolitan humanity.

Although critics often repeat his term of the "household," its significance to his poetic has remained largely uninvestigated.[15] "Our whole American Way of Life," Duncan writes in his extended essay "The Truth and Life of Myth" (1968), "is designed to save the householder from his household myths, from the lifestory of working in which he has his communion with the house; as in the factory, the worker, no longer a maker, is removed from his work" (*FC* 24). Recuperating a bygone era's hybrid space of domesticity and labor for aesthetic production, he links an artisan ethos to a feminine tradition of "folk and fairytale [that] have their home in the gossip of old wives and little children, stories about the cooking-hearth and the nursery bedside" (*FC* 26). Folklore had opened domestic spaces to public eyes through narratives about socially inscribed individuals who represent a people's fears and desires. "The lowly folktale was populated irremediably by kitchen sluts and begging women and broom vendors and soldiers home from the wars and the like and their wish-phantasies and fear-delusions" (*FC* 26). Modern art might function similarly if it represented the private North American home more like a semipublic, artisan household. Through this strategy, Duncan violates Cold War norms of privacy by transforming the home from a site to be guarded, or a border in need of patrolling, into a space where poetry can challenge capitalism's fetishism of consumer goods and its alienation of labor.

Through Duncan's trope of public domesticity, homosexuality is brought into the public eye. This visibility would not feed into the general populace's Lavender Scare; instead, it would encourage some citizens' "wish-phantasies" and so generate connections with readers who, once inspired by his work, might challenge compulsory privacy and a cultural containment of sexual and gender differences. In fact, Duncan was attracted to feminine householder traditions later in his career precisely because they offered a desirable alternative to keeping homosexuality locked behind the doors of private poetic coteries. Even in the 1950s he and Spicer desired to move homosexuality into public consciousness: "Our people were the people of a dream secretly at work in the nation without, of an other nation within and below and behind and above the public identity of America; even as we felt *our* language to be that of a meaning striving to come into existence within the public exchange" (*Caesar's Gate,* xix; emphasis in original).[16] By striking at the Cold War's domestic front, his household reworks conventions of the home to create a public workspace which left open the front door—perhaps more appropriately, the back door—so that male homosexuality might come into full view for the reading public. Such visibility let Duncan evade the sort of autonomous agency and self-expressive voice later associated with liberal gay and lesbian identity politics. But more than queer closets are thrown open in this scenario. *All* homes became public sites of a creative desire, and thus the queer household leads the way toward the constitution of a new form of inclusive commonality. That does away with a liberalist logic which fashions the contained home front as a metonym for both the idealized citizen-subject's contained ego and the state's impermeable boundaries. In a householder's world, there are no closed doors to contain the home's policed contents. Everyone remains vulnerably, but joyfully, exposed in their work. Thus, the whole citizenry becomes a bit queer.

The concept of the "household" has a certain degree of biographical verisimilitude. It can easily be imagined as any of the domestic spaces Duncan shared from 1951 until his death in 1988 with his partner, the collagist and painter Jess Collins (known in the art world simply as "Jess"). The physical spaces inhabited by the couple were varied, ranging from the first room they shared in a Berkeley artists' residence (known as the Ghost House) to the nineteenth-century Victorian house they purchased in 1967 at 3267 20th Street in San Francisco. But the household is more a spatial imaginary, an aesthetic trope they shared rather than a poetic representation of any of their actual homes. "Finding Jess made a householder of me," Duncan claims in a 1976 interview ("Conversation," 1: 90). He proceeds to explicitly differentiate their partnership from a marriage by describing it as more like a "conventional fairy-tale idea" (ibid., 91). Of course, he means his idiosyncratic interpretation of the fairy-tale convention, as fostering a different sense of publicity rather than more usual understandings of fairy tales as promoting private, bourgeois romances. In 1966, Duncan described his household construct as "a lone holding in an alien forest-world, as a campfire about which we gathered in an era of cold and night—a made-up thing in which participating we have had the medium of a life together" (quoted in Bertholf, "The Concert," 80). The Cold War backdrop of "an era of cold and night" is never far removed when the trope appears in his texts, so it is difficult to equate Duncan's trope with Michael Auping's characterization of it as a "decidedly middle-class, domestic household" providing "insulation" from the social world ("Jess: A Grand Collage," 39). Even though it was not oriented toward a public in the same way as the Beats' bar counterculture, Jess and Duncan's household was still a visible and public arrangement. It was a "made up thing," a communal concept equated with art and the imagination, and into which they openly invited other artists, texts, and readers. That publicity was just as unconventional and disruptive of liberalist norms as was the homosexual nature of the couple's partnership.

Duncan's relationship with Jess is not at the center of my analysis, however. Instead, I am interested in how he begins to articulate the household as more than a gay construct by connecting it to gender. This alliance between primary identities would reinforce the effectiveness of his poetry's deconstructive, vulnerable ethic. This development originated in his exchange of poems and letters between 1959 and 1961 with the modernist poet H.D. (Hilda Doolittle). Although he probably culls ideas about the household from a number of sources, ranging from Dante to Gaston Bachelard, I read H.D. as his primary influence. Her work led him to associate the trope with vulnerability and with gender and textual structures, rather than just with sexuality or his own biographical narrative.[17] A longtime admirer of and sometime correspondent with H.D., Duncan realized that their relationship reached a new level when she asked him to be the temporary caretaker of some of her manuscripts. In a letter dated August 21, 1959, she wrote him: "I would be glad if you would 'house' these two sets of poems ["Sagesse" and "Ave Vale"] for me, for the moment" (*GA* 15). Recovering from a broken hip in London, H.D. turned Jess and Duncan's home into a way-station for her typescripts before they were forwarded to Norman Holmes Pearson, her curator at Yale University's Beinecke Rare Book and Manuscript Library.

At the time, the couple was living in Stinson Beach, California, physically removed from the poetry scenes of Berkeley and San Francisco. Although their household was moving farther from the outside world, Duncan and Jess were eager to turn their home into a public and literary site by "housing" H.D.'s typescripts. At first, the arrangement simply initiated the development of a small coterie of poets. Duncan wrote H.D. that he and Jess read the poems as soon as they arrived "for the immediate delight"; and he then "housed the typescript in a clip-binder with heavy end-boards," an architecture or ark improvised to protect the coterie's covenant (*GA* 18). He concludes his letter by marking the affective and erotic intimacy awakened by H.D.'s literary gift: "In love's name, as he attends our art" (*GA* 18). By requesting that Duncan and Jess "house" her manuscripts, H.D. transforms their home into a semipublic space. As one of the residents of this transformed space, Duncan is assigned the role of receiver and reader. Their coterie's private dimensions are overshadowed by the fact that these texts (and the story of their keeping) will ultimately become public; the "private" household, then, is opened to other members of that public, as well as to their texts. While he had already long defined his poetic as "derivative" and dependent on the writer's role as reader, H.D.'s actual presentation of a gift had a profound effect on how he conceived the household as a "feminized" structure that renders the poet more receptive and vulnerable, as both a writer and a reader. In December,

Duncan forwarded the poems to Pearson, per H.D.'s request, and confessed at the start of the new year that "the light you gave to my house long ago reamins [*sic*]" and that "once guests in my house, they [i.e., her long poems "Vale Ave" and "Sagesse"] have left their imprint upon my heart—where the mind best reads" (*GA* 23, 22). Oddly, he then likens that "imprint" left on his "heart" to an impregnation. Since "a man" can "receive one or more souls that unite themselves with his own if they are related to it," H.D.'s poetic gift is both a companionate soul and a "light" figuratively inhabiting Duncan's own receptive, reading body and his poetic field (*GA* 22). "'Poetry' is a womb of souls," he claims (*GA* 22). Reading is a passive activity that perforates the subject's bodily boundaries and turns the subject's attention inward. Within one's male self, a domestically "maternal" space is accessed. A commonality queerly gestates there, thus redefining private spaces as media for public and literary exchanges (*GA* 22).

A problem ensues, though, because Duncan's deconstruction through the household trope is still mediated by Cold War discourses categorizing his own embodied experience of male homosexuality. The threshold through which the "light" of H.D.'s poems gains a point of entry into his reading body is associated with the "heart" (the seat of passion, corporeality, and eroticism), rather than with the eyes or the brain (the seats of identity, consciousness, and psychology). In order for Duncan to house her poetic word, even as a reader, her texts must enter an erotic passage to the younger poet's soul. Indeed, in his *H.D. Book*, Duncan likens the self-discovery born of reading as revealing and grounded on a *hole*, an opening, "As if I were a gap, making up my self" (*HD* 2.6: 28). "Making up" has several connotations—a constructivism or self-fashioning, an imaginative fancy, even a form of drag—all of which imply that one cannot re-create oneself in Cold War America without an initial surrender and a bit of cross-gendering. The ability of his and Jess's household to render them properly receptive to H.D.'s texts, then, depends on the sexually unconventional nature of this domestic-yet-public space, a queering of readership that is in no small part imaginable as queer because of the supposed gender inversion of male homosexuality, the possibility of sexual receptivity, or the prospect of both partners' sexual versatility. In May 1960, Duncan forwarded H.D. his long poetic suite "Apprehensions" (*Roots and Branches*, 30–43). His struggle in that poem to divorce homosexual topicality from a general queering of containment structures leads me to conclude that the hole through which "Sagesse" must enter in order to reach Duncan's heart-womb is his anus. Try as he might, homosexuality contains his queer and anarchist critique of liberalism.

## Apprehending the Difficulty of Queering the Home Front

Each of the five lyric movements constituting the long suite of "Apprehensions," the first of Duncan's householder poems inspired by H.D., works through different tropes of passivity or receptivity. It begins with a scene of receptive readership to divorce such a vulnerable, passive subjectivity from sex. The narrator slips into a reverie as he reads a translation of Paul-Henri Michel's "Renaissance Cosmologies," which Duncan carefully notes as published in the eighteenth issue of *Diogenes*. His "mind fell away / or disclosed a falling-away," and he happens upon "an excavation—but a cave-in of the ground" that—"hiding in showing, or showing in hiding"—reveals "a glass or stone, most valuable." Egoistic agency is immediately troubled. This reading figure has no certainty about what his mind "disclosed" to him, or even whether that disclosure is truly unconscious ("a falling away") or the product of the unconscious's assumption of agency (as the subject of the transitive verb "disclosed"). The diction augments the indeterminacy about who possesses agency and what that agency is. The hole could be an excavation, the product of an active digging; or it could be a "falling-away," merely ("but") a sinkhole caused by natural forces beyond human control. In a third interpretation, this geographical site might possess its own unfathomable agency that makes the narrator uncertain as to whether it is disclosing ("showing") or occluding ("hiding") an object from him.

These questions about agency raise new ones about epistemology and identification, for what is concealed or revealed in or by the hole is left ambiguous as well. Although it is deemed "most valuable," what the narrator discovers is described in an unspecific way as a "glass or stone." These designations could signify either a precious gem or even some material with little economic value: a common rock, a piece of costume jewelry, a shard of window glass, a fragment of a mirror. If it is just a common thing, then what kind of value does it have? Associated with a possible excavation, it might have historic or social value. If that excavation is really just a happened-upon hole, though, then the basis of all value is entirely subjective, a matter of the narrator's own pronouncements. The will to formulate ethical, social, or any other kind of value is thus challenged by the passion that sets the scene. Ironically, the only unambiguous element in the reverie is the narrator's *inability* to determine what he sees. He glimpses just a reflection, "only a gleam" off the object's surface. This glint, caused by a light source he does not direct, prevents him from discovering the identity of the object: "I did not bring the matter to light." Indeed, this "matter"—whether we interpret this word as the actual substance in question (the "glass or stone") or as a topic of poetic discourse—is still in the pit's dark depths. Consequently, the narrator is estranged from rationality's "*Eidos,* Idea," "to which" he notes "we gain access through sight." Since sight "defines the borderlines of the meaning," and since all he sees is an indefinable "gleam," the narrator who perceived these objects is not boxed in by meaning either. Giving himself over to the associations spurred by reading, then pursuing new associations evoked by a mere reflection off an unclear object rediscovered during a reverie, he is no longer bound by the need to throw reason's revelatory light on everything. He seems free of preexisting identity structures.

Despite the liberties it affords, however, his imagination still operates within some bounds. Even in a reverie, he cannot escape the context's material contingencies through which he filters his experience. At first, the narrator compares the cave housing the object to a bestial goddess from European folklore (a "toad-mother") and Tiamat, the Babylonian dragon-goddess of chaos; however, these initial speculations prove unsatisfactory because, even in a state of poetic reverie, he cannot evade the actuality that he is looking into a "most real" pit, which could be the "washt out" product of a recent rainfall's erosion of "the shit-yellow clay." Prompted to abandon his unreal and mythological impressions, he reasons that the cave was produced by a storm. Such realistic conjecture opens other possibilities, colored by his momentary reflection on folkloric figures. He parenthetically wonders about the unearthed texts of the Dead Sea Scrolls, "fragments of an old way / stored out of sight." Although this last association seems as digressive and removed from the immediate scene as his more fabulous imaginings, his final speculation actually resembles the circumstances of the poem's composition. H.D.'s long poem "Sagesse" was archived in Duncan's home at that time. Like the Dead Sea Scrolls, her text, published in bits and pieces in various magazines during H.D.'s lifetime, is a fragmentary narration of "an old way." Its twenty-six sections are connected only by the thread of a reading figure's consciousness, which glides from a present moment when she reads a magazine article in *The Listener* to remembrances of a male lover code-named Germain to childhood memories of reading fairy tales.[18] Derived from but independent of H.D.'s model, the reverie in "Apprehensions" founds a feminized household poetic in which reading opens possibilities of a more passionate and less egoistic consciousness.

The narrator muses that the matter he glimpses might be an organism, a "living thing," because he believes it has "moved in the muck." Organic and seemingly animate yet unidentifiable, this "thing" seems to live beyond categorization. But a compulsion to identify reasserts itself. Here the deconstructive element of reading-in-itself comes to an end, and the limits of queering—a *social type* of deconstruction aiming specifically to undo the liberalist citizen-subject—are exposed. The narrator is drawn toward epistemological certainties, confronted no longer by some vague and undefined "thing" or "gleam" but by his own "soul." It is through this Freudian Narcissus motif that identity generally, and homosexuality specifically, creep into the poem. This "soul" is no ethereal thing: it is a projection of his self into what had been described earlier as "*shit*-yellow" clay. This ego-image enthralls him and solicits his "rapt" attention in spite, or perhaps because, of its scatological associations. The scene is so perverse that the narrator does not just face a mirror image, returning his gaze from beneath him. Instead, it is a *mise-en-abîme* like a Magritte painting: he faces the backside of his double, who, like him, is "looking *down* into the six-foot pit where . . ." (ellipsis in original; emphasis added). As in Freud's classic narrative, the narcissist is faced with an *unheimlich*—an unsettling and, literally, unhomey—image as he peers into this improvised gravesite ("a six-foot pit"). In the projection of himself below, he recognizes that submission to passions could lead to the death of him. Though he is "Fearful," he is also "rapt" and cannot tear himself away.

This realization is enough to bring an abrupt end to poetry, as is signaled when the narrator's lyric reverie concludes, jarringly, with the line's sudden ellipsis. Yet, both Duncan and his narrator *need* this deathly experience to further their shared lyric ambitions. When the narrator recovers his tongue, he reverts to a speculative frame of mind. These subject-centered ratiocinations begin to articulate a value for the object that lured him to this disturbing vision of himself, face down in the pit. Even when embedded in a web of scatological, homosexual, and morbid associations, the narrator believes it is "a stone that is most rare." Although this noncommittal description refuses to peg the object with a fixed identity (it could be either a base rock or a valuable gem), it still ascribes some kind of value to it. This "jewel," left behind and "hidden" by another, is the harbinger of a new poetic form. Born of external factors ("pressure") and an internally originating desire ("inner fire"), this object—whether a found text, a thing, or an image of himself—originates in a process driven by both passivity and activity, self-dissipating passion and self-assertive agency.

The generally queer possibilities of being both vulnerable and originary, both acted on and acting, however, are undercut by a homosexual allegory. In the second movement of "Apprehensions," Duncan foregrounds the fact that he is exploring an alternative poetic tradition. His longed-for "architecture of the sentence" provides a rudimentary structure a poet can inhabit, a structure synecdochally presented as "the house and hearth." For one of the first times in his oeuvre, Duncan identifies these domestic terms as "the rude elements of my household." The construction of that household depends on earlier writers' cultural and discursive production, though. Any deconstruction is predicated on an identity it seeks to unwrite because a work is produced through engagements with, and exposure to, external forces. Like the object in the pit, they are the results of "pressure" as much as they are of "inner fires." That is to say, they are produced out of material constraints and circumstances that come to identify them; they cannot simply grow out of a desire to defy categorical logics. A "landscape" is first produced by members of an unnamed group ("they") who have "ploughd the given fields in rows, / prose and / versus." This is no pastoral agricultural scene but a scene of conflict and aggression, overwrought with gendered readings enabled by a longstanding tradition in which men are figured as the cultivators of a feminine landscape. Poetic fields are not sites of lines (*verses*) but of prosaic conflicts ("versus" and "rows," as when rhymed with "ploughd"). His transformative household, then, is built on others' battles. So, even though it grows out of a desire to found a site that is not so egoistic or agentic, it risks perpetuating the same sort of subjective antagonisms and defensiveness we saw Duncan oppose in Beat writing. He realizes that he cannot wholly disavow such agency, but the result of his inability to evade that pressure means that his texts cannot escape the externally originating strictures of identification. The "grove" produced by these poetic cultivators inflects ("interpreting and / interpreted by") the queer household Duncan builds at that site; as such, a fertile possibility for reimagining poetry anew actually can lapse into "a grave expectation." It does not produce a death of self or death of poetry, as Duncan's narrator originally feared; but it does *reproduce* a dead end, the ineluctable expectation of using poetry to secure a recognizable self and social agency. Homosexuality still haunts that gravesite, back where Duncan thought he buried it. Identity morbidly lingers where poetry digs a foundation for its vulnerable household.

Admirably, Duncan chooses not to ignore that haunting gravesite. During the suite's third movement, he delivers a bracketed instruction that directs the reader back to the first movement. This signals a recapitulation of the narrative of the cave, with all of its excremental, narcissistic, and deathly perverse associations. Rewriting that earlier scene, he tries to deal head-on with the limits that the patriarchal orders of his historical moment have placed on his project. Standing before the pit once more, the narrator now muses that what he sees is a paternal figure's body, imagined as a cross between the Freudian primal father torn apart by his progeny and an Osiris figure, reconstituted "member by member remember." An embodied, reproductive masculinity has been torn asunder and reconstituted at this hole. Floodwaters have "passionately dug out / his substance," though; so all that remains are traces of his body's outline. In order to avoid re-membering masculinity by restoring the paternal phallus, the narrator fixates on a particular outline in "the bottom" of the cave. He associates it with the missing male body, whose present insubstantiality makes it bereft of reproductive associations. Looking down at the outline of a figure positioned "head downwards," the narrator can assert: "I have seen the jewel."

What had been an elusive object, only an unidentifiable gleam, is now definitively identified ("*the* jewel"). The narrator's certainty about the identity of this object ends up defining him, too. In the first movement, he had misrecognized it as his own "soul" and, later, as his own double in the six-foot pit. No longer is he vulnerable to this valuable object, though, because it is no longer understood to be an extension of his self. Yet the very distance put between him and it causes his own identity to emerge all the more clearly. Both the jewel and its discoverer are defined by all of the connotations of where it is found, at the pit's "bottom": a designation of spatial orientation; a cheeky synonym for the buttocks; gay slang for the passive male partner's position during anal intercourse. In the depths of a six-foot pit, found in the outline of a patriarch who is buried upside-down, the "jewel" in the "shit-yellow clay" would be the primal father's anus. This anus supplies "the body to my soul," or reifies the narrator's identity. This is no heteronormative moment, to be sure, since the narrator's identity is not the product of his interpellation by the patriarch's phallus (or even the family jewels). Nonetheless, Duncan does reproduce conventional identity logics because his narrator is interpellated as gay by another synecdoche of the patriarchal body, the anus. Thus, homosexuality *limits* the poem's generally deconstructive possibilities because it keeps in play, rather than queerly deconstructs, normative Cold War gender and sexual binaries. Those limits play themselves out in the rest of the poem.

The fourth movement introduces the Lover, the allegorical personification of the household's resident, to account for the association of vulnerable passivity with homosexuality. The Lover exclaims that he wakes up from his own reverie "a new, a workt figure of joy." This receptive figure is not merely an instrument played on by tradition, like a Stevensian guitar or a Shelleyan lyre. His "soul" has been "fingerd" by the night, and this digital penetration—both metaphysical and physical—has affected the "Spectral images of manhood" that "took shape in me" since childhood, a masculinization akin to a supernatural gestation. Upon awakening, the Lover directly addresses the reader as a potential partner: "I saw in your eyes—sudden, waiting, empty—a place I was to fill." Anuses are replaced with eyes, the seat of epistemology where ideas and identity form. Predicative identification will be reworked by future eroticized, mutual submissions as those passive encounters become further removed from bodies. Given the bibliographic history of "Apprehensions," as a poem that documents H.D.'s influence on Duncan, it would seem that the anality experienced earlier by the Lover can be read as queer without reducing that queerness to biographical homosexuality. H.D.'s writing inverts her, imbues her as a female subject with the masculine ability to penetrate Duncan and transform him with her authorial digit. However, the Lover's account of his transformation forecloses possibilities of our separating the queer from the homosexual. He explicitly likens the process that recreates him to *cire perdue*, the making of hollow bronze statuary with wax casts. Although what results is a "river of me that flows away, melted from cast after cast," an image suggestive of a continual dissolution of identities, the name of the procedure evokes Marcel Proust's classic about inversion, *À la recherche du temps perdu*. The wax then reads as an image of spent ejaculate. As the mold of the Lover's seminal male corpus melts away through the heated passion of a homosexual encounter, left in its stead is an ecstatic, joyful substitute. But this artful memorialization literally reifies the dissolved identity and re-presents the hole and organ that made the queer dissolution possible in the first place. We are left with a hollow rectum whose anus provided the opening through which the other could finger, and thus transform, the Lover. The artwork left behind bears the "fingerprint-fine intensions" of "the *man* of the world that is a worker *in men*" (emphasis added). The other man's "shaping hand" undoes a preexisting masculinity, melting away inculcated phantasmic gender ideals; yet he leaves behind markers of his own identity and will, his fingerprints and intentions. This displacement of identity from one male into the interior of another does not deconstruct Cold War containment logics so much as queerly reproduce them. Like a forensic investigation, inescapable identities—the bases of any liberalist logic—do not just constitute what the Lover calls a "previousness to passion"; they are also queerly reproduced through one's vulnerable surrender.

By the end of the suite, Duncan works through why the queer household must be founded on such a homosexual anality. More than a patriarchal or heteronormative discursive architecture is to blame. Ultimately, *his body* cannot be withdrawn from the context of its historical location and discursive construction. The second part of the final movement reprises the suite's opening scene by introducing receptivity in the context of a narrative about reading. What are read this time are Tarot cards, not philosophical treatises. Unlike Madam Sosostris and her "wicked pack of cards" in T. S. Eliot's "The Waste Land," this occultist reading does not divine a possible future (the Eliotic fortune of "death by water") (*Collected Poems*, 54). Instead, oddly enough, Duncan's diviner reveals *the past.* As the narrator reads the cards with the addressee, he remains open to an external force, "an angel of time" whom "we are reading." In the shadow of that angel and "among his power," reader and narrator-poet "are meeting." The act of reading, then, demands passivity to a masculine force, which opens the possibility for the narrator to form a new kind of community with his addressee. Modalities of speech and writing produce a "distribution of words" that leaves it up to the emergent community of readers to discern new meanings and possibilities for themselves; but Duncan seems dubious that openness to others' treatment of language is sufficient for an unrestrained questioning of identification. Centers may move, they may be redistributed, but they still function as points that organize and set limits to poetic and social meaning. Even if language is a material entity that can be manipulated like cards held in one's hands, readers are still compelled to arrive at a single meaning since "There is only one event" responsible for linguistic production.

The final part of the last movement is significantly titled "Close," and that title is itself enclosed by parentheses. Here Duncan seals the container and exposes, without qualification, how the poem's logic has been overdetermined by a singular event linking its composition to his own embodied experience. Like the bizarre divination of the past read through the Tarot cards, a prose account retrospectively gives the entire suite coherence: "March 27th: We found after the rains a cave-in along the path near the rosemary and thyme, disclosing the pit of an abandoned cess pool." Included in a line of dated prose, the narrator's reminiscence obviates any of the earlier ambivalences about the nature of what he discovered in the pit while daydreaming. With this coda, the whole suite is inserted firmly into the realm of fact and biographical history. Since the simple act of dating "Apprehensions" brings the narrator's persona even closer to the poet's person, the distance between lyric fiction and confessional verse collapses. Even if Duncan's reader is unaware of the unconventionally public artistic and homosexual household he shares with Jess, the final anecdote reveals that the poem's "distribution of words" ultimately leads back to, or anticipates, a singular event and material site from which we cannot dissociate vulnerability from scatology and anality. The very *foundation* of Duncan's household and its queering of liberalism is a cesspool, through which his poetic stand-in comes to recognize the valued object of his own desire. Although the mainstream might imagine this site as metonymically pointing to a particular sort of homosexuality associated with abjection and waste, Duncan does queer it as a trace of a (past and future) same-sex home and even a queerly anal (rather than phallic) source of power and patriarchal resistance. Thus, the poem's lessons of vulnerability and receptivity do help refashion a new poetry continuing, while contesting, a previous line to transform a field aggressively plowed by previous writers, and thus "Apprehensions" does challenge containment systems. However, the cards Duncan holds—the tropes he deploys and the context in which he writes—circumscribe the possibilities for a queer critique of American nationalism and liberalism. If the site for the vulnerable household's foundations is a cesspool, and if its scatological anality is what is valuable, in the final analysis his poetic subject remains enclosed in a male homosexual frame. The author's own body proves to be an impervious container, what limits readers' own abilities to passionately queer not just the poetic landscape but also the national one.

## The Containment of Bodies; or, the Theoretical Limits of Vulnerability

Robert Duncan's work illustrates the value of testing and queering those systems of meanings that trap us within containing identity structures. His essays point us to the recognition that the interconnection of identificatory rubrics—of the field of social discourses and ideological narratives that structure our understandings and experiences of gender, sexuality, and nation—can frustrate the systemic logic from which their individual meanings and recognizable natures originate. We might even extend this coalitional queering logic of similarities to include other primary identity categories, such as race and class. Realizing a provisional and alternate universalism does depend on what Judith Butler calls "a translative project," an attempt to articulate a common language for different groups' visions of social transformation ("Competing Universalities," 168). Duncan helps us envision who the agent of that translative project is, as well as what the agency necessary for promoting it looks like. He even anticipates Butler's own claims elsewhere that vulnerability might be the basis if not for a new humanism (a possibility she is more wary of than he is), then at least for a different idea of ethical encounter and civic responsibility.[19] His refusal to associate the household—his preferred trope for signifying this universalism—exclusively with either gender or sexuality points to the fact that cultural translators who instantiate this democratic effort must divest their selves of a liberalist idea of originary agency, and they must resist the temptation to affiliate their selves with one identity group. Instead, they must look for some other public and human possibility that encourages intimacies, refashions our most familiar and supposedly private sites (our homes), and encourages us to move beyond immediate boundaries.

Yet, even if such modes of critique move beyond a liberal affirmation of identity, our queering of a nation and its population cannot escape our own bodies' material inscriptions in, and our singular experiences' dependence on, the systems we seek to disrupt. This is the limit of his poetic ethic, as exposed in "Apprehensions." Our primary identities, as Étienne Balibar argues, constitute the "kernels of resistance to integration" into a hegemonic, exclusive national identity. "The heart of this conscious or unconscious ability would seem to be the body or the body image" (*We, the People of Europe?* 28). "Apprehensions" demonstrates that a supposedly more inclusive project of queering liberalist logics generally, and Duncan's Cold War milieu specifically, is likely to find resistance in the source of its own resistant energies: the body. Founded on his writing body's experience of same-sex desire, his resistance to identificatory structures cannot help but repeat the norms by which homosexuality is recognized. Thus, when Cold War or contemporary readers house Duncan's poem by opening their selves to his text, they are also compelled to experience vulnerability in the same way as the persona of the narrating householder and the embodied person of the gay author.

Duncan implicitly teaches us that such limits should be celebrated by queer theory. They help answer the nagging question of what's so "queer" about a "queer theory" that disavows the importance of same-sex content as either the adequate reason or apt object for analysis. Queerness is not just a deconstructive process but an *extension* of an identificatory marker inscribing our bodies and circumscribing our desires even as it deconstructs those limits. We need to struggle to redefine queerness apart from sexual identity, inclusively rather than particularly, so as to understand queerness as part of a *social field*, a means of connection across identity rubrics and a basis for similarity rather than a marker of absolute difference. Even when drawing figurative alliances in order to "queer" the nation or identity constructs, then, homosexuality shadows queer critiques. This occurs in a fashion similar to what Butler remarks on when she notes that the disenfranchised subject's "otherness" is the limit that "haunts its [i.e., universalism's] boundaries, and that threatens to enter the speakable through substitutions that cannot always be detected" (*Undoing Gender*, 191). Elaborating on Butler's point, I would urge us to see that haunting presence as a paradoxically *material specter* since a queer ethic—whether conducted by a critic or an artist—is rooted in a struggle with one's embodied experience of language, norms, and social codes. What emerges is a *bodily* supplement or, in the least, the supplement of hegemonic representations of *queer bodies*. It is that supplement which speaks; and though its speaking distorts some norms, they still re-contain many queer projects' more radical potential. Supplements do not just open boundaries, in an absolutely liberating deconstructive move. They can also close boundaries again: a deconstruction of the deconstruction caused by the critical body that *insists* on making its historical experience heard. The resultant image of queer commonality thus does not necessarily expand the parameters of who may or may not be included in humanity's new cosmopolis. In the case of the production and reception of Duncan's poetry, subjects who are vulnerable enough to household here must be *like* the embodied homosexual male, must accept an ontologically ethical or politically civil passivity allegorized as gay anality. This vision introduces a form of similarity which insists on a kind of relation that begins to unsettle the identity/difference binary, even though it also inherently excludes other models—erotic or otherwise—of citizenship.

Is such a queer ethic always consigned to political failure, then? I do not want to dismiss it out of hand. After all, "Apprehensions" does supply us another lesson, one much more successfully executed: *even in art, the production of a queer nation can never be completed.* Even in the space of a single poem, Duncan sets out to revise his attempts to queer the American household. Revising is not just a rewriting, but a revisiting—a return to one's foundations. Staging that return in the poem, he models the need for a continual openness and struggle with the "previousness" and "pressure" that form us. One must reprise the struggle to achieve a more inclusive universalism and to revise prevailing liberalist understandings of subjectivity and agency. One must continually note how and why our deconstructive, resistant efforts keep falling short. It may be impossible to definitively upset those primary categories that are violently managed to give the secondary category of nation its sense of stability; however, this is no reason to lose hope. Duncan's career attests to a lifetime of provocatively reimagining the possibilities for a queer*ed* nation that transforms our perceptions of a collective life, a commonality set apart from the nation-state that uses identity logics to manage its citizens' lives and to curb their freedoms. Politicized aesthetic and linguistic processes are always emerging and leaving behind traces of a history of change. Today, we might turn to that evidence, like those traces Duncan gifts us through his poetry and essays, to uncover their ambitions and shortcomings. Instead of denigrating his work for its shortcomings, we should value it, as well as the various failures of other resistant artists, who remain vulnerable by leaving their unsuccessful attempts in plain view, for us to see.

That self-exposure to criticism is what is most remarkable about "Apprehensions." The poem's conclusion registers Duncan's own awareness of the incompleteness, contradictions, and weaknesses of his own critical and ethical effort. Following a trajectory from universalist imaginaries (of Mesopotamian mythology, Renaissance cosmology, etc.) to queer romance (the

Lover), the poem ends up returning readers to a site of homosexual abjection: a cesspool. The normative discourses and traditions limiting Duncan's writing and his critique recur here, nakedly. For that reason, "Apprehensions" is more than a poem that exemplifies how an antiliberalist agency is rooted in forms of passion and passivity, in a vulnerability to texts and language. It also valuably documents the crucial lesson that *we must struggle publicly with the socially and culturally derived limits to which we are always vulnerable.* Moreover, *we must date those struggles*—just as Duncan dates his poem's revelatory final episode—in order to locate them in our own personal histories, in the histories of our embodied experience. Only in this way can we bring private points of consternation, as well as private joys and pleasures, into a public milieu. By negotiating the shortcomings of "Apprehensions" and other queer projects, we can learn what it takes to continue *our* work of forging political—not just poetical—coalitions between primary identity groups, in order to move toward a queer*ed* nation and a queer*ed* humanity. Our challenges of the identity structures that still reify, bind, and contain our bodies, persons, and communities are part of ongoing embodied historical struggles with liberalism and its nation-state. 30 July 2005 / 17 August 2007 / 7 February 2008.

CHAPTER 4

# A Baroque Revolution

## Severo Sarduy's Queer Cosmology

Because queer theory draws on concepts of power (Foucault), *différance* (Derrida), and desire (Lacan, Deleuze), its critiques of identity politics and heteronormativity continue a tradition of what Louis Althusser famously termed "antihumanist thought."[1] Rather than subscribe to a liberalist idea of the *person* whose dignity and rights are determined by an *a priori* human status, a clear identity, and an ability to intervene directly in ethicopolitical domains, queer theorists presume that other forces—language, discourse, ideology, desire, the unconscious, power, history, class, or some combination thereof—mediate social relations and shape the impersonal *subject.* When these concepts are used to further a democratic project via narratives about the lack of meaningful identity and the liberation discovered in shattering the ego, the resultant theories take antihumanist thought to an extreme. Stripped of all personhood and most social substance, the queer subject appears to be a lone actor, trangressively opposed to the society that denies her bliss. In contradistinction, the field of queer studies tends to reject theory in favor of a more sociological approach to identity and community. Yet, it does so because it misconstrues theory's antihumanist premises as only allowing for abstracted, ontological work, at the expense of analyses that accommodate very real differences affecting socially and culturally distinct experiences of queerness. Models of a monolithic queer subject risk racism, ethnocentrism, sexism, gender normativity, and classism because they privilege what Hiram Perez calls a *transparent white subject* (Perez, "You Can Have My Brown Body and Eat It, Too!").[2] Although such a metaphysics is undesirable, problems still inhere in queer studies' own adoption of a sociologically informed epistemology that stresses identities and communities as they exist. Despite the fact that its proponents say they offer "the most innovative and risky work on globalization, neoliberalism, cultural politics, subjectivity, identity, family, and kinship," queer studies tends to leave unexamined the liberalist tenets framing how we understand each of those social elements (David L. Eng, Judith Halberstam, and José Estaban Muñoz, *What's So Queer*, 2). Positivistic treatments of identity and community are therefore as unsatisfactory as queer theorists' determination to unravel or jettison those terms.

There is an alternative, however, and it comes in revisiting antihumanism as a theoretic dialogue about ethics and collectivity that originates in, and that is responsive to, the exigencies of a particular sociopolitical milieu. In this way, ontology meets sociohistorical realism in a critical fashion. Through the Cuban writer, painter, and art critic Severo Sarduy, I offer one narrow point of entry into such a rereading. Exiled in Paris from 1960 until his death in 1993, Sarduy imagined queerness and commonality as beginning in the *absence* of a national homeland or even of a household, such as the one valued by Robert Duncan (chapter 3 above). Rather than a geopolitical premise for commonality, he strives to transform *language* into an eroticized and power-driven space one might inhabit to work through the limits of identity and difference. Such an ambition demanded that he undermine the propriety and individualism supporting liberalism's formal fiction, a task for which Sarduy depended on his own appropriations of French antihumanism. Below I read a brief period in Sarduy's poetics and poetry—from 1969 to 1974, from the essays of *Escrito sobre un cuerpo* (*Written on a Body*) through the poetry of *Big Bang*—as a distinctly *postcolonial* and *queer* contribution to antihumanist discourse. Never did he imagine himself as just applying structuralist or poststructuralist thought to his writing. As he put it in a 1991 interview, "I had to invent another language, a metalanguage in order to talk about my work and not fool around, so to speak, with those terms that are purely tautological, purely useless with respect to my fiction" ("Mudo combate contra el vacío," 364).[3] The resultant "metalanguage" constitutes a critical bridge between French theory, a post-Revolutionary Cuban condition, and a thinking of difference through queer erotics. Sarduy's project furthers our sense of how literature contributes to the cultivation of an eroticism that produces a vulnerable openness to human actors *and* impersonal forces through one's body.

At times the connections Sarduy makes between ontological ethics and material realities may seem vague and indistinct, but ultimately those links render his queer antihumanism especially important to *particular* sexualized and geopolitically marked bodies. Concentrating, as I do here, on his interest in embodiment and materiality already runs contrary to how most have read him. The majority of critics comment that *the baroque* is his central conceit, and that it culminates in the quintessentially "postmodern" concept of the simulacrum, as he develops that concept in the essay collection *La simulación* (*Simulation,* 1982). The few critics who have been interested in Sarduy as a queer thinker usually begin with *Simulation*'s contestation of identity structures through the figure of the transvestite and through his elaboration on the Lacanian concepts of the gaze and anamorphosis. For instance, Ben Sifuentes-Jáuregui has remarked recently that Sarduy's "transvestite narrative defines the homographetic markings in his work." This transgender account supposedly supplies the point from which Sarduy engages an unrestrained, queer metonymic play that demonstrates the "privileged position that the author enjoys" (*Transvestism, Masculinity, and Latin American Literature*, 135). Invoking (and misrepresenting) Lee Edelman's concept of *homographesis,* Sifuentes-Jáuregui erroneously attributes to Sarduy the capacity for an agentic, performative resignification of identity scripts.[4] The author himself is read as in absolute control of the text. By no means are such assessments of a paradoxically sovereign simulation new. Long before *Simulation* appeared, Sarduy was either reproached or praised by critics for the seemingly autonomous and transgressive nature of his ludic style.[5] If queer theory were to settle for such readings, we would be using this Cuban forebear simply to reproduce the field's frequent, problematic slippage into a metaphysics based on fluid performativity.[6] We also would end up overlooking *Simulation*'s thin postmodernism, which Emilio Bejel rightly warns evinces Sarduy's stubborn persistence in trying to overcome history and the Symbolic despite his own recognition of how those forces limit and define his queer body.[7]

A careful reading of *Simulation* that continues where Bejel leaves off would reveal that, even in the late writings' predominant rhetoric of postmodern play and its theoretical focus on virtuality and appearance, the body actually does function in Sarduy's thought as a material site, limited and affected by social norms. Instead of lost or dissipated, bodies resurface as haunting presences that challenge the apparent naturalness of the symbolic order, including normative liberalist ideas about agency and will. Take the following passage from *Simulation* as a case in point: "Relating transvestites' *corporal work* to a simple cosmetic mania, to feminization or homosexuality, is simply naïve: these things are nothing more than the apparent borders of a limitless metamorphosis, its 'natural' screen" (*OC* 2: 1298; emphasis in original). Bodies are the screens, the media on which performativity occurs. By rejecting an originary ontology that ties the signifier *feminine* to a particular kind of bodily signified, *Simulation* presages Judith Butler's argument in *Gender Trouble* that "acts and gestures, articulated and enacted desires create the illusion of an interior and organizing gender core." For Butler, as for Sarduy, drag exemplifies how "the gendered body" actually "has no ontological status apart from the various acts which constitute its reality" (136). Oscar Montero usefully characterizes such a performativity modeled on the simulacra of drag as allowing Sarduy to "rescue the banished body, not in its specular totality but as a fragment" and as "a by-product, a residue, of writing" ("The Signifying Queen," 170). In Latin American contexts, queer subjects "seek fables of origin, on which and against which to write" but instead are confronted with "omissions and absences" of bodies marked as queer (165). Sarduy's performativity supplies such origins. At the same time, he emphasizes their fabulousness—in both a literal and campy sense—due to the fragmentation of bodies and egos. In this way, his emphasis on baroque style consciously furthers Lezama's theorization of that aesthetic style as rooted in an ethical appreciation of the fragmentary (chapter 2 above). Even more importantly, his predecessor taught him that that ethic is founded on how the fragment solicits a mode of *passionate*, rather than agentic or transgressive, engagement.

If we read Sarduy against the grain of his own later rhetoric about "postmodernism" and "simulation" and "revolution," we can discover how antihumanism paradoxically helps him *ethically rehumanize* the subject by bodily locating it in an expansive textual universe that is as material as it is linguistic. His tropings seduce us, invite us not just to read his texts with pleasure but also to *cruise him*. On the scene of the page, we become newly aware of our own embodied condition and conscious of our erotic and material ties to both the text and the outside world. My unorthodox reading necessitates focusing on an *earlier* moment in Sarduy's career, when his nonfiction prose was less focused on topically queer issues like transvestism and struggled more with issues of agency, resistance, and eroticism. His readings of the period's French antihumanist thinkers, who were his friends and teachers, are historicized engagements with an intellectual and political phenomenon. The recurrent motif of revolution helps situate his oeuvre in a site encapsulating the shift in post-1968 French activism and philosophy from political radicalism to a reformist ethics.[8] Sarduy's preferred sense of the word "revolution" hinges on its secondary meaning: *a turning of one body around another.* This astronomical metaphor is politicized insofar as it opens new imaginings of home and collectivity. Much gay and lesbian politics, as well as queer thought, assumes that disenfranchised subjects desire a place among a nation's citizenry. Sarduy, though, signals that such a home is *always* an imaginary experience for the marginalized, just as it was for him and other exiles. When one imagines home, one need not embark on a nostalgic return to what was once known. Instead, one perpetually departs to discover new cosmologies where others' bodies echo one's self.

## The Structuralist Resignification of "Revolution" for Postcolonial Writers

Through French theoretical discourse, Sarduy queerly reflects and distorts the conventionally humanist precepts governing Latin American ideals of independence, as well as North American (and conservative French) liberalist ideals of democratic citizenry. Both of these factors had produced an incorrigible Cold War drive toward contained nationalism. In his own experience, post-Revolutionary Cuba, with its totalitarian and repressive and bureaucratic administration, was the nightmare reality of such a nationalistic attitude. He uses French thought to scrutinize and reveal the flaws of liberalist idealizations of the citizen's dignity, of a national collectivity that reflects an undivided social body, and of heroic manhood (particularly as theorized and exemplified by Ernesto "Che" Guevara). Contrary to what René Prieto has argued, I do not read Sarduy as "caught in the prison of the master texts" written by his continental contemporaries (*Body of Writing*, 172). No, his project purposefully *distorts* both the antihumanism he appropriates and the liberalism that philosophy opposed. In this way, he transforms that body of critical thought into a nearly unrecognizable theory of eroticized exilic or postnational writing, which better reflects the postcolonial roots of his own thinking, its Cubanness.

Rolando Pérez's admonition is worth repeating: "The failure to take Sarduy's opposition to nationhood seriously is perhaps the worst form of betrayal" ("Severo Sarduy," 131). Sarduy's interest in originary catastrophes and subsequent dispersals—including the loss of a unitary language, the proliferation of simulacra, and the cosmological Big Bang theory—are metaphorical displacements of the historical event that led to his exile and thus motivated his literary production: the Cuban Revolution. Forbidden from reentering Cuba after the government refused to renew his passport in 1966, charged with treason as early as 1968, and accused of being a CIA operative in the 1970s, Sarduy had every reason to be critical of the Cold War Cuban state. Roberto González Echevarría has read him as continually working through the "catastrophe" of "exile, ex-isle, of leaving the island" to work his way back home (*La ruta de Severo Sarduy*, 5). Sarduy's writing does register his distance from Cuban historical actualities. Neither realist nor positivist, the critique of the nation-state he develops is *ontological* in nature and is informed by French structuralism and ethnology.[9] However, rather than read him as González Echevarría does, as engaging a parodic and nostalgic recovery of his missing geopolitical center, I see Sarduy as using that distance to his advantage to comment on modern subjects' ontological condition as *generally exilic.* In other words, his particular experience provides him with a point from which he expands, even universalizes, a theory of subjectivity befitting his postcolonial world. In that expansion from a limited sociohistorical critique to an ontological one, Sarduy leaves his ideas open enough so that others might find their similarities with his own subjectivity; yet, he leaves behind sufficient material traces to make it impossible to forget the motivating factors of his project. Instead of going back to Cuba, of contracting to a missing and irrecoverable origin, his work explores how *expansion* might help him find a home *elsewhere.*

The very act of writing that dispersal constitutes a re-visioning of political possibility. "El barroco y el neobarroco" ("The Baroque and the Neobaroque," 1972), an essay Sarduy wrote for the Mexican collection *América Latina en su literatura*, abruptly closes with the fragmentary phrase: "Baroque of the Revolution" (*OC* 2: 1404). The essay opens as curiously as it ends, with Sarduy's proviso that he is not continuing the tradition of an "irrepressible metonymization" which has rendered the definition of *baroque* vague. Instead, he expresses greater interest in outlining a "restricted" meaning for the aesthetic term, one that "reduces it to a precise operative scheme" with particular relevance to Latin American arts (*OC* 2: 1386). He uncharacteristically classifies types of baroque writing in such a schematic fashion that the essay verges on the boring, a term Sarduy, not so incidentally, uses to describe the style.[10] A theoretic playfulness, even seductiveness, enters the conclusion of the piece, though, where that odd final phrase surfaces. This ending supplies "The Baroque and the Neobaroque" with what Sarduy would describe two years later in *Barroco* (*Baroque*, 1974) as the second center that gives the aforementioned style its elliptical structure. "Something is decentered, or even better, duplicates its center, doubles it; now the master-figure is no longer the circle with a unique, radiating, luminescent and paternal center, but the ellipse which opposes that visible focus with another equally functioning one, equally real but obstructed, dead, nocturnal, the blind center, the reverse of the Sun's germinating Yang, the absent" (*OC* 2: 1223). The presumed authority of the center, of the sovereign, is disrupted by a second focus that demands equal attention, even if it remains in the master-signifier's shadow. The opposition of the circle and ellipse allegorically represents what Sarduy once called "the underlying battle" of "Western civilization" (Interview with González Echevarria, 42). As the preferred style for Latin American arts, the baroque and its elliptical revolution does not just overthrow master forms. Rather, it maintains a productive struggle between two foci: between a dominant colonizing discourse and an occluded, postcolonial one.

A key contributing factor to the postcolonial resistance of the baroque is the style's *eroticism.*[11] "The baroque space is that of overabundance and waste. Contrary to communicative, economic, austere language reduced to its functionality—serving as a vehicle for information—baroque language indulges itself [*se complace*] in the supplement, in the excess and partial loss of its object" (*OC* 2: 1401). Predicated on a wasteful, even onanistic and self-pleasuring, expenditure of words, Sarduy's baroque is an erotic mode of linguistic contact that need not *communicate* anything. Instead, it heaps signifier on signifier in an "obsessive repetition of a useless thing," an excess he analogically compares to both Derrida's supplement and Lacan's *objet petit a.* "This game" discovers and promotes a nonutilitarian and noncommunicative eroticism in its exposure of the artifice of culture, its refusal to participate in language's "reproductive elements," and its pursuit of "waste, in the function of pleasure." Such linguistic play aims for "total rupture at the denotative, direct, and natural level of language—*somatic*—, like the perversion that implicates all metaphor, all figuration" (*OC* 2: 1402; emphasis added). Although seemingly immaterial language practices are the source and site of such erotic play, they really are quite embodied pleasures. Expanding on Lacan, however, Sarduy clarifies that such pleasure is not willful transgression but merely "a structural reflection of a desire that cannot reach its object." Moreover, the supplements it disseminates do not clearly articulate "the disharmony, the rupture of homogeneity" of a supposedly "absolute" *logos*; they merely expose "the lack that constitutes our epistemic foundation" (*OC* 2: 1403). Through an ontological, rather than properly political, operation, the baroque's stylized but unwilled proliferation of language to interrupt norms has the effect of shifting receptive, embodied subjects' consciousness.

The postcolonial force of "The Baroque and the Neobaroque" owes to this brief and performative concluding section, this second center, where Sarduy is both theoretical *and* elliptical. Combining the seemingly irreconcilable theories of Lacan and Derrida, his obtuse theorizations fall short of clearly communicating his own ideas. More interestingly, this has the effect of frustrating his own essay's earlier, meticulously outlined explanation of how other Latin American artists have fabricated baroque styles. Thus, Sarduy performatively demonstrates—not just schematically describes—how the baroque can be "at times strident, boring, and chaotic" (*OC* 2: 1404). By his essay's own example, revolution is tied to a textual eroticism, a performativity that draws the reader in. It is quite distinct, then, from the agentic voluntarism with which projects of democratic liberation are usually associated. Voiced by a Cuban exile, the essay's final phrase—"Baroque of the Revolution"—cannot help being read as a deflating invocation of the *fidelistas'* (and for his Mexican audience, the *Zapatistas'*) political cry: *¡Viva la Revolución!* It is a distorting echo. With it, Sarduy renders Latin America and its citizen-subjects unrecognizable, for his ideal revolutionary is erotically invested, playful, and wasteful. This erotic and passionate subject avoids the prerogative of (socialist) realism and *testimonio.*

Even when he was involved in the resistive Cuban vanguardist publications of *Ciclón* and *Lunes de Revolución,* he was indifferent to politicized radicalism per se.[12] Sarduy's sense of *revolution* is closer to Michel Foucault's notion that "the real political task in a society such as ours is to criticize the workings of institutions, which appear to be both neutral and independent," a praxis of unveiling otherwise hidden mechanisms of power (Foucault and Noam Chomsky, *The Chomsky-Foucault Debate on Human Nature*, 41). Writing is key to that praxis. *Tel Quel* introduced a brand of antihumanist commitment that appealed to the young Cuban exile. In a 1966 interview (published only in 1977), Sarduy comments that Philippe Sollers and the other authors associated with the journal "rejected [the idea of] literature as something backed by 'what's said,' what's described, the *message,* etc. They do not think, as is very often thought by storytellers from our America, that the message is enough for writing well. . . . Later Sollers and his friends came to think that writing, even when it seems to say something else, is really writing, the first thing it reflects is that, precisely that: the *act of writing,* with its own structures and what I believe is its own ontological dimension" (*OC* 2: 1809; emphasis in original). As he would note elsewhere around the same time, literature is an "an art of tattooing," "the art of proliferation," and "the language that thinks us" (*WB* 41, 42). In other words, literature re-marks existing bodies (thus causing a loss of "natural" identity), forms new subjects, and makes possible self-reflexive thought. Comprising an ethical practice, an *ascēsis,* writing is an alternative mode of social commitment.

Sarduy's linking of revolution to writing expands on other *Tel Quel* authors' critiques of Jean-Paul Sartre's understanding of writing and engagement. In this way, he explores how the second life of existentialist philosophy at the heart of postcolonial nationalism limits the possibilities for creating new subjects. If we read his baroque aesthetic as he asks us to throughout most of his career—that is, as an extension of Lezama's poetics—and if his predecessor's baroque also draws on María Zambrano's own contestations of Sartre's ideas (chapter 2), then Sarduy ought to be read as using a French critical idiom to elaborate a *distinctly Cuban* critique of revolutionary existentialism whose emphasis on sovereign action also resonated with a *norteamericano* imperative of liberalist individualism. For an exile like Sarduy, Sartre's name also would have been associated with a betrayal of revolutionary possibility. In 1960, the French philosopher awarded Fidel Castro a certificate of good conduct, which, in the global South's eyes, conferred philosophical legitimacy on the Cuban leader's past as well as future policies. According to Jacobo Machover, the memory of this event would haunt later generations of Cuban authors. It seemingly authorized Castro's later declarations that Cuban literature must support the Revolution, an edict in line with Sartrean notions about realism and positivism as the only truly "committed" forms of literary writing ("La memoria frente al poder," 41). Sarduy would hold no truck with such conservative ideas about literature. Indeed, the Cuban state would not renew his passport when he terminated his medical studies in Europe because the first novel he published in France, *Gestos* (1963), was declared "counterrevolutionary." This refusal effectually forced him into exile. Existentialism thus presented more than merely a theoretic problem for Sarduy. It also implicitly endorsed a problematic *political* program of agency, sovereignty, and insularity that alienated writers like him either from their homelands or, if they capitulated to the state's prescriptions, from their own aesthetic sensibilities.

Sarduy's rethinking of existentialism begins with his extension of structuralism's own early opposition to Sartrean notions of the relation between writing and political or ethical engagement. Following Jean-Michel Rabaté's lead, we should date the full appropriation of antihumanist thought by literary theory to the publication of Roland Barthes's *Writing Degree Zero* (1953), portions of which appeared in journals the same year as the publication of the essay that spurred it, Sartre's *What Is Literature?* (1947).[13] Barthes valued style as a key feature of literature for reasons similar to those cited by the existentialist in his devaluation of it. Style is "always secret" and "is recollection locked within the body of the writer" (*Writing Degree Zero*, 12). Rather than believing that such secrecy and embodiment causes the writer to withdraw from politics, however, Barthes argued that style is tied to the writer's singularity. Thus, it causes her to register her individualism in "a general choice of tone, of ethos," that signals how she "commits himself [*sic*]" to the world around her (ibid., 13). Her self enters History (with a capital "H") and her writing assumes a worldly relevance because she makes choices while composing, choices that insert her work into a history of literary styles. Such decisions implicitly lead to "the affirmation of a certain Good" because they perform "an act of historical solidarity" with others' precedents (ibid., 14). Style—what is proper to the individual—thus entails a social consciousness. It brings the writer into a historical continuum that challenges tradition and demonstrates freedom, albeit a freedom that lasts but "a mere moment" because the individual always contends with the History (capital "H") that co-opts her work and reduces it through socially understandable interpretations (ibid., 17).

Modern poetry presents the most stylized language, which asymptotically approaches a *zero degree* of signification.[14] Each word is a thing in itself that "obscures the relations existing in the world"; its objectivity disrupts all relational norms. Barthes warns that "these poetic words exclude men: there is no humanism of modern poetry" (50). Poetry does not re-present the world as humanity defines it: it is a primordial Nature, in which every relational potentiality between things is revealed and exemplified by language's own indifferent, inhuman objectivity. Barthes held little hope for writing—especially modern literary writing—to be political, conventionally speaking. At its extreme, zero degree writing would not even be ethical: words' "violent drive toward autonomy destroys any ethical scope" (51). Such a poetic absolute, though, is actually an impossibility that only theory can imagine. If this absolute limit is never actualized, even according to Barthes's own logic, then writing is *inevitably* committed. Although he is caught up in the ethereal dream of degree zero, Barthes is well aware that literary writing invariably incorporates the author as an ethical actor, even as a person, into the fabric of history. It cannot be helped. The momentary freedom the author's body discovers in writing demonstrates a constrained, yet necessary, solidarity with past writers and future readers. That alignment offsets the writer's ability to disappear into an indifferent, impersonal linguistic order.

Interested in finding some way of addressing the status of the postrevolutionary Cuban citizen-subject while speaking in a structuralist fashion so as to supersede a particular geopolitical context, the young Sarduy was drawn to the possibilities of extending Lezama's antiliberalism through antihumanism's own critique of existentialism. In a section of *Written on a Body* published in 1967 in the journal *Mundo Nuevo*, he makes the following aside: "Writing about the *subject* is writing about *language*, which is to say, thinking about the relation or coincidence of the two, knowing that the space of one is the space of the other, that language is never (as Sartre believed) just a *practico-inert* used by the subject to express itself, because, on the contrary, the subject is what constitutes language—or, if you prefer, both are illusory" (*WB* 17–18). Here he extends an ongoing critique of Sartrean concepts and even anticipates by one year Barthes's formulation of the subject's constitution by the act of writing in "The Death of the Author": "The modern *scriptor* is born *at the same time* as his text; he is not furnished with a being which precedes or exceeds his writing, he is not the subject of which his book would be the predicate" (Barthes, *The Rustle of Language*, 52; emphasis in original). As Sarduy continues with his analysis of the Marquis de Sade and Georges Bataille and Giancarlo Marmori, he argues that, for centuries, modern literatures have investigated ontology through a stylized language that aids authors in their inquiries into the nature of "man." In this tradition, "in spite of the resistance they faced man is placed on a plane of literalness previously off limits, thereby formulating that question about his own being, about his *humanity* that is above all the question about the being of his writing" (*WB* 22; emphasis in original; translation emended).[15] Through their language practices, these authors open routes of ethical inquiry that can produce previously unimaginable subjects. Humanist traditions and definitions of personhood are consequently thrown into question.

Alongside the aforementioned notable Europeans, Sarduy adds contemporary Latin American writers Julio Cortázar and Salvador Elizondo. This new canon establishes Southern literature's role in the radical reconceptualization of humanity according to an antihumanist ethic realized through eroticized stylistic writing, rather than a Sartrean politics realized through the person. Implicitly, Sarduy struggles to render the embodied postcolonial writer, as well as the bodies her work calls into being, less transparent. Then they can be used to revise late modernity's general ontology. Still enamored of a "subject" (albeit an embodied one), though, Sarduy dangerously flirts with a structuralist line of thought that threatens to erase the postcolonial subject's visibility and difference. That risk would be remedied in the years that followed.

## May '68 and Sarduy's Distorting Turn from Revolution to Revolving Bodies

*Written on the Body* was published in 1968, the same year that social actions erupted in France. Like the structuralism informing that first nonfiction project, Sarduy's poetic was changed by those events. In May and June, Paris was immobilized by a general strike. Nonviolent protests and other, more violent incidents occurred in the streets. Students took over high schools and universities, while workers seized control of factories. *Comités d'action* were established to inaugurate self-management and participatory democracies in institutions ranging from schools to factories to hospitals. Self-published pamphlets called for further actions. Broadsides and posters, as well as graffiti, plastered the walls of buildings declaring a new cultural and political era, a time when, as one famous slogan put it, *It is forbidden to forbid.* President Charles de Gaulle responded by ordering the erection of barricades and the deployment of police forces to the Latin Quarter. The National Assembly was dissolved, and de Gaulle ordered new elections for parliamentary representatives. In this brief period of insurgency, traditional politics, based on a prohibitive law and an economic conservatism, were revealed to be insufficient. A change was sought. Another slogan encapsulated this revolutionary moment: *Be realistic, demand the impossible.* Inspirited by Situationism's anarchism, many believed "that a liberated politics could only emerge from liberated interpersonal relationships and that structured, impersonal political organizations could not respond to the problems of alienation in an over-structured society" (Sherry Turkle, *Psychoanalytic Politics*, 63). The actions registered a discontent with the routes of resistance open to radical party politics through such organizations as the PCF (Parti Communiste Français). To call May '68 a cultural revolution misses the point. *Culture is the inversion of life,* another slogan ran. Clearly, it was imagined as life's revolution.

Initially, the connections between the political actions and the intellectual scene dominated by French structuralism were tenuous at best. Militants espoused a liberalist humanism, and, as Sherry Turkle notes, "Structuralism was associated with mechanistic determinism" that activists regarded "unfavorably" (*Psychoanalytic Politics,* 72). Consequently, as the skeptics Luc Ferry and Alain Renaut have cynically claimed, it seems that only a "rather unlikely blindness," a willful ignorance of the strikers' anarchism and voluntarism, allowed antihumanists to ally themselves and their theories with the May events (*French Philosophy of the Sixties*, 32). "How can we view the coexistence of this philosophy . . . with a historical movement where the claims of the Ego against the System are at the most basic level of conviction?" (ibid., 64) Equating the individualist spirit of the resistances with liberalism is misguided, however. Julian Bourg, for one, sees May '68 as evidence of the critical disjunction between liberalism and democracy: "In gross terms liberalism sees the individual and rights at the heart of political life, and democracy focuses on legal and social equality" (*From Revolution to Ethics,* 39). This fine distinction causes him to qualify the activists' individualism as an ethical pursuit of collective democratic ends, what we might call a means of *living together.*[16]

After the resistances of May '68 failed to produce a successful and lasting revolution, many became less skeptical about antihumanism. Perhaps, after all, it did not simply embrace impersonal institutions and bureaucracy. Lacanian psychoanalysis, which began to influence Sarduy even earlier, was especially important to this general change of attitude. Activists in the late 1960s and early 1970s appreciated its "theory of the construction of a symbolic order, when language and law enters man" because it "allows for no real boundary between self and society: man becomes social with the appropriation of language that constitutes man as a subject" (Turkle, *Psychoanalytic Politics*, 74). Naïve celebrations of complete autonomy, humanistic dignity, and liberalist possibility were questionable. The failed "revolution" had proven that humanity could not be facilely dissociated from social discourses and institutions. A more nuanced belief in "the power of the word" emerged (ibid., 80). That nuance extended from activism into antihumanist thought. Rather than wholly dismiss the individual, French theorists' antiliberalist critiques more nakedly *reassessed* individualism and humanism. Language may have limited personhood and agency, but it also produced new possibilities for ethically understanding both; and with those possibilities came new political freedoms. Although Sarduy was more inclined to parody the Maoism of May '68 than hop on its bandwagon as other *Tel Quel* contributors did, his longtime belief in the ethical power of the word now had more cultural and political legitimacy. This setting also enabled him to cultivate and refine elements of his literary structuralism. Sarduy would begin to imagine language as wielding a *cosmological* force. That is, literary writing can create new universes that may be shared between writer and readers. Sarduy was still wary of equating such vitalist concerns with a liberalist or existentialist emphasis on the person, rather than an antihumanist emphasis on the subject. Yet May '68 helped illuminate how subjectivity and personhood coincide at the site of the body. Sarduy stresses bodies' *materiality* to account for agency without unduly emphasizing liberalist or existentialist personhood, all while minding the contextual exigencies and individual singularities that compel writing.

To negotiate this fine line, Sarduy's post-1968 writing, beginning with the extended essay *Baroque* (1974), thematically concentrates on celestial, rather than human, bodies. We can imagine several reasons why he would find astronomical figures attractive. For one, their orbital movements add a new connotation to the word *revolution*. Rather than connoting political upheaval, the term now primarily signifies the turning of one body around another. As he outlines in his opening discussions of the move from Galileo's and Copernicus's centrist models of revolution to Kepler's elliptical one, astronomy helps us see how revolution—in all its senses—experiences paradigmatic changes. Also, because cosmology entails concerns with the universe, this conceit refigures the universalism condemned by most structuralists and poststructualists. As a postcolonial and queer thinker, out of necessity Sarduy is concerned with expanding the parameters of the human universe; but he persistently conceives of universality in his preferred ontological terms, rather than in liberalism's particularistic and humanistic ones. The treatise's last sections move from astronomy to cosmology, as Sarduy outlines two contemporary models of the origin of the universe: the theories of the Big Bang (an originary event that produced atomic matter to form a continually expanding universe) and the Steady State (matter and energy are neither created nor destroyed, merely transformed). From the latter, he would go on to develop his more famous "postmodern" theories of simulation in the early 1980s. In the 1970s, though, Sarduy was more concerned with the parallels between the elliptical astronomical model informing baroque style and the cosmological Big Bang model of material bodies that appear, then disappear as they withdraw from their origin.[17] Those analogies suggest that his embodied ethic sits on the cusp of humanism and antihumanism, political revolution and ethical ontology.

Echoing May '68 revolutionary rhetoric, Sarduy distorted it enough to accommodate his ontological theory. My metaphor of the echo resonates with *Baroque*'s epigraph, where Sarduy redefines *retombée*—the French for landing, rebounding, or falling again—as: "achronistic causality, noncontiguous isomorphism, or a consequence of something that has not even been produced, a likeness with something that does not even exist" (*OC* 2: 1196). Changes in how people imagine planetary rotation or the beginnings of the universe are not chronologically progressive "revolutions" that affect only one discourse community.[18] Instead, the history of verbal, visual, and architectural arts demonstrates stylistic shifts that echo scientific theories about the universe, and vice versa.[19] Neither is originary; only analogies exist between roughly contemporaneous discourses. These epistemological similarities reveal a way of thinking shared across different fields of experience. They even show how power operates in a fashion that can be ontologically generalized to establish similarities between different institutions and contexts during a historical epoch. If the world of art echoes the world of astronomy, it is not such a logical leap to assert that a postcolonial revolution might echo the recent French one. As the arc of his astronomical and aesthetic discussions highlights, though, such echoing does not merely reproduce or transplant ideas or praxes. This *retombée* of analogous ideas in unrelated discourses and fields distorts both foci just enough in order to reveal their differences.

Sarduy subjected his own work to this same displacing and supplementary logic. Part Five of *Baroque* reproduces the earlier "The Baroque and the Neobaroque"'s conclusion, in its entirety. By titling this section "Supplement," Sarduy does more than indicate that it is an appendix. He also invokes Jacques Derrida's deconstructive theory and calls on his readers to use it to connect his two texts while deconstructively ascertaining their differences. Thus contemporary Latin American literature, which was the explicit focus of his earlier essay, is related to his present consideration of European baroque art and the discoveries of baroque astronomy. In this fashion, *Baroque* instantiates an echo that distorts the geopolitical limits of the first text: the postcolonial specificity of his earlier discussion of an aesthetic style is now ontologically abstracted. That universalism—rooted in a *materiality*—also implicitly signals a need to consider spatial and temporal forms of particularity, context, situation, location. On the one hand, this move seems to let Sarduy irresponsibly skirt issues of identity by concentrating on material bodies and general models that are ineffective for postcolonial thought. On the other hand, it also lets him gesture toward the idea that universalism need not promote only the primacy of a metaphysical and transparent (North American or European, white, straight, bourgeois) subject.

Another effect is registered in this distortion of his earlier work. As we have already seen, "The Baroque and the Neobaroque" appropriates Derrida's concept of the supplement and aligns it with Lacan's *objet petit a*. This configuration refigures the supplement as the site at which eroticism enters the scene of writing. When that earlier discussion of eroticism, revolution, and supplementarity later supplements a cosmological and aesthetic discussion meant to trope a French revolutionary ethic, the revolving bodies in Sarduy's oblique narrative about postcolonial universalism via *Baroque*'s discussion of astronomy and cosmology is transfigured into an ethical narrative about the resistive force of *eroticized bodies*. Literature provides a revolutionary and eroticized universe lying beyond the looking glass; it is a supplement, or an alternate ontology, that lets us see our bodies and social lives differently. Writing is a mode of commitment that queers the common, so as to render humanity more perversely different though not necessarily inhuman. Antihumanism is important insofar as it indicates that the queerness of this transformative process is detached from sexual identity and community, as they're known. But personal elements do creep back in because two bodies, two persons, are involved in a codependent relationship, a turning about one another, which resignifies and distorts revolution, collectivity, and personhood. The full implications of that distortion can only be fully appreciated if we read *Baroque* as Sarduy's performative echo and expansion of yet another origin: the post-'68 queer and ethical turn of his structuralist mentor, Roland Barthes.

## The Pleasure of the ~~Text~~ Author's Body

In a late interview, Sarduy maintained that homosexuality is just a matter of "personal taste" and so should not be associated with "any special connotation or value, either positive or negative." He regarded it as neither a "subversion" nor "a virtue" ("Una autobiografía pulverizada," 38). Given his antihumanist and antiexisentialist leanings, his refusal to politically identify as gay and his resistance to the idea of the inherently transgressive nature of homosexuality are not surprising. What is striking, though, is his persistent characterization of *writing* as subversive, transgressive, and revolutionary—terms that do resonate with the rhetoric of the gay revolutionary politics that emerged in France alongside the antipsychiatric movement in the early 1970s. The principles of that sexual movement are perhaps best known from Guy Hocquenghem's *Homosexual Desire* (1972), a lengthy manifesto for the Front Homosexuel d'Action Révolutionnaire (FHAR). Reading sexual politics through Gilles Deleuze and Félix Guattari's *Anti-Oedipus* (1972), Hocquenghem upholds male same-sex practices—particularly anal sex—as transgressing phallocentrism: "Only the phallus dispenses identity; any social use of the anus, apart from its sublimated use, creates the risk of a loss of identity. Seen from behind we are all women [i.e., subjects who lack a proper 'personhood' since they are lacking access to the identity-granting phallus]; the anus does not practice sexual discrimination" (*Homosexual Desire,* 101). Anality supposedly leads to revolutionary universality, but Hocquenghem problematically relies on a homosexual identity defined and circumscribed by heteronormative ideologies. Consequently, even he is more reformist than revolutionary.[20]

A more astute reader of Deleuze and Guattari than Hocquenghem, Sarduy would have recognized that their idea of revolution actually consists of something other than the liberation of the individual or an identity group. Instead, *Anti-Oedipus* promotes the liberation of *desire*, which is otherwise contained by a liberal idealization of personhood. Such an impersonal revolution inheres in the libidinally driven production of language and a "deterritorialization" of extant sociocultural codes.[21] Sarduy's fellow *Tel Quel* contributor Julia Kristeva positively appraised Deleuze and Guattari in *Revolution in Poetic Language* (1974), applauding their idea of the unconscious's revolutionary force but criticizing their social theory as overly dependent on literary examples. What is needed, she argues, is a literary theory *distinct* from politics: "The text is a practice that could be compared to political revolution: the one brings about in the subject what the other introduces into society" (17). Texts are revolutionary only insofar as they introduce a different experience of desire to disrupt social norms and train, and thus subjectivate, new revolutionary subjects. Rather than subscribe to any belief that writing could liberate homosexuals, Sarduy, like Kristeva, was interested in literature's liberation of desire. Writing might act as an impersonal force to facilitate queer subjectivation. Insofar as his hypothetical writer is a "subject" rather than a "person," and insofar as his likening of human bodies to astronomical ones seems to strip them down to their ontological foundations, Sarduy could be called an antihumanist. Yet even though he favors "impersonal" concepts like eroticism and pleasure over a "personal" rhetoric of sexual identity, the distinction is difficult to sustain. Both the impersonal and the personal intersect at the site of the *body*, to which Sarduy does not hesitate to call our attention. At once private and public, person and subject, the written re-presentation of the writer's body causes readers to rethink prevalent liberal and liberalist attitudes. Writing ushers in the emergent singularity of the author who, despite actual physical absence, becomes virtually present through the text. Readers, seductively enticed by the text, help along this process of realizing the writer's body by engaging the writing.[22] Consequently, there is a human element, an *amorous intimacy*, accompanying the impersonal erotics of writing and reading. A curious combination of humanism and antihumanism, this intimacy is the unintended strength of Sarduy's queer ethic. We might call it his ethicopolitical unconscious, an unarticulated link supplementing the resistant French political climate.

That link surfaces immediately in *Baroque*, with Sarduy's naming of Roland Barthes as its dedicatee (*OC* 2: 1196). Jacques Lacan imagined his subject as a perversion of the Cartesian *cogito*: "I am not wherever I am the plaything of my thought; I think of what I am where I do not think to think" (*Écrits*, 168). Similarly, the Cuban insists that the baroque subject "is not where it is expected—in the site where an I visibly governs the discourse that is enunciated—but there where no one knows to look for it—under the elided signifier that the *I* believes to have expelled, in that *I* believed to be expelled" (*OC* 2: 1237).[23] In *Baroque*, Barthes's name is that elided signifier. Together, he and Sarduy make up "the subject in its constitutive division," the Lacanian split subject that emerges with the reversal of the ego's repressions and suppressions of otherness (*OC* 2: 1237). Sarduy thus literalizes Charles Baudelaire's dictum that the reader is the author's double, an embodied similarity (*mon sembable*). Unlike Baudelaire's *frère*, though, Barthes supplies a queer charge. As D. A. Miller argues, the queerness of his own writing resides in its dual performance of "sublimating gay content" and "undoing the sublimation" through form. So, queerness for Barthes is less a matter of identificatory practices than the stylized production of an eroticized "paradigm" (*Bringing Out Roland Barthes*, 27). If Lezama gifted Sarduy a model for the Latin American baroque as a committed postcolonial resistance to existentialism and liberalism, then Barthes helped him link the eroticism of that style to a queer ethic.[24]

In light of what Sarduy writes about baroque astronomy and art as organized around the elliptical figuration of two foci, one of which partially suppresses, occults, or represses the other, the essay's dedication obliges us to read his relation to Barthes in the following way: the supposedly sovereign author is doubled in the suppressed figure of the reader. The suppression of his presence as the essay's second center is not an erasure. Sarduy's specification of Barthes as his intended audience makes *Baroque*'s argument all the more elliptical. His name forces us to displace the author's authority, to read Sarduy's tenets about the revolutionary eroticism of baroque writing against themselves. After May '68, affected by the revolutionaries' rhetoric of liberalist and personal politics but unwilling to surrender antihumanist ideas about structures and systems, Barthes had opened a space for thinking critically about the personal and intimate experience complementing writing: reading. This shift in emphasis from authorship to reception marks what I see as his personally vested turn from a scientistic, impersonal structuralism to a curious blend of antihumanism and humanistic hermeneutics, all in order to appeal more to audiences in the wake of '68.[25] In "Writing Reading" (1970), Barthes complains that "we have been overly interested in the author and insufficiently in the reader. . . . We try to establish *what the author meant,* and not at all *what the reader understands*" (*The Rustle of Language*, 30; emphasis in original). Such understanding could not be wholly systematized because of individual readers' idiosyncrasies. He does develop an account of how reading, *as an embodied experience*, still can be thought ontologically, however. "To read is to make our *body* work . . . at the invitation of the text's signs" (ibid.; emphasis in original). Thus, through the bodywork of reading, Barthes ethicizes and somewhat personalizes antihumanism. This personalization provides the back door through which the underlying vulnerability of antihumanist thought enters.

Addressing the Big Bang and the Steady State in *Baroque*, Sarduy elaborates how these cosmological theories elucidate "an instantaneous event, without origin or any trace: the springing forth [*surgimiento*] of the body, immediate disappearance" (*OC* 2: 1241). Bodies are now imaginable as simply happening and, in time, disappearing. From the time of their eventful emergence, the distance between heavenly bodies widens. "The universe is dilated: its bodies are separating [*se separan*], fleeing from one another" (*OC* 2: 1245). This separation is at once willful and inevitable: the reflexive verb structure of *se separan* and the bodies' flight from one another suggest that they themselves are responsible for enacting this distancing; yet, because cosmological expansion is a force, it cannot be willfully initiated. Paradoxically, thanks to that distancing, long after their disappearance celestial bodies are still present. After all, even long-dead stars are virtually present since they continue to be visible. Moreover, the light that belatedly arrives from stars is not just the evidence of their having existed in the past; for the viewer, that light is a quantum body doubling for the heavenly bodies' existence, even after their deaths. If contemporary cosmology offers an analogy that illuminates how bodies are imagined to function in other fields, Sarduy implicitly uses his narrative about the stars and the universe to spur a rethinking of how bodies are also virtually present in writing. Similar to the way light functions as a quantum medium attesting to the author's existence or having-existed, a literary text acts as the evidentiary light signaling the presence of the author whom structuralism had declared dead. It ties us, the readers, to the writing body long after the author has disappeared from the scene of writing. Through the word we share, we restore body and life.

If *Baroque* is read as an echo or *retombée* of Barthes, the dedicatee who embodies the other center lurking in the shadows and around whom Sarduy's thought elliptically revolves, then it is possible to see how Sarduy's analogy about the tie between the reader and the author's quasi-stellar and virtual presence is implicitly suffused with a queer eroticism. In *The Pleasure of the Text* (1973), which appeared one year before *Baroque*, Barthes mentions Sarduy's novel *Cobra* as exemplary of the dynamic whereby literary *pleasure* is transformed into *bliss* (8). *Pleasure* connotes an erotic relation between reader and text (or writer and text), in which just enough contact with culture and conventions remains so that the experience can be described. In contrast, *bliss* is akin to a Lacanian idea of *jouissance*, an ecstatic loss of self. It is wholly atopic and asocial, experienced in solitude. It results from an intransitive literary use of language, an encounter occurring entirely in the present and outside cultural or narrative conventions. In brief, "Pleasure can be expressed in words, bliss cannot" (ibid., 21). Pleasure can be critically described, but bliss can only be experienced. At most, it can be simulated for others. The distinction between pleasure and bliss is not a matter of absolutes, however. Barthes admits from the very start that, "terminologically, there is a vacillation" and "a margin of indecision" between the two: "The distinction will not be the source of absolute classifications, the paradigm will falter, the meaning will be precarious, revocable, reversible, the discourse incomplete" (ibid., 4). Even though Barthes plays with a Lacanian idea of *jouissance*, he does not celebrate total self-dissolution. Instead, he establishes an ethical compromise between the antihumanist impersonality of desire and the humanist intimacies of erotic attachment.[26]

The only distinction that matters is not the one between *pleasure* and *bliss*, but what divides both from more banal textual encounters. Barthes addresses some unnamed nonliterary author whose unstimulating work he is reading: "For you I am neither a body nor even an object . . . but merely a field, a vessel for expansion. It can be said that after all you have written this text quite apart from bliss; and this prattling text is then a frigid text, as any demand is frigid until desire, until neurosis forms in it" (ibid., 5). In contrast to such "prattling" and "frigid" ventures, stylized literary writing evinces both bliss and pleasure. Barthes enjoys reading such literature—texts like Sarduy's *Cobra*—because they restore his body to the scene of reading; and they do so by heightening his sense of the writer's embodied pleasurable or blissful experience. The joy an author evidently has had while writing reassures Barthes that he, as a reader, exists as either a body or an object of desire. The writer writes for him, to him. Such textual pleasure brings to our attention the fact that we cannot know our bodies in an unmediated fashion. To know ourselves, we first must become conscious of our relations to others' bodies and their experiences of pleasure and bliss. As Barthes puts it, "The pleasure of the text is that moment when my body pursues its own ideas—for my body does not have the same ideas I do" (ibid., 17). Taking advantage of this statement's ambiguity, an uncertainty that leaves it unresolved whether Barthes is speaking as a reader or a writer here (he oscillates between both positions throughout the book), I argue that pleasure disrupts liberalist conventions of identity and personhood for *both readers and writers*. It causes one to think multiply: as an embodied "I," reading (or writing) alone, as well as a body intrinsically linked to the alien one of the writer (or reader). In literary joys and pleasures, the self is split, expansive, extensive beyond its own corporeal shell. But because such pleasure preserves the other's objectivity and difference, it is an expansive pleasure that does not colonize.

When the textual encounter causes the split between *cogito* and body, one finds one's self subject to the text, to language, and to the other body at the end of the line. Here a strange humanism—or, at least a sense of the encounter's humanness—creeps back into Barthes's antihumanist narrative (if it ever really left). It eroticizes, almost sexualizes, the encounter. Writing in pleasure also "guarantee[s]" a reader's pleasure; it necessitates that the author pursue the audience, as one would pursue a john for anonymous sex. As Barthes writes: "I must seek out this reader (must 'cruise' him) *without knowing where he is.* A site of bliss is then created. It is not the reader's 'person' that is necessary to me, it is this site: the possibility of a dialectics of desire, of an *unpredictability* of bliss" (ibid., 4; emphasis in original). Notwithstanding his reversion to gay male slang (*cruising*), Barthes is not narrating the pleasures of the text as a product of his own homosexual orientation. However, a personal element is still at play in this eroticism. *It is not, however, the typically liberalist "human" person who is integral, independent, identifiable; instead Barthes offers a personhood reconfigured.*

Toward the end of *The Pleasure of the Text*, Barthes explains that his theory of reading and its eroticism is part of "a theory of the materialist subject," which brings materialism back to its most foundational unit: the body (61). The desired "site" supplied by a literary text between the reader's and the writer's bodies is the materialization of the bond *and* the distance between them. Thus, the text supplies a space, a universe, they might coinhabit, if only virtually. This is the locus of a peculiar condition, what Barthes calls "a drift, something *both revolutionary and asocial*, and it cannot be taken over by any collectivity, any mentality, any ideolect" (ibid., 23; emphasis added). Despite his insistence on bliss and pleasure's "asocial" nature, the materiality of this bond and this drift figure an intensely intimate form of sociality, one that is "asocial" only insofar as it is different from conventional communality. Occurring in each other's absence, but predicated on the founding of an alternate space where humanity and commonality might be redefined, this relation moves Barthes's thought toward a thought-provoking paradox: a new sort of love growing out of an impersonal vulnerability. That vulnerability comes in imagining another's embodied desire for one's self. Such imagining renders one's own self unrecognizable. We never know how we look in our lovers' eyes. The new humans, readers or writers, produced out of such intimacy are always different from their selves. They are split by the others to whom they are pleasurably linked by a text and to whom they must remain open and potentially vulnerable. Barthes reads Sarduy in this fashion, and Sarduy reads Barthes in this way, too. When we restore this elliptical intimacy between them, and when we let *The Pleasure of the Text* revolve out of the shadow *Baroque* casts on it, the planetary bodies of Sarduy's postcolonial antihumanism are infused with a rather queer eroticism and a strangely human vulnerability.

## Beginning a Queer Universe, with a Bang

What are only echoes and traces in *Baroque* of the author's vulnerability, the intimate and pleasurable link to others, surface as explicit tropes in Sarduy's poetry. Little has been written about his verse, in spite of his insistence that poetry is the first of his arts and "the generator of everything" ("Mudo combate," 365). Perhaps critics avoid it precisely because it demonstrates a lyric sensibility that calls attention to the embodied authorial presence that we presume, in good antihumanist fashion, is dead. While railing against Romantic lyricism, especially as it was rewarded in communist Cuba, Sarduy wrote to Manuel Díaz Martínez that "in the center of a society structured around the notion of 'unity,' of a *monolithic* thought," poetry presented "the only transgression" (*Cartas*, 41; emphasis in original). Disruptive of conventions and staid ideas, it alone exposes the power of the word. Yet his sense of poetry's uniquely transgressive powers qualifies what "transgression," or revolution, actually entails. Not to be confused with the act of an existentialist or with romantic self-expression, poetry is a stylized action that heightens readers' awareness of their intimate relations to the author who addresses them.[27]

*Big Bang* (1974)—the companion volume to *Baroque*—mixes lyric with concrete poetry and heteroglossic forms. This combination foregrounds the transformative nature of intimacy while calling attention to language's mediation of eroticism. The page supplies a material universe, where reader and writer cruise one another and find a new home. This textual space is governed by a new sense of universalism that can accommodate each party's corporeal singularity. The volume is divided into four sections. *Flamenco* consists of what could be described as objectivist poems that simulate dance movements by repeating architectural tropes, and stock phrases to underscore the relation between space, the writing body, and the text. *Mood Indigo* gathers concrete poems printed in a block font reminiscent of newspaper headline type. Each shares the title of a Duke Ellington song ("Moon Mist," "Echoes of Harlem," "Mood Indigo," "The Mooche") and together they pay homage to the departed Afro-Cuban singer and guitarist Beny Moré. By connecting Ellington to Moré, Sarduy implicitly imagines art as forming a bridge between North and South, even though the Cuban musician actually had cut his ties with his North American record label RCA and did not leave the island or his people after the Revolution. This section features writing as constituting a body whose racialization helps give body to the reader as well ("the music the page : black layers"; "a map your black body"; "the face a text / written with gypsum / ebony") (*OC* 1: 153, 152, 161). Reading is like dancing. As readers are led by the poems through the volume, they simulate the author's "ESPIRAL NEGRA" (*OC* 1: 158–59), his concrete poetry's representation of black music's transnational movements between Harlem, Havana, Río, Paris, and Africa. The next section of *Big Bang*, which I analyze below, is a long, multipart poem that lends the entire volume its title. *Otros poemas* closes the collection with lyrics written in Indonesia. Here Sarduy thematically connects East and West with topics ranging from cinematic representation (part 1), to reminiscences of Cuba ("Sexteto habanero"), to the visual arts ("Páginas en blanco [Cuadros de Franz Kline]," "Pavo real de Carlo Crivelli," "Cubos de Larry Bell"), to traditional Indonesian dance ("Ketjak").

Connecting East and West, North and South, while urging readers to interact bodily with his texts, *Big Bang* clearly has a cosmopolitan vision. Key to that vision is the intimate link forged between reader and author. "Ketjak," which finishes the entire volume, puts it most nakedly: "I teach you how to dance. I take you close to me. Close to my body. / I model arms and fingers for you. Fingers for feet. [*Te modelo brazos y dedos. Los dedos de los pies.*] / Follow me. Skin against skin. Touch my black skin" (*OC* 1: 196). We are seduced to come into contact with Sarduy's own queer multiracial (Afro-Cuban, Sino-Cuban, and *criollo*) body, via his text. His lyric anamorphically distorts body images and forces us to correlate the digits with which he embraces us (fingers) with those on which we dance (toes). Our rendezvous with him occurs through a close attention to another sort of foot, then, the metrical feet constituting both poetic lines and musical phrases. In the absence of Sarduy's actual body, his darkened skin is re-presented by the black type whose foot drives us and mediates his caresses. This dance is a cooperative effort, even if one partner—the author—inevitably must lead. Sarduy's verb *modelar* ("te modelo brazos y dedos") has a double sense: this literary dance, this intimate form of reading and moving with his poems, simultaneously *models* what a body can be and *forms* or *shapes* readers' bodies anew. "The page and, above all, the poem are, for me, like bodies in space," Sarduy would note later about *Big Bang*. "They begin with an initial explosion of a primitive verbal atom, which does not yet actually exist and will continue to expand" ("Severo Sarduy," 21). Conceived as a cosmological explosion and structured like a dance, these poems reimagine intimacy to move both reader and writer across a recognizable globe, into new worldly spaces.

It is the eponymous third section of the collection, though, that concretely establishes the echo between *Baroque*'s cosmological theory and this volume. In the long poem "Big Bang" (*OC* 1: 164–75), ethico-aesthetic theory becomes poetic praxis. Originally published by Fata Morgana Press as a chapbook with facing French translations (1973), the seventeen-part poem features a lyric eroticism that disrupts scientific narratives about heavenly bodies and cosmological beginnings.[28] Thus, Sarduy reminds his readers of the ability of poetry to generate a new sociopolitical universe by bodily provoking new intimacies. The constitutive sections alternate between brief explanations of cosmological and astronomical concepts (Big Bang, red giants, white dwarfs), lyrics (typographically set in italics), combinations of the two (verse following astronomical exposition), and uncaptioned reproductions of graphs from the French scientific journal *La Recherche*. Much like T. S. Eliot in *The Waste Land*, Sarduy closes the section with a citation of his sources. Sarduy leaves many traces of his body in the poem, and his citational strategies alert us to his efforts to *craft* a narrative out of his passions, readings, and imaginings. In Barthesian fashion, then, Sarduy strives to stylistically lay bare, to *materialize*, the pleasure he takes in recounting theories about the universe's origins and its astronomical bodies. This pleasure may produce a fragmentation, but, unlike Eliotic modernists, he does not yearn to shore up the pieces and secure a unified self. Instead, he capitalizes on the foundational premise of the Big Bang theory: "The universe is expanding (*OC* 1: 165). Like celestial bodies, Sarduy exists in a dilating space and time, constantly expanding beyond his own boundaries. Decentered by a constant distancing from his origin, he nonetheless remains materially and lyrically connected with the other, the "you" [*tú*] he informally addresses.

The first of these lyrics surfaces as the second half of "Isomorphism," the third canto of "Big Bang." The piece begins with a prose paragraph that continues the colloquial prose accounts of the Big Bang theory that make up the first two sections. The astrophysicist Allan R. Sandage is noted to have attested that, in June 1966, the Mount Palomar observatory witnessed the explosion of a quasar, an extremely bright quasi-stellar object. This discovery added new knowledge about that type of celestial body, which had only been discovered and classified three years earlier. As Sarduy recounts, Sandage theorized that, given the Earth's light years of distance from the star, the event of the explosion actually could have happened billions of years earlier, shortly after the "initial explosion" with which the universe was born. The section's title suggests that this astronomical narrative exists in an isomorphic relation to the lyric that immediately follows. If that is true, one would expect the complementary verse to shed light on how universes begin out of explosions; however, the lyric has nothing to do with stars. Instead, it depicts a cruising encounter in the Moroccan baths of the Hotel de la Confianza. The setting is luridly described with earthy, not celestial, tones. A "mustard cone" of light from a "stained chandelier" casts the "shadow of the shower pipe" on a nearby "reddened wall," as desert sands batter the windowpanes. In a parenthetical aside, our attention is directed "Outside." Random details are disclosed about the world just beyond the baths' walls: sandals tossed aside, the sound of a radio, whirlwinds. Inside, a naked water-bearer appears. The reader finds himself folded into the poem's scene of action: he is rendered male by the narrator and is directly addressed with the familiar "*tú.*" "You" push small containers of "putrid water" to the ground, thus breaking them, while "you" draw out "your" cock and squeeze it. While "you" are masturbating to the sight of the naked visitor, you "stain" your genitals with "saffron" from your hands. A rather anticlimactic microscale version of the Big Bang happens. "Cum [*La leche*] on the wall, dense point, white sign that spreads [*se dilata*]." After "you" gather your djellaba, presumably to cover up, we hear a simple but cryptic statement, all the more unintelligible because it lacks quotation marks or an explicit attribution to a particular speaker: "I, the impermeable." A final aside quickly returns us to the world beyond: an overheard film dialogue, a blinking neon sign (*Luxor*), the subway. A closing notation locates the lyric as composed between the sites narrated in each of the two parenthetical asides that send us "Outside" the baths: *Tiznet / Barbès-Rochechouart.*

On the surface, the lyric component of "Isomorphism" appears to be an unremarkable narration of public sex and sexual tourism. Ultimately, though, the text resists such reductions. Much like the astronomers who witness a quasar's explosion billions of years after it occurred, Sarduy's reader is brought into proximity with what is now absent: the writer's past encounter with a Moroccan water-bearer. We share his position, inhabiting his memory of his experience in the Tiznet baths as we identify—admittedly, somewhat forcibly—with the second person "you" who jerks off while gazing at the object of his desire. The final aside draws our attention to yet another time and place from which we are removed, that of Sarduy's writing in view of the Barbès-Rochechouart stop of the Paris Metro. Space and time have both dilated, much like the ejaculate on the wall. In this "dense point" of lyric—a seamy, but bright, spot in "Big Bang"—boundaries are crossed, on multiple levels. Through the mnemonic peregrinations of an individual writer, a North African periphery becomes a train stop in the European metropole. Sex—particularly, the supposedly private and solitary act of masturbation—is now part of the baths' public space and involves more than one body. Reader blurs into writer; the latter's erotic past informs the reader's present textual experience.

But that cryptic statement, attributed to no one—"I, the impermeable"—haunts the scene. Perhaps the narrator states it, but it could also be victoriously pronounced by the Moroccan water-bearer, the one who provokes, but is untouched and not soaked by, the poet-narrator's onanistic pleasures. In this ambiguity, Sarduy reminds us that, like the Moroccan, he is also a postcolonial subject. Their similarity is reinforced by the fact that, in reading the poem, we gaze like sexual tourists on Sarduy touching himself, a gaze akin to his own as he watches the naked water-bearer. This declaration of impermeability—voiced by either or both of these postcolonial subjects—however, is not to be confused with a claim of independence. As is illustrated by the asides linking the events in the baths to the world beyond their walls, no boundary is wholly invulnerable to crossing and penetration. At the same time that someone—Sarduy, Moroccan, or both—claims that he is not penetrated by a colonizing gaze, the poem encourages us to trespass boundaries and collapse the distance between inside and outside, North Africa and

Paris, self and other. As voyeurs of Sarduy's past erotic transgressions, we are erotically bound to him. Our reading pleasure hinges on the *mîse-en-abyme* structure of the lyric scene, which calls on us to find our "identities" in a dilating, extensive fashion. Just as he is like the object of his own desire, just as he is the Moroccan's double, we, too, are forced—even at the level of the poem's second-person address—to see our selves *as* Sarduy. The resultant sharing of a body between the reader and the writer opens a new universe that challenges conventions of identity and difference.

Most importantly, this blurring of subject boundaries, this critique of the mechanisms of identity that support colonial inequities, occurs through a queer encounter. It is not queer because it is same-sex; rather, its queerness owes to its autoerotic nature: *we are compelled into a new relation with ourselves by confronting our desire for the other; there we find a desire for our selves to be other.* Identity shades into difference, and an episteme of similarity—mediated by the written word—emerges. It is not incidental that geopolitical zones collapse into one another as identities and discrete subjects blur. Nor is it incidental that all this is read in a splatter of cum, a perverse writing on the wall. Depicted in Cuban slang, the semen is similar to female emissions, to milk (*la leche*). Androgynous, this nonheteronormative and nonreproductive ejaculate creates a new universe, produced in a miniature explosion resulting from an encounter with self and difference. Reading about that sordid spreading of milky semen after three prose pieces about the Big Bang and the expansion of the universe, we cannot help hearing an echo in the description of the emissions the name of that galaxy we call home, the Milky Way (*la Vía Lactea*). The cum is the evidentiary trace of a world where correspondence and simultaneity between supposed opposites exist. A simulacrum of the actual expansion of the universe and of that perverse ejaculatory writing, "Isomorphism" mediates the production of a universe where we fully understand what it means for bodies to be "fleeing / to the borders / of space," as Sarduy puts it in "Oriente/Occidente," the final part of the poem "Big Bang." Other borders—geopolitical, subjective, and ideological—are incidental. Liberalist Cold War logics of identification, nationalism, and containment are all undone by the eroticism of the literary encounter.

The virtual nature of writing materially unsettles the reader as well as the author, and that disruption drives future encounters. It is the pleasure of the text that we long for. The twelfth part of "Big Bang," the lyric canto "Cuerpo divino" ("Heavenly Body"), invites the blurring of the boundaries between Sarduy and his readers' bodies. He remarks that he feels "The weight of your body / on my body / skin suture coded." Language binds reader to lyricist, suturing us with a code written on both our bodies. But this soldering code weighs heavily on Sarduy, burdensomely reminding him of his own materiality so that it is not so easy for him to disappear. We are zipped up back-to-back, "vertebra between vertebra." His body presses against ours, too, a reminder of our own materiality. This suture is less a burden or a discomfort than an immobilizing stitch designed to promote a healing. Think of it as language's cosmetic surgery to improve our embodied condition, to redistribute the weight we otherwise would have to bear alone and in isolation. The suture (*sutura*) of our bodies rewrites tomes about erotic unions (the *Kama Sutra*). Though we are stitched back-to-back, together we form a heavenly body with no backs. Although the union is not like that of the copulative beast with two backs, Sarduy and his reader reciprocally penetrate each other, "entering" one another "greased" as if engaging in anal sex. This impossible buggery, zipping ourselves up with him in our mutual reading and writing, signals the coming of a new world. With this union, "volumes are being articulated." We come to inhabit Sarduy (he contains multitudes), or he inhabits us, or together we share a universe with him inside our respective realities. However we imagine this cohabitation, these voluminous expanses usher in a cosmopolis where "unos en otros / unos en otros." This repeated (or echoed) phrase is literally rendered as "some in others / some in others." Sarduy's exact wording reminds us, though, that the collective "some" always consists of multiple individuals, several *unos* or many ones. (He could have simply written *algunos en otros,* which would have lost the connotation that one always comprises several.) In our multiplicity, we are entangled; we recombine to form a new body extensive with the other with whom we are similar-yet-different. In this commonal condition we are queerly vulnerable.

Lyric ushers in a new, expansive universe apart from the contained one imagined by a Cold War liberalism. No longer does intersubjective distance signify a gulf, identity's unsurpassable boundary between individuals. Here vulnerability facilitates intimate connections in spite of material distances, an eroticizing invocation of bodies and differences to accompany us. And poetry is that discourse which best realizes that pleasurable, queer lesson. As Sarduy imagines in the conclusion of "Heavenly Bodies," that universe-begetting union may be impermanent, a short flash of ejaculatory "brilliance" that trails down the wall, like "dead stars falling," to the bedclothes' funereal "marble." Nonetheless, that passionate connection still pleasurably engenders an ethical universe queerer than the one that either Sarduy or we have ever lived in, off the page. It supplies the poetic space where we're free to pursue those echoes that let us experience the joy of being expansive, extensive, and similar yet wholly individual.

# EPILOGUE

Two concepts have recurred throughout this book: *queerness* and *cosmopolitanism*. Many now find them unsatisfactory buzzwords, rather than viable critical or theoretical concepts, because of their vagueness and imprecision. In *Queering Cold War Poetry* I have worked toward a definition of the first—*queerness*—by associating it with a resistant yet vulnerable subjective attitude. In the process, a working definition of the second term—*cosmopolitanism*—has implicitly emerged as an effect of that attitude. We might say that *cosmopolitanism is the horizon of vulnerability that grows out of poetic and queer resistances to the constructions by modern biopolitics of liberalist individualism and nationalism.* Poetry constructs and inhabits its own world republic, as Pascale Casanova calls it. That cosmopolitan space is structured by the nationalistic political world's actualities and power dynamics, yet it provides enough autonomy for authors and readers to more freely reimagine restrictive definitions of nationhood and the predominant *ethos* of each writer's respective *polis*. The poets discussed here—Wallace Stevens, José Lezama Lima, Robert Duncan, and Severo Sarduy—achieve that end by working against the same ontological foundations. Their expressions of vulnerability and a poetic cosmopolitanism are quite varied, though, because liberalism itself, as an ontological or formalist ideal, is articulated differently in particular historical and social contexts. Stevens's hemispheric ideas about cosmopolitanism are very much a product of his time and his national setting, and they differ significantly from Lezama's, Rodríguez Feo's, and the other *origenistas*' ideas about it. That difference is due to the fact that, unlike the *norteamericano*'s narcissistic conception of extending one's self into the world, their antinationalist postcolonial project depends on founding a global community of friends through a technology of reading world literatures. Similarly, Sarduy's qualifiedly antihumanist ideas about queerness, or what he terms "desire," are significantly different from Duncan's more humanistic ones about what he calls "love." The differences between their projects are due to more than Sarduy's struggling with (a foreign) structuralist theory in rethinking social relationality outside the terms of national citizenry. They are also due, in no small part, to the fact that his exilic life led him to be critical of liberalism's romantic foundations in a way different from what Duncan, the archetypal householder, could be. Read together, then, these poets' writings offer only a small sampling of ways of imagining how vulnerability might help the contemporary reader reach toward more cosmopolitan horizons, beyond the containing logics of late modernity and its entrenched need for the security of identity and clear-cut difference.

What is not coincidental, however, is the fact that these writers' poetic investigations of the limits of modern nationalism are accompanied by notions of various forms of vulnerability which give rise to pleasure, eroticism, attraction, and joy. Edward Said reminds us that literature affords readers opportunities to move beyond the boundaries of their respective homelands into foreign spaces and pasts. By moving into the "provisional homes" provided by texts, the reader can enter "that precarious exilic realm" where one can "truly grasp the difficulty of what cannot be grasped and then go forth to try anyway" (Said, *Humanism and Democratic Criticism*, 144).[1] In this displaced terrain of reading, our private lives are a bit shaken up because literature uses language as a tool to model an understanding of agency—namely, that one acts only after being acted on—at odds with the (limitedly) sovereign one imagined by biopolitical, liberalist paradigms. Thus, the reader awakens, joyfully, to the sense that it is possible to live differently, in ways that deepen our attachments to others without normalizing our behavior. With that discovery, we move beyond the constraints not only of the modern rational subject but also of collective national forms that overemphasize security to ensure that populations remain easily managed and governed.

Poetry, that most unlikely of discourses, thus allows us to circumvent the classic means by which cosmopolitanism is usually imagined as a form of stability and peace. As Immanuel Kant originally postulated in "Idea for a Universal History with Cosmopolitan Intent" (1784), cosmopolitanism is the rationalistic goal of humanity's evolution toward "a cosmopolitical state of public security" that uses the middle ground of culture and law to create an artificial "concord" (*Basic Writings*, 128, 123). His better known treatise "Toward a Perpetual Peace" (1795) specifies that this development, though occurring through cultural means, is both teleological and natural: "Nature's mechanical course evidently reveals a teleology: to produce harmony from the very disharmony of men even against their will" (ibid., 450). Although Kant interestingly resignifies volition, and also blurs the lines between nature and culture in a way that would appeal to all four poets I have studied here, his secure and harmonious vision of cosmopolitanism is quite unlike the queer ethic we have been exploring. Experimentation and openness to change, rather than conformity and ensuring the security of the self-same, are to be pursued. Since life's unforeseeable disruptions must be valued, a *perpetual process*—rather than a perpetual peace—is most desirable. Holding out for a static "peace" only promotes an ideologically motivated illusion whereby particular parties and biopolitical logics govern our lives according to *a priori* rationalities that preserve an inflexible state and a sociocultural status quo.

At the heart of a dynamic in which individuals' lyric encounters supply the gateway for rethinking the nationalist and popular parameters circumscribing life is *difference*. Moreover, that difference traverses identity and points to the perpetual division and multiplication of the self. It compels us to find resemblances, similarities that invite us to be reflexive about our selves. This reflexivity is not a process of finding out *who we are* but instead is one in which we discover *what we can do*. What potentials can we realize when we recombine with others, in unexpected fashions? Where this difference resides, at the center of this process of perpetual discovery, is the body. One of the general difficulties of addressing the nature of cosmopolitanism is due to a recurrent failure to take notice of how our singular embodied living mediates our experience of a common condition. In this way, the sort of cosmopolitan difference I am gesturing toward here bears similarities to how Gilles Deleuze reads Spinoza's concept of *common notions*, particularly those of the "less universal" kind that realize "a similarity of composition between bodies that directly agree, and this from their own viewpoint[s]" (*Expressionism in Philosophy*, 276). Deleuze urges us to realize that when we think of commonality "we must begin from the least universal," our singular embodied experiences. "When we encounter a body that agrees with our own, when we experience a joyful passive affection, we are induced to form the idea of what is common to that body and our own" (282). That is to say, passivity—what I have called *vulnerability*—produces joys that compel us to think differently about how we can connect to, and are already connected to, others. This is a different kind of reason, one predicated on a desire that comes to be rationalized: "Desires of reason thus replace irrational desires" (284) This is a different kind of action, one predicated on passion: "There is a whole learning process involved in common notions, in our *becoming active*" (288; emphasis in original). With such an affirmation of joy at the center of cosmopolitan thinking, the desiring discovery of new commonalities does seem quite queer indeed.

Because the body is the specific site of that singular perspective from which common notions are realized, we should hesitate to associate a Deleuzian or Spinozan idea of cosmopolitanism with a celebration of abstract networked societies.[2] All of the body's relations, including the actualities of the nation-state, form an assemblage that contributes to the formation of a cosmopolitan perspective that frames interpretations of any vulnerable and passionate experience of queerness, whether it occurs in the street or on the page. As Pheng Cheah reminds us, the freedom engendered by a so-called postnational spirit is actually a product of "an interminable negotiation with and responsibility to the forces that give us ourselves instead of the transcendence of the given" (*Inhuman Conditions*, 79).[3] The Deleuzian premise that any ethic is based on what a body can do necessitates an account of the material limits constituting and situating that body. Manuel DeLanda, for one, has argued that such a material and posthumanist rendition of social assemblages necessitates moving past models of social constructivism: "Language should be moved away from the core of the matter, a place that it has wrongly occupied for many decades" (*A New Philosophy of Society*, 16). However, the cases of Stevens, Lezama, Duncan, and Sarduy indicate that *language itself is a material* that not only constructs us but also poses necessary limits mediating our embodied relations. In many ways, it will always be "the core of the matter." Lyric, and one might imagine other verbal arts, provide further material for embodied negotiations with language and ideas so as to move toward a freer, less nationally and egoistically constricted, condition. Thus, the queer cosmopolitan ethic that I am elaborating here is, at the heart of it, always a *cultural* project. Contrary to the Kantian assertions of some, culture does not just bring about the consolidation of cosmopolitan norms.[4] Rather, it furthers a project wherein, according to Paul Gilroy, we attain a degree of "self-knowledge . . . acquired through the proximity to strangers." Culture supplies the mediated forms through which we achieve such proximity. Thus it is a necessary tool in "the principled and methodical cultivation of a degree of estrangement from one's own culture and history" (*Postcolonial Melancholy*, 67).

If estrangement is an underlying queer objective for much modern art, then it is already far removed from the classically humanist project that liberals like Kwame Anthony Appiah imagine when they characterize art as encouraging a mode of "connection not *through* identity but *despite* difference" (*Cosmopolitanism*, 135; emphasis in original). Modern poetries, in their queering of ethical modalities, supply models of a cosmopolitan vision that account for the situated and ecological nature of subjects' relations with an inhuman world, a world that is material because of both linguistic representation and political and economic institutions. Bodies function as the boundary where one comes into contact with that world; through them, difference is inevitably introduced. So, Appiah is right in saying that art does not work by encouraging connection "*through* identity," but it is a more precarious situation than trying to connect to others "*despite* difference." Indeed, the lyric arts encourage us to connect *through difference*, to struggle with the mediations that ultimately make us strangers even to ourselves. The pursuit of self-estrangement in the name of growing closer to others is an ethical strategy for realizing what Gilroy provocatively calls a "systematic form of disloyalty to our own local civilization" (*Postcolonial Melancholy*, 71). If we are good ethicists, we risk being read as bad humans. We set out to betray the identitarian logic that forecloses possible actions and imaginable collectives because it favors the security of the known. Through a never-ending process of opening to others in order to rearticulate, reflexively, our selves and our relations, however, we might offer a broadened account of what humanity is and, perhaps more importantly, what humanity can do. Experience, not essence or existence, is the new ontological foundation of such an ethic.[5]

Because I see myself as working outside postcolonial studies, I cannot speak responsibly to how this connection between *cosmopolitanism* and *queerness* might change that critical discourse. However, I will close by pointing to how it can begin to expand the critical horizons of queer theory. Most significantly, if our cosmopolitan potential always entails a negotiation of our embodied experience of national living, we will be heartened to learn that the idea of the *queer nation*, one of our most resistant tropes in queer activism, has a great deal of potential. We have gone about imagining its character all wrong, however, because we presume a transformation based on our identifiable difference *as queers*. Queer nationalism tends to be read as: a "camp counternationality" that resignifies commercial mainstream culture (Lauren Berlant and Elizabeth Freeman, "Queer Nationality," 214); an ontological plateau in which coming out into a sexual and gender minority community lets individuals realize particular practices and create an "ethical agency" that is "lived and acted beyond the community, carried into the larger world as ethics" (Mark Blasius, *Gay and Lesbian Politics*, 203); a resistance to a "normalized homoeroticism" that strives "not for a simplistic rejection of publicity dynamics as they are currently constituted [in sexual minority communities], but rather for progressive ethical and political reworkings of them" so as to reconfigure, through a trickle-down effect, other public institutions, the civil sphere, and markets (Eric O. Clarke, *Virtuous Vice*, 30–31, 170); and even the desired milieu of a queer "stranger" whose more passionate mode of citizenship "requires [of the heterosexual majority] an active encounter with difference and a willingness to understand differences as fruitful and enhancing rather than as threats to bodily, social, or political integrity" (Shane Phelan, *Sexual Strangers*, 147). Such imaginings presume that an *a priori* queerness, cultivated in a community set apart from the rest, introduces a transformative radical difference into the general national consciousness.

In many ways, such conceptualizations of queer nationalism paradoxically begin with a mode of recognition that, as Alexander García Düttmann has argued, obstructs the ethical change or social justice pursued by their advocates.[6] Fallacious identitarian premises implicitly endorse the liberalist condition and the liberal state to which we are tied. "The vast infrastructure of voluntarist culture—from churches to twelve-step programs—interprets itself through an identitarian discourse to which [the] queer is rapidly becoming assimilated," Michael Warner warns. He goes on to add, "The state also contributes more directly to the intelligibility of queerness. The modern state claims to be the agency of our wills and the site of our reason; that's why it works so well with a culture of voluntarism" (*Publics and Counterpublics*, 214). Because of this situation, Warner "distrust[s]" the "metanarrative of queer theory" as "a fundamental critique of liberal individualism, where the latter is understood as a belief in voluntarism and the ego-integrated self" (ibid., 219). The general claim of queer theory that it opposes strong individualism is impossible to sustain because it cannot extricate itself from the voluntarism supported by both the state and society. Even though Warner titles his essay "Something Queer about the Nation-State," his chief concern might really be said to be that there is something "nation-state" about "the queer." If the stranger is not truly strange, or if the queer is not really unexpected and eventful, the queer cannot realize the very transformation of social consciousness that the stranger promises. Instead, the field promulgates a critical discourse suspiciously reminiscent of the sorts of social "conversation" esteemed by more liberal figures like Appiah. Not to be confused with the communicative rationality found in theories of deliberative democracy, "Conversation doesn't have to lead to consensus about anything, especially not values." It does have some potential for dissensus, but, as Appiah helps us see, conversations really are not all that queer or eventful. Rather, it renders difference *habitual*: "It's enough that it helps people get used to one another" (*Cosmopolitanism*, 20). Queer theorists' own conversations about queer nationalism really only habituate the general national public to identity-based differences, as Warner fears.

If transformation is to occur, it must do so through *continuing struggles* with established parameters of identity and nationhood. In some way, each of the poets featured in *Queering Cold War Poetry* gives us an admittedly unsatisfactory answer to the dilemma we face. Lezama remains stubbornly secret. Stevens persistently clings to an imperialist and narcissistic worldview, despite his protestations otherwise. Duncan was unable to make even a gay household seem something other than normal without resorting to scatology. Sarduy hyperbolically claimed the disappearance of his body and buried the human intimacies of his project in obtuse echoes of others' work. At the core of each supposed failure, though, is a conflict cutting across an embodied subject who remains vulnerable to the very biopolitical proscriptions and prescriptions contested by his poetic. In their work, then, nationalism is very much present and is even queer. But each of their respective failures is itself an indicator of a difference that has emerged in the uneasy and insecure process of contention. I have brought these differences to light to help us see each project as even less secure, less integral than the authors themselves believed. Even these writers who were so conscious of the necessity of vulnerability, dependency, openness, connectedness, similarity-in-difference—even they were tempted to shore up their identities and to narrate their successes. So, even if they expressly acknowledged a universal or cosmopolitan vision from time to time, that vision very much remains on the horizon. It is up to us to be open enough to the traces of themselves they left behind so that we might find our own deconstructive agency for continuously drawing closer to some queerer cosmopolitan possibility. Perhaps someday that vision will be actualized in material institutions of politics and economy. Until then, though, we can realistically labor to make a cosmopolitanism grounded in difference part of at least one small facet of our material lives: a function of the language in which we imagine, share, and, indeed, live.

# NOTES

## Prologue

1. See S. Neil MacFarlane and Yuen Foong Khong, *Human Security and the U.N.: A Critical History*, especially 61–138, 202–24.

2. As I detail in the introduction, *liberalism* is central to my understanding of security, too. My inclusion of Cuban authors in this study is not paradoxical, though. I derive my definition of liberalism from a Foucauldian approach to operations of biopower and the management of populations, not from a political economic framework. The distinctions between the political forms of U.S. "liberalism" and Cuban "communism" are also not as clear-cut as they initially seem. Before and after the 1959 Revolution, Cuba had a changing relationship to American liberal ideals. Many conservative U.S. liberals (i.e., liberals who opposed communism and socialism as suppressions of democratic individualism) supported Fidel Castro between 1956 and 1958 because of his heroic image (Van Gosse, *Where the Boys Are: Cuba, Cold War America, and the Making of a New Left*, 60–135). Similar support came from both politically and culturally conservative papers such as the *Chicago Tribune, Coronet, Look, Time, Life,* and *U.S. News and World Report*. These media outlets contributed to a public discourse that paradoxically equated Cuban populist resistance with a North American strong individualism. Thus, prior to the establishment of a socialist government (later declared communist), the U.S. mainstream perpetuated a paradoxical romance of the anti-American revolution against Fulgencio Batista. That romance even inspired conservatives to become "Yankee *fidelistas*" and fight alongside the same Castro who also was admired by the New Left for embodying an ethos of personal politics. Unfathomably, American liberalism—in both its conservative and liberal/New Left varieties—resonates with the distinctively Cuban ideal of the communist hero.

3. For other work on the neoliberal privatization and mainstreaming of the gay and lesbian movement, see Rosemary Hennessy, *Profit and Pleasure: Sexual Identities in Late Capitalism*; Urvashi Vaid, *Virtual Equality: The Mainstreaming of Gay and Lesbian Liberation*; Leslie Feinberg, *Trans Liberation: Beyond Pink and Blue*; Samuel R. Delany, *Times Square Red, Times Square Blue;* Alexandra Chasin, *Selling Out: The Gay and Lesbian Movement Goes to Market*; Richard Goldstein, *The Attack Queers: Liberal Society and the Gay Right*; and Paul Robinson, *Queer Wars: The New Gay Right and Its Critics.*

4. For ACT UP's mission, see the website for the NYC branch (http://www.actupny.org) and its Oral History Project (http://www.actuporalhistory.org). One could criticize U.S. chapters of ACT UP for their largelyAmerican, even local, focus. A French chapter does exist in Paris. It is still quite active, whereas many American chapters are less so now. (See: http://www.actupparis.org.) Consequently, its actions have not fostered enough of a consciousness of the uneven developments of the HIV/AIDS pandemic and the resources allotted to globally address the crisis. In any cultural ecology, accounts of differences are necessary for imagining ethical and politically viable programs to redress those conditions that affect seropositive subjects globally. For a critical account of the unequal discursive conditioning of HIV/AIDS worldwide, see Cindy Patton, *Globalizing AIDS.*

5. For critical accounts of Queer Nation's resistance to queer citizens' economic and political exclusion by reimagining the nation as a cultural, rather than state, entity, see Lauren Berlant and Elizabeth Freeman, "Queer Nationality," and Henry Abelove, *Deep Gossip*, 29–41.

6. The CLAGS participants upheld a classically humanist sense of coalitional politics. In contrast, the idea of commonality I outline in chapter 1 would be called "posthumanist" by theorists. Both are cognizant of an inherent ecological relationality, but I would differentiate a humanist politics as more invested in the human citizen-subject's ability to act as a civic agent. A posthumanist ecological model would *also* account for the roles of "inhuman" factors—such as discourses, language, desire, even nature—in the shaping and conditioning of possibilities for political resistance. For a posthumanist ecological model, see Félix Guattari, *The Three Ecologies.*

7. I want to thank Belkin Gonzalez and Patricia Meona-Picado for this eloquent and concise formulation of queer politics' changing historical relationship to vulnerability.

8. See Judith Butler, *Excitable Speech: A Politics of the Performative*; *The Psychic Life of Power: Theories in Subjection*; *Precarious Life: The Powers of Mourning and Violence*, especially 128–51; *Giving an Account of Oneself.* Below I explicitly and implicitly address these texts.

## Introduction

1. On the politics and "cost" of Foucault's philosophy of power, read as a continuing into his philosophy of biopolitics, see Jefffrey T. Nealon, *Foucault beyond Foucault: Power and Its Intensifications since 1984.* For Foucault's key discussions of biopower, biopolitics, and governmentality, see *The History of Sexuality, An Introduction, volume 1*, 133–59; *"Society Must Be Defended": Lectures at the Collège de France*, 239–63; the essays "Governmentality," "'*Omnes et Singulatim*': Toward a Critique of Political Reason," "The Subject and Power," and "The Risks of Security," in *Essential Works*, 3: 201–22, 298–325, 326–48, and 365–81; "The Ethics of the Concern of the Self as a Practice of Freedom," in *Essential Works*, 1: 281–301; and *Security, Territory, Population: Lectures at the Collège de France, 1977–1978.* See also *Naissance de la biopolitique: Cours au Collège de France, 1978–1979*, where Foucault discusses the relationship of liberalism to neoliberal economics.

2. For a brief example where sovereignty is discussed as part of biopolitics, see Foucault, *Security, Territory, Population*, 23. Roberto Esposito explores this relation in great depth, and he characterizes it as "a copresence of opposing vectors superimposed in a threshold of originary indistinction" (*Bíos: Biopolitics and Philosophy*, 40). The translation of his crucial contribution to this discussion was made available only as this book was going to press, so I do not treat it in detail here.

3. See Agamben, *Homo Sacer: Sovereign Power and Bare Life*, esp. 119–80, passim.

4. For accounts in queer theory that correlate biopolitics to Homeland Security, see Jasbir K. Puar, *Terrorist Assemblages: Homonationalism in Queer Times*; "Abu Ghraib:

Arguing against Exceptionalism"; "On Torture: Abu Ghraib"; and Puar and Amit S. Rai, "Monster, Terrorist, Fag: The War on Terrorism and the Production of Docile Patriots." Also pertinent to my discussion of Foucault in relationship to security and risk is Randy Martin, *An Empire of Indifference: American War and the Financial Logic of Risk Management.*

5. In Foucault's account, capital and resources, rather than people, move through populations. Consequently, his ideas of movement are quite distinct from the nomadic circulations imagined by Gilles Deleuze. This tension is registered in Deleuze's *Foucault* (esp. 23–44, 70–93), in which he forcibly imagines power operating through a disciplinary apparatus that neglects Foucault's late turn to biopolitics and governmentality. In the future, it would serve queer theory well to read Deleuze in tandem with Foucault. This would let us more productively rethink the former's attempts to explain modalities of resistance through Deleuze's metaphors of traversal, the diagrammatic, and topography in his reading of Foucault. Those figures correspond with Deleuze's better-known concepts of nomadism, lines of flight, and deterritorialization.

6. I am also working with, but establishing a strong distinction from, Noberto Bobbio's understanding of liberalism as "a particular conception of the state" with "limited powers and functions" (*Liberalism and Democracy,* 1). This kind of state-form establishes a social contract based on an unquestioned "imaginary reconstruction of a presumed original state of man" as free and sovereign (ibid., 6). As I detail below, my conceptualization of liberalism does not tie it to a specific state or economic form; however, we must criticize its mythification of individualism as an absolute sovereignty. We can do so by investigating how liberalism is articulated, in particular epochs, by state, economic, and other institutions.

7. On the difference between comprehensive and political liberalisms, see Rawls, *Political Liberalism,* xxvii–xxx, xl–lxii, 37–46. Historicity is the fundamental element distinguishing the two. Contrary to his own intentions of elaborating how a public consensus necessary for meting out political justice changes over time, however, Rawls's concentration on political liberalism is not as historical as he makes it out to be. Because he works with the transgenerational democratic principles of equality and liberty, he problematically glosses the exclusivist nature of the common language established by these constant "principles" and "ideals" (liii). Particular, incommensurable perspectives are sacrificed to establish a consensus. Furthermore, procedural debate presumes a shared standard of rationality that lets citizens perceive "one another as free and equal in a system of social cooperation over generations" (xliv). A rationalistic imperative actually limits procedural debate by instituting moralistic, transcendent norms that must be legible across generations. Individuals "know" they are free if they subscribe to an unthreatening normative paradigm evacuated of passions. Rather than critically reading and historicizing civic debates' premises (*liberalism can "become" because it is in a historically dynamic relationship with commonality*), Rawls only superficially isolates some of its ontological dimensions in order to let others remain unexamined (*liberalism "is"*).

8. Kwame Anthony Appiah reads Mill this way in *The Ethics of Identity,* esp. 1–35 and 141–65.

9. My critical turn toward ontology engages a methodological strategy that Foucault likens to modern thought's own potential to move past a classically categorical logic of identity and difference by engaging "a dialectical interplay and an ontology without metaphysics" (*The Order of Things: An Archaeology of the Human Sciences,* 340). For Foucault, putting ontology back into history allows us to think the subject in the absence of the human person. For me, though, this methodology is less a part of an antihumanist project and more a means of facilitating a critique of humanism's exclusionary premises. Rather than say there are no persons bearing their own agency, we must inquire as to what forces determine who and what *count* as human or as citizens in particular moments. Here I am working with Jacques Rancière's theorization of the *count* in *Disagreement: Politics and Philosophy.* A supposedly democratic consensus is monitored by "a count whose complexities may mask a fundamental miscount" that is corrected only when the excluded raise their voices to call attention

to a social order's contingencies (6). A politics inheres in "a multiplicity of speech events" (37) in which a collective (or, as Rancière terms it, a "world," 42) voices its dispute with a dominant order (or "world"). What is more, that political "disorder" entails a troping of the language structuring a dominant political paradigm. "The modern political animal is first a literary animal, caught in the circuit of a literariness that undoes the relationships between the order of words and the order of bodies that determine the place of each" (37). As I argue below, lyric is such a literary form through which a politicized disorder between words and bodies, order and disorder, transpires. For Rancière's work on lyric as a political form, see *The Flesh of Words: The Politics of Writing*, 9–40.

10. Connolly delineates a third category: civic liberalism (or, liberal communitarianism). He aligns this form with identity politics and multiculturalism, which are based on exclusions made in the interest of a so-called "common good" (see *Identity/Difference*, 87–92). I am glossing over this category because I feel that, if we read his liberal individualism more closely in light of Foucault's notions about the population, it is difficult to distinguish liberal communitarianism from liberal individualism. Both are premised on exceptions (the liberal individualism of some is secured by excluding others from the social order), and both render the individual's sovereignty a function of the population's common will (which secures its status as "common" via normalizing apparatuses).

11. Foucault reminds us that statistics, that mechanism instrumental to governmentality's biopolitical management of populations, precisely means "science of the state" (*Security, Territory, Population*, 101).

12. Dewey's historicized and politically motivated treatment of the tension between collectivity and individualism warrants more attention than it has received. For key works constituting that phase of his interwar thought, see *Individualism Old and New* (1930), *Liberalism and Social Action* (1935), and *Freedom and Culture* (1939).

13. The coexistence of liberalism and commonality are articulated in a manner aptly described by Chantal Mouffe as both paradoxical and antagonistic (*The Democratic Paradox*, especially 1–16, 99–105). A liberal grammar of equality and liberty exists alongside a hierarchy that stabilizes liberties and thus limits freedoms. A rhetoric of freedom impossibly coexists with neoliberalism's reinforcement of an antagonistic pluralism that determines what identity groups are most entitled to the rights measuring such individual equality. Thinking through other facets of the democratic paradox depends, in part, on examining other moments' articulations of aporetic dynamics.

14. Eric Paras's discussion of the "strong subject" (*Foucault 2.0: Beyond Power and Knowledge*, 101–23) opens a useful way of thinking about *ascesis* that relates to what I imagine for queer theorists' ethical relationship to crisis. His account pertains to Foucault's critical relationship to but continuing involvement with liberal politics, and I find it useful for correcting others' uncritical appropriations of Foucault for their own liberal projects (see, for example, Kwame Anthony Appiah, *The Ethics of Identity*, especially 1–35). One can develop a politicized ethic that lets one work more freely in a liberalist system, without merely reproducing its transcendent, exclusivist categories.

15. Thomas Keenan (*Fables of Responsibility: Aberrations and Predicaments in Ethics and Politics*, 27–42) expresses a similar view of ethics as originating in the interruption of an unknown that threatens the individual's coherence. For Badiou, that change-incurring alterity is a singular "event" to which one becomes a subject by remaining faithful to it. In contrast, Keenan's subject is produced out of a negotiation of conflicting calls.

16. See Badiou, *Manifesto for Philosophy*, esp. 79–88.

17. Despite queer theorists' and activists' attraction to revolutionary models, historically in the United States the connection between revolution and queerness has been tendentious at best. A famous case in point: Huey Newton, the Black Panthers' Minister of Defense, urged his brethren to overcome "personal opinions and insecurities" about gay and women's liberation movements. While laudably calling for a coalition between racial and sexual politics, Newton's public letter actually tempers one form of violence by urging his fellow revolu-

tionaries to shore up some of their defenses, in the name of sympathy. Rather than giving in to "our first instinct" of "want[ing] to hit the homosexual in the mouth because we're afraid we might be homosexual," he instead directs his audience to "gain security in ourselves" so as to generate the appropriate "respect and feelings for all oppressed people" ("Manifesto," 89). In the final analysis, the revolutionaries' own security was to be ensured. A coalition based on such security, articulated through a rhetoric of tolerance, only preserves *a priori* definitions and thus is limited in its ethicopolitical potential.

This limit is an effect of the surprisingly disciplined nature of revolutionary articulations of desire. When reassessing Newton's seductiveness, Robert Reid-Pharr notes that "revolutionary desire is not undisciplined. On the contrary, the revolution enforces a narrative of desire that ultimately denies the realities of individuals involved in their blind pursuits of pleasure" (*Once You Go Black: Choice, Desire, and the Black American Intellectual*, 141). In this case, queerness is devalued and disciplined so as to promote a revolutionary idea of blackness. That racial ideal is tied to a mythologized tradition borne by an ahistoricized body that maintains ages-old dichotomies such as straight and gay, black and white. Reid-Pharr tries to rescue Newton, though: "I would argue that his willingness to address topics as seemingly out of character for a black nationalist leader as sexual liberation and gay rights acts itself as evidence of a will to break the hold that the logic of black historical and cultural profundity holds within the American imagination" (144). I am not convinced of this conclusion, though. Newton expressly articulates his desire to link black and sexual and gender revolutionaries so as to defensively maintain a secure sense of (reproductive) blackness. The narrative of what is "acceptable" for black nationalism may be changed, but the identitarian and liberalist logics underlying it remain untouched.

18. For a sampling of key texts from this archive, see: Valerie Solanas, *The S.C.U.M. Manifesto*; Martha Shelley, "Gay Is Good"; Charlotte Bunch, "Lesbians in Revolt"; Seymour Krim, "Revolt of the Homosexual"; and Charley Shively, "Indiscriminate Promiscuity as an Act of Revolution."

19. For critical responses to Edelman, see John Brenkman, "Queer Post-Politics" and "Politics, Mortal and Natal: An Arendtian Rejoinder," and the position papers by Robert L. Caserio, Judith Halberstam, José Esteban Muñoz, and Tim Dean constituting "The Antisocial Thesis in Queer Theory." Edelman's own responses to each are published at the end of this dossier of position papers, too.

20. See Douglas Crimp, *AIDS: Cultural Analysis, Cultural Activism*, and *Melancholia and Moralism: Essays on AIDS and Queer Politics*; Cindy Patton, *Inventing AIDS*; and Paula A. Treichler, *How to Have Theory in an Epidemic.*

21. Many theorists imagine that queer subjects illustrate an ontological condition of vulnerability because they live in proximity to an outside force (power, desire, the death drive, the Real, *jouissance*, attraction, hegemonic narratives) beyond one's control. However, because this attitude often produces a disruption that affirms identity-based difference even as it opposes the rhetoric and logics of community, queer theory often comes dangerously close to reproducing, rather than challenging, the biopolitical liberalist logic of a seemingly autonomous openness to risk-taking (as elucidated by critics such as Martin; see note 4). For a representation of queer theories that walk a fine line between vulnerable passion and the affirmation of an identity-based difference, see Leo Bersani, "Is the Rectum a Grave?" and *Homos*; Tim Dean, *Beyond Sexuality*; Jonathan Dollimore, *Sex, Literature, and Censorship*; Elizabeth A. Povinelli, "Sexuality as Risk: Psychoanalysis Metapragmatically"; and John Paul Ricco, *The Logic of the Lure.* Other queer studies more responsibly consider the realities of loss, injury, and shame without deploying a rhetoric of risk. However, they frequently evince an identity-based communitarian impulse, rather than what I call a similarity-based idea of commonality-in-difference. They use either shame or injury to remedy the exclusions brought about by the standards defining present minority communities or implicitly (and, in some cases, explicitly) express a romanticized yearning for impossible communities. A small sampling of work in this vein includes Heather Love, *Feeling Backward: Loss and the*

*Politics of Queer History*; Kathryn Bond Stockton, *Beautiful Bottom, Beautiful Shame: Where "Black" Meets "Queer"*; Judith Halberstam, *In a Queer Time and Place: Transgender Bodies, Subcultural Lives*; José Esteban Muñoz, *Disidentifications: Queers of Color and the Performance of Politics*; and Christopher Nealon, *Foundlings: Lesbian and Gay Historical Emotion before Stonewall.* I do not treat vulnerability as a trauma to be worked through or as what sets queerness absolutely apart from heteronormativity. Instead, I see it as articulated in some subjects' specific material experiences, which do result from their differences from the norm, but as ultimately supplying the basis for a more universalizing possibility. In this way, my theorization is closest to Judith Butler's (especially in *Undoing Gender*), but with significant caveats that I elaborate below.

22. Winnubst concentrates on liberalism's classic political form, as first articulated by John Locke. As such, it promotes what she calls the neutral individual's "phallicized whiteness." She uses an alternative idea of sovereignty modeled by Georges Bataille and his philosophy of the accursed share to counter such exclusivist forms of liberalist privacy.

23. Harper still holds out for a transformative social agency discovered by queer subjects who "seize and interpret the meanings of 'public' and 'private' in a way that enhances, rather than hinders, our free subjectivity" (*Private Affairs*, 82). Although the redefinition of the public–private divide may not transpire through an agentic seizure of opportunities as easily as he implies, it is worth noting that shifts of power in liberalism's biopolitical order are owing to the two spheres' relatively uncontrollable and fluctuating division.

24. In *Giving an Account of Oneself*, Butler also notes the corporeality of this condition, but she ends up foregrounding rhetoric, or what she repeatedly terms the "structure of address." In *Undoing Gender* (esp. 17–39), she primarily concentrates on embodiment and so gives a fuller account of a "condition of primary vulnerability" (24). My work here tries to make more of an explicit connection between these two modes of embodied and linguistic vulnerabilities. Butler does not explicitly formulate them as analogous modes; however, because she treats them separately she does end up aligning language's improper qualities more with an epistemological and ethical enterprise than a civic one. These should not be treated as separate projects, though: the epistemological, ethical, ontological, and civic dimensions of these inquiries are interrelated. In the midst of those connections, the line between theoretic subject and civic person are blurred. We are thus called on to reformulate queer theory's antihumanist foundations.

25. Deleuze's reading of Whitman focuses on how an American whole (a "web of variable relations" that preserves the integrity of each of its constituent parts; *Essays Critical and Clinical*, 60) arises from the combinative fragments of relations between individuals, groups, and histories. "Relations are not internal to a Whole; rather the Whole is derived from the external relations of a given moment, and varies with them" (59). Individuals are not atomistic and self-contained Wholes, but only *approximations* of such. Resemblance arises from their various, fragmentary, contingent senses of self, which derive from their relations with others.

26. Butler has developed her recent thinking about responsibility largely in light of her sense of the precariousness of life and the necessity of risk. For her, an ethical stance entails questioning the norms of social recognition, of subjecting one's self to impersonal standards and an impersonal language that challenges our egos' self-containment and integrity. It "involves putting oneself at risk, imperiling the very possibility of being recognized by others" (*Giving an Account of Oneself*, 23). Butler uses vulnerability as a conceptual fulcrum to shift our political sensibilities about nationalism, gender definition, or embodied life from an immobilizing melancholic frame to one that allows for hope and healing by permitting the mourning of injury and losses. "Perhaps . . . one mourns when one accepts that by the loss one undergoes one will be changed, possibly for ever. Perhaps mourning has to do with agreeing to undergo a transformation (perhaps one should say *submitting* to a transformation) the full result of which one cannot know in advance" (*Precarious Life*, 21; emphasis in original; repeated virtually verbatim in relation to transgender politics in *Undoing Gender*,

18). The gravitas of mourning is itself a first step in reclaiming hope. It historically connects us to a past that is lost and to a future potentiality that comes from working through that loss. As I elucidate below, however, we need not associate vulnerability only with mourning to critically appreciate certain forms of this fundamentally ontological condition.

27. On courage and the risk of the polis, see also Arendt, *The Human Condition*, 28–37.

28. Badiou's theory of the joyful nature of poetry differs from mine insofar as he sees the poem as a threshold or a Heideggerian opening. For him, poetry merely "waits"; it does not think actively of (and thus enact) the future (*The Century*, 21–22). But if poetry is truly active, and if that activity is the reason for its joy, we ought to remember that it is *composed* by an embodied subject. Badiou's metaphysics disembodies poetry and renders it an ahistorical text that only welcomes history when it eventually arrives. While it might not manifest a direct action, a poem, as I see it, does not merely wait. Its action, as I detail below, is a kind of seduction. Through the text, the author calls us to receive and complete what (and who) the poem voices.

29. To this extent, I imagine queer theory's ethical project as proceeding along the lines of a Foucauldian archaeology. In that methodology, texts from various discursive archives provide a "positivity" that "defines a field in which formal identities, thematic continuities, translations of concepts, and polemical interchanges may be deployed." Historical work is based on an analysis of what is "given" and of "things actually said" (Foucault, *The Archaeology of Knowledge*, 127). That is to say, we work with a legible discursive field from the past; but our textually mediated engagements with that past bear the potential to unsettle our selves, as historical actors. In *How to Do the History of Homosexuality* (1–23), David M. Halperin outlines a similar Foucauldian methodology as crucial for escaping the tautology of much post-Stonewall gay and lesbian historiography. Maintaining such archaeological dimensions that contribute to what Halperin (after Foucault) terms "a history of the present" is key for preserving the ethicality of our work.

30. For a different formulation of such incommunicative articulations (as socially originating "lines of flight" and "expression machines," rather than Adorno's immanent encroachment of a Hegelian world spirit), see Deleuze and Guattari, *Kafka: Toward a Minor Literature*, esp. 28–42.

31. Although I disagree with his assessment that Wallace Stevens and other high modernists endorsed a conservatively liberalist ideal of privacy, Joseph Harrington's reading of some lyricists as asserting the need for their work to be read as forms of public discourse, rather than as private expression, is worthwhile. Interestingly, he also notes that the public nature of lyric comprises the poet's "ethical duty toward an audience, or anyone else" (*Poetry and the Public*, 13).

32. In *Giving an Account of Oneself* (30–40), Judith Butler makes a similar move in relation to Cavarero but does so by emphasizing the risky vulnerability that subjects assume in their struggles for recognition with linguistic norms. Like Cavarero, Alphonso Lingis posits a similarly othering mode of intersubjective contact that begins with the voice. While his model allows for one's own voice to introduce a continual, repeated disruption of selfhood, that disruption ironically introduces some coherence and renarrativization. One might think of it as shifting strategies for aesthetically fashioning one's self by, as Lingis terms it, *honoring* one's word (*The First Person Singular*, 37–44). The risks attending one's living encounters with others, the inherent violence of that contact (by encountering what he terms their interior "visionary space"), and their challenges to the narrative one honors about one's self risk sliding into dishonor and, ultimately, death.

33. Mladen Dolar illuminates possibilities for thinking of the text as a third body. Revising Lacan's concept of *extimacy*, he theorizes the *object voice* as "the pivotal point precisely at the intersection of presence and absence" through which one "recogniz[es] oneself as the addressee of the voice of the Other," but "at the same time . . . inherently lacks and disrupts any notion of a full presence" (*A Voice and Nothing More*, 55). This voice functions "as an [assumption of] authority over the Other and as an exposure to the Other, an appeal,

a plea, an attempt to bend the Other. It cuts directly into the interior, so much so that the very status of the exterior becomes uncertain, and it discloses the interior, so much so that the very supposition of an interior depends on the voice. So both hearing and emitting a voice present an excess, a surplus of authority on the one hand and a surplus of exposure on the other" (80–81). Through this mediating voice or virtual body, one is brought outside one's self and into relation with the Lacanian Other, thus complicating the divisions between public and private, exterior and interior, submission and sovereignty.

## Chapter One

1. Perhaps that career division overstates Stevens's early aestheticism. As James Longenbach (*Wallace Stevens: The Plain Sense of Things*, 41–82) details, that volume's later poems—including "The Death of a Soldier" and "Sunday Morning"—respond to an interwar condition, but their "ambitions [are] circumscribed" because of Stevens's "awareness of the frightful unreality that may arise from a poetry that tries to be political" (63).

2. For his complete discussion, see Alan Filreis, *Modernism from Right to Left*, 12–45.

3. For excellent readings of Stevens's ethical reflections on various sociopolitical concerns, see Angus J. Cleghorn, *Wallace Stevens's Poetics: The Neglected Rhetoric*, and Jacqueline Vaught Brogan, *The Violence Within, the Violence Without: Wallace Stevens and the Emergence of a Revolutionary Poetics.*

4. I do not have the space to do so here, but reappraising Stevens's investment in, and critique of, liberalism could be more thoroughly historicized as engaging Dewey's rethinking of democratic individualism in the 1930s (see introduction, n. 12). Dewey and Stevens published in the same magazines, including *The Partisan Review* and *The New Republic*; and the poet found the philosopher's work "valuable," as he wrote Henry Church in 1941 (*LWS* 441).

5. I am thinking specifically of a 1949 letter to José Rodríguez Feo where Stevens remarks that "one is always desperately in need of the fellowship of one's own kind" as well as "the fellowship of the landsman and compatriot" (*SM* 165). The question remains, though, whether he easily equated that "kind" with "compatriots." What is evident is Stevens's *ambivalent* relationship to his affective connections with the U.S. people. He both longs for his "kind," yet is critical of settling for the sort of security provided by the steadfastly liberalist nationalism of the Cold War.

6. The few other existing investigations of the exchange between Stevens and Rodríguez Feo focus on the letters' "camp" and gender elements (David R. Jarraway, "'Creatures of the Rainbow': Wallace Stevens, Mark Doty, and the Poetics of Androgyny"); its imperialist asymmetries (Roberto Ignacio Díaz, "Wallace Stevens y el discurso en la Habana: Palabras de José Rodriguez Feo"); or the poet's criticism of the young editor's indiscriminate reading of other national literatures (Alan Filreis, *Wallace Stevens and the Actual World*, esp. 187–206).

7. I am not suggesting that Stevens was a queer subject or even that he was politically or culturally a homophile. (Quite the opposite is true: he tended to be paranoid about the effeminacy of queer men, including Rodríguez Feo.) However, there are affinities between his ethical reappraisal of liberalism and queer writers' resistances that highlight similarity, commonality, and even cosmopolitanism. I am not alone in sensing the "queerness" of his project. Jarraway (*Going the Distance: Dissident Subjectivity in Modernist American Literature*, 1–17), for one, has made explicit links between an idea of "distancing" (i.e., the subject's internal division) in Stevens's work and some queer theories. His concept of distancing is akin to the effects of resemblance explored here; however, I read Stevens as less interested in the subject's internal division than in the subject's relation and connection. The queerness

of this dynamic is owed to the embodied nature of relationality and its resultant eroticism, what Stevens calls "pleasure."

8. See Eric Keenaghan, "A Virile Poet in the Borderlands: Wallace Stevens' Reimagining of Race and Masculinity."

9. In chapter 2, I discuss the Platt Amendment more. For the text of the Jones-Shafroth Act, including articles added with the Nationality Law (1940) and later emendations (1950), see <http://www.lexjuris.com/LEXLEX/lexotras/lexactajones.htm>. Accessed July 23, 2007.

10. See Frederick R. Pike, *FDR's Good Neighbor Policy: Sixty Years of Generally Gentle Chaos*, 11–38.

11. On nativism as the drive to cement essentialist identifications in interwar American literature, see Walter Benn Michaels, *Our America: Nativism, Modernism, and Pluralism*. During the interwar period, pluralist thought had an ambivalent relationship to nativist policies; often both reinforced liberalist ideologies of privatization and personal autonomy. For example, see Everett Helmut Akam's discussion of John Collier and the Indian New Deal of 1934 in *Transnational America: Cultural Pluralist Thought in the Twentieth Century*, 126–28. For an account of how that ambivalence was worked through by American intellectuals in the 1940s and 1950s in order to address the realities of international markets and the inadequacies of domestic cultural pluralism, see David W. Noble, *Death of a Nation: American Culture and the End of Exceptionalism*. Stevens's later career is marked by the influence of earlier pluralist thought and its ambivalences, while demonstrating his own commitment to reassessing American exceptionalism.

12. See also Benjamin D. Rhodes, *United States Foreign Policy in the Interwar Period, 1918–1941: The Golden Age of American Diplomatic and Military Complacency*, 123–24.

13. See Bryce Wood, *The Making of the Good Neighbor Policy*, 118–55.

14. See Bryce Wood, *The Dismantling of the Good Neighbor Policy*, 191–209.

15. On the conservatism of Cold War liberalism, particularly in regard to its consolidation of heteronormative and nationally exceptionalist ideologies, see Robert J. Corber, *Homosexuality in Cold War America: Resistance and the Crisis of Masculinity*, 160–89, and *In the Name of National Security: Hitchcock, Homophobia, and the Political Construction of Gender in Postwar America*, 19–55.

16. The Good Neighbor Policy promoted a dependence sustaining the singular differences between North and South; ultimately, though, the resultant diplomatic model was conservative. It *reinforced* national asymmetries based on a persistent faith in cultural purism, security, and U.S. exceptionalism. Pike criticizes the policy's merits, based on FDR's personal antipathy toward Latin America (*FDR's Good Neighbor Policy*, 216–26). As he argues, FDR used the hemispheric model to win credibility from the European nations on whom he focused his diplomatic attentions and energies. However, he does not note that this pan-American enterprise is also motivated by a nationalism common to FDR's policy of nonintervention and Herbert Hoover's earlier, more openly conservative presumption of the superiority of U.S. political and cultural systems.

17. Badiou's model of a poetic disruption of the "we" hinges on his opposition of the "eloquence" of St. John Perse to the murmuring of Paul Celan (see *The Century*, 90–97). Stevens's lyric falls closer to Perse's style than Celan's, but our American also importantly avoids the sort of "nihilistic epic" evident in the former's oeuvre. Significantly, Stevens models the sort of lyric thinking Badiou is interested in, even if this poet avoids the avant-garde ruptures the philosopher esteems in figures like Celan, Bertolt Brecht, Samuel Beckett, and Osip Mandelstam.

18. Perhaps Rodríguez Feo was drawn to Stevens's phrase "the major men" because he believed it specifically addressed the *gendered* and *sexualized* dimensions of national belonging. After all, in the same paragraph in which he asks Stevens about the meaning of the major man, he proceeds to complain about Ernest Hemingway's *machismo*. Although Rodríguez Feo brings Stevens's attention to the trope, his hints about possibly queer content did not register.

19. See Eric Keenaghan, "Wallace Stevens' Influence on the Construction of Gay Masculinity by the Cuban *Origenes* Group."

20. This suggests a difference that distinguishes Stevens's project of reordering the world from much interwar American aestheticism. Russ Castronovo reads the cultural and philosophical proponents of aestheticism between roughly 1890 and 1930 as metaphorically substituting the order of culture for the anarchy and violence of politics. At one point, he draws on Foucault to note that a more ethical "aesthetics of existence" could develop an aesthetic practice that does not "aestheticize life but rather politicizes it by revealing the subject as ethically—but not morally—situated among others" (*Beautiful Democracy: Aesthetics and Anarchy in a Global Era*, 59). Castronovo's implicit point about politicized art's preservation and cultivation of violence and disorder puts into relief the ethicopolitical dimensions of Stevens's project (which deems both chaos *and* order necessary). Moreover, Stevens's example shows that in this late modernist moment a transformative aesthetics of existence was imagined as including, not precluding, metaphorical strategies. Metaphor is (dis)figuration, rather than mere substitution and beautification.

21. Pressing the point, Stevens can be said to cling too much to an idea of "private resemblance" here. If perceptual proclivities are bodily and social, the resemblances a poet discovers are *never* truly private. Acknowledging this lack of privacy and proprietorship would complicate his reproductive metaphor ("the mind *begets*"). This presents a cautionary lesson for any theorizing out of poetry: Stevens provides a point from which we can begin to think about similarity, not an ethical template we should adopt without revision or criticism.

22. For Deleuze on "the middle," see Gilles Deleuze and Félix Guattari, *A Thousand Plateaus: Capitalism and Schizophrenia*, 3–25, 492–99, and Gilles Deleuze and Claire Parnet, *Dialogues*, 36–76.

23. In chapter 2, I discuss a key essay from *Orígenes* where Lezama explicitly mentions the centrality of Stevens's influence. In my analysis of Duncan in chapter 3, I do not go into any depth about similar influences. This is largely because his critical prose does not focus on Stevens, though he did regard him as one of his "masters" (alongside Gertrude Stein, H.D., Ezra Pound, William Carlos Williams, and Laura Riding Jackson). Much like Stevens, Duncan rejected group identification on the grounds that it separated the writer from the rest of human commonality. While his anarchism is not exclusively influenced by Stevens, Duncan found in Stevens's work a useful model for an individualized poetic opposition to *a priori* communities and identity groups. Stevens's thematic emphasis on poetic freedom as deriving from reading and reflection also resound in Duncan's poetics of derivation (from his readings of others) and rewriting (from rereading his own previous work). The centrality of reading to both may result from the influence of Ralph Waldo Emerson that they share. Duncan pays explicit homage to Stevens in one late text: "*Structure of Rime XXVIII* In Memoriam Wallace Stevens" (*Ground Work*, 60). Significantly, this poem singles out "Desire" and "Imagination"—two Stevensian tropes—as the means of resisting the imperialist and nationalist effects of the Vietnam War on identity.

24. If we accept Edward Said's classic definition of literary imperialism as perpetuating a representational logic "which not only misrepresented them [i.e., colonized peoples] but assumed they were unable to read and respond directly" (*Culture and Imperialism*, 31), Stevens is not a hard-and-fast imperialist. After all, he did respect the *origenistas'* intellectual and aesthetic integrity. Despite Stevens's requests for "little vistas" of Cuba, Rodríguez Feo also never saw Stevens as an imperialist. Instead, the editor openly accused others, such as Charles Henri Ford, of "that stupid, tourist-exotic vision of our tropics" and "the silliest, most unintelligent bit of Americana" (*SM* 60). In contrast, he singled out Stevens as "an almost legendary amigo of us Cuban writers" (*SM* 190).

25. In my study of Lezama (chapter 2), it becomes clear why Stevens's presumption that the Cubans are not concerned with nationalism and the state actually misses the mark. His conclusion also ignores all the other global contributors to *Orígenes*. Given that he himself published in the magazine, this is a remarkably strange oversight. Setting these criticisms

aside, though, Stevens's comment still can help refine our understanding of his poetic ethic.

26. See Benedict Anderson, *Imagined Communities: Reflections on the Origin and Spread of Nationalism.*

## Chapter Two

1. All translations from the Spanish are mine, unless otherwise noted. Here I have translated the title of Lezama's essay with the English preposition "about" to capture his diction's spatial dimensions. *Alrededor* signifies the direction of an approach, or proximity, but one still remains on the outskirts of one's destination.

2. The core members of *Orígenes* consisted of poets (Lezama, Baquero, Gaztelu, Piñera, Solís, Justo Rodríguez, Fina García Marruz, Cintio Vitier, Eliseo Diego, Octavio Smith, Lorenzo García Vega); painters (Mariano Rodríguez, René Portocarrero); musicians (Julián Orbón, José Ardévol); and other writers (Rodríguez Feo, Bella García Marruz, Agustín Pí). Later issues of the publication involved younger poets, such as Roberto Fernández Retamar and Fayad Jamís.

3. Unruh's subscription to conventionally existentialist ideas about vanguardist resistance is evident in that she gives some attention to the *minoristas* but ignores the *origenistas* altogether.

4. James Buckwalter-Arias addresses how some contemporary Cuban authors glorify the *origenistas* as pre-Revolutionary predecessors. Many regard Lezama and the rest of the *Orígenes* group as using art to realize "the highest expression of true, individual liberty," an alternative to the later Revolution's recasting of liberty "in explicitly collective terms" that is believed to be still capable of resisting the global market ("Reinscribing the Aesthetic: Cuban Narrative and Post-Soviet Cultural Politics," 364). In contrast, my project unsettles such an easy attribution of individualism to the *origenistas,* who were known for their emphasis on *amistad* or "friendship." Such an amicable—indeed, amorous—model can resignify both resistance and collectivity without reading their aesthetic in overly individualizing, transcendental terms.

5. Gustavo Pérez Firmat's "The Strut of the Centipede: José Lezama Lima and New World Exceptionalism" is one of the few pieces about how Lezama's poetic connects Northern *and* Southern identities.

6. The Platt Amendment is transcribed in full at http://www.fordham.edu/halsall/mod/1901platt.html. Last accessed 8 January 2008.

7. Since the Missouri Compromise (1820) and the annexation debates before the Emancipation Proclamation (1862), the United States had desired to possess Cuba. Those debates heated up again during the colony's first attempt to win independence from Spain (the Ten Years' War, 1868–78) and before the War of Independence (1895–98).

8. The Cuban Colonization Company's ads to attract prospective settlers are reproduced by Louis A. Pérez, *On Becoming Cuban,* 112–13.

9. Rojas specifies that Cuba's political Right identified with the liberalist imperative of an individualistic pursuit of happiness, and the Left pursued liberalist independence through a collective form of nationalistic sovereignty.

10. For Nuez's complete discussion of "confrontation," "reproduction," and "appropriation," see *La balsa perpetua,* 21–40.

11. One of Lezama's more famous poems is "Para llegar a *Montego Bay*" (*Orígenes* 35, 1954; reprinted in *Dador,* 1960). Julio Cortázar's essay "Para llegar a Lezama Lima" ("To Reach Lezama Lima," 1967) plays on the poem's title, as does the *origenista* Cintio Vitier's late essay collection *Para llegar a Orígenes* (1994). Neither deals with the trope of *approaching* as I do here, as ultimately maintaining distances rather than achieving a goal because the *telos* itself is the limit, a pure impossibility.

12. Elsewhere Lezama names that arche-image the *imago*, thus distinguishing the desired image from what is produced by poetic metaphors. An image (*imagen*) is thus only the approximation or fragmented re-presentation of the *imago*'s ultimately unknowable *telos*. See "Introducción a un sistema poético" ("Introduction to a Poetic System"; *Orígenes* 36, 1954), in *TH* 9–36.

13. See de Man, "The Epistemology of Metaphor," in *Aesthetic Ideology*, 34–50.

14. This is not to say that metaphysics always precludes social ethics. Emilio Bejel (*José Lezama Lima: Poet of the Image*, esp. 16–69, 124–47) offers an excellent reading that connects the metaphysical and postcolonial dimensions of Lezama's poetic. Brett Levinson (*Secondary Moderns: Mimesis, History, and Revolution in Lezama Lima's "American Expression,"* esp. 159–81) supplies a strong postcolonial account of Lezama's critical engagement with Aristotelian and Platonic metaphysics. Neither connects postcolonial and queer critique, though. I facilitate that link here by focusing on less-discussed essays that work through the principles outlined in their shared primary text, Lezama's well-known "Introduction to a Poetic System."

15. For another reading of Zambrano on the "pre-natal" nation's innocence and Lezama's secret, see Carlós Barbáchano, "La Cuba secreta o la íntima historia de un encuentro inacabable."

16. For her full discussion, see Zambrano, *Persona y democracia*, 162–65. Not incidentally, she theorizes that individuals experience overlapping forms of temporality (esp. 11–25, 59–92). Because love, family, and commonality are experienced in different temporal registers, what is called "history" should be seen as just one kind of temporality. This notion of different experiences of time resonates with Lezama's distinction in "The Dignity of Poetry" between historical and poematic time. If read in light of Zambrano's philosophy in *Persona y democracia*, which appeared at about the same time, his elaboration of two forms of temporality can be read as *overlapping* and *mutually affecting one another*.

17. Despite their ontological vocabulary, Lezama's and Zambrano's opposition to Sartre is distinct from that posed by Martin Heidegger in the form of the ecstatic metaphysics elaborated in "Letter on Humanism."

18. See Barthes, *Writing Degree Zero*, 9–18. In his response to Sartre, Barthes argues that "style is never anything but metaphor, that is, equivalence of the author's literary intention and carnal structure. . . . So that style is always a secret; but the occult aspect of its implications does not arise from the mobile and ever-provisional nature of language; its secret is recollection locked within the body of the writer" (12). His concern with the writer's body and its secretive nature connects Lezama's poetic to Severo Sarduy's, who was influenced by Barthes and his differences from Sartrean existentialism (as I discuss in chapter 4).

19. The little magazines published either separately or jointly by Lezama, Gatzelu, and Baquero prior to *Orígenes* were: *Verbum* (1937), *Espuela de Plata* (1939–41), *Clavileño* (1941–43), *Nadie Parecía* (1942–44), and *Poeta* (1942–43).

20. José Quiroga (*Cuban Palimpsests*, 25–50) argues that such an idea of the "redeeming force of history" continues to be important to the post-Revolutionary Cuban state. It rewrites history in terms of "a cohesive set of symbols geared toward a future teleology," a mythopoeic symbolization overwriting the actualities of cultural fragmentation in order to generate a false sense of security in the present order (4).

21. In *The American Expression*, Lezama describes Eliot as "essentially pessimistic and crepuscular," settling only "to repeat" old narratives because "he believes that the ancient masters cannot be surpassed." In contrast, a baroque use of myth and history more optimistically strives to create something new by recombining old materials. "Everything will have to be reconstructed, invented anew, and the old myths, upon reappearing, will offer us their conjurations and enigmas with an unfamiliar face" (*EA* 286).

22. This point is made all the more poignant by the fact that the poetry collection where this essay originally appeared was sponsored by the Cuban government, published by the Council of National Culture, only six years after the Revolution. It is quite powerful that

Lezama's piece surreptitiously undermines the state's official hermeneutic strategy and instantiates an antinationalistic ethic by implicitly encouraging Cuban readers' sympathetic identification with Columbus, the preeminent colonizer.

23. Cinito Vitier (*Para llegar a Origenes*, 18–34) narrates the politicized shift in Lezama's poetics differently. He reads *The American Expression* as beginning to promote Lezama's idea of "the image as creator of fact" (29). This change in Lezama's poetic supposedly responds to the "full insurrectional struggle against Batista" (29). Vitier's full response to Lezama constitutes part of his lectures at Havana's Lyceum, *Lo cubano en la poesía* (*The Cuban in Poetry*).

24. Martin Jay ("Scopic Regimes of Modernity," in *Force Fields: Between Intellectual History and Cultural Critique*, 114–33) similarly argues that the Enlightenment de-eroticized relationality by introducing distances between self and other. As he argues, baroque aesthetics seek to restore intimate points of contact to rectify that situation.

25. In "Discurso origenista y Cuba postsoviética," James Buckwalter-Arias warns against such approaches to Lezama's work, especially by post-Soviet Cuban gay writers. Willful misreadings reduce Lezama to a homosexual martyr persecuted by a homophobic totalitarian system and are used to endorse market logics and identity politics. Ironically, he has become an icon, rather than a critic, of liberalism.

26. "It is not only identifications *across* definitional lines that can evoke or support or even require complex and particular narrative explanation; rather, the same is equally true of any person's identification with her or his 'own' gender, class, race, sexuality, nation" (Sedgwick, *Epistemology of the Closet*, 60–61).

27. Quiroga distinguishes between silence and the secret in his analysis of another *origenista*, Virgilio Piñera. The secret refuses disclosure, but silence—the one associated with Piñera—entails a "coding [that] calls attention to itself: it plays with the full spectacle of the disclosure" (*Tropics of Desire*, 103). I would argue that that sort of seduction flirts with identity and thus begs to be deciphered in a liberalist manner. This befits Piñera, who left *Orígenes* to found *Ciclón* with Rodríguez Feo so as to explore more overtly queer, resistant expressions in art.

## Chapter Three

1. Allan Antliff (*Anarchy and Art: From the Paris Commune to the Fall of the Berlin Wall*, 113–32) gives a good historical account that reads Duncan's early essay on sexuality, as well as an attack on the gay poet Charles Henri Ford's surrealist magazine *View*, as part of his anticapitalism and anarchism.

2. Ekbert Faas (*Young Robert Duncan: Portrait of the Poet as Homosexual in Society*, 146–60) provides an overview of the composition, publication, and reception of "The Homosexual in Society."

3. See Alexander Berkman, *What Is Anarchism?* and Emma Goldman, *Anarchism and Other Essays*.

4. In his edition of *A Selected Prose*, Robert J. Bertholf published the expanded 1959 version of Duncan's "The Homosexual in Society." This version includes an "Introduction" and a "Reflections 1959" conclusion that frames the 1944 original. Duncan also included additional footnotes that provide running commentary, as a kind of palimpsest, about the context and ideas prompting the essay fifteen years earlier.

5. For example, in the first edition of *Leaves of Grass* (1855), Whitman introduces his poetic persona as "Walt Whitman, an American, one of the roughs, a kosmos." In the fourth edition (1865), he amends the potentially exclusivist nature of this self-introduction by dropping the masculinist identification with the "roughs" and the nationalist one with "America": "Walt Whitman, a kosmos, of Manhattan the son" (For the two versions, see the Norton Critical Edition, 52).

6. Levertov complained of the hypocrisy of Duncan's disapproval of her politicized antiwar poetry by pointing to "Up Rising" (see *LRD* 664–86). Although he portrayed it as an apolitical piece, the poem's bibliographic history does suggest otherwise. "Up Rising" was solicited by Levertov for a 1965 issue of the liberal periodical *The Nation*, and the next year Duncan included it in *Of the War*, a small chapbook locally distributed by the Berkeley-based Oyez Press. The national reader would not be able to dissociate "Up Rising" from *The Nation*'s antiwar articles and editorials. In fact, the poem was singled out as exemplary for its antiwar position in its readers' letters (*LRD* 515). *Of the War*'s local readers arrived at similar conclusions. Although the metaphysics of his poetic can be read in the chapbook's title, which is akin to that of an eighteenth-century philosophical treatise, his ontological perspective is in tension with the visceral cover image: a negative exposure of a body dragged behind a tank. That image would have been read by many in the Bay Area—the hub of U.S. antiwar activism—as a clear indictment of Vietnam War atrocities. As Duncan recounts, Robin Blaser, for one, found "Up Rising" and the rest of the chapbook to be politically didactic "examples of bad verse and the public corruption of my talents" (*LRD* 573). Elsewhere ("The Queerness of Poetic Action during Vietnam") I consider the political dimensions of his Vietnam-era poetic as encompassing a critique of the biopolitical state rather than a protest of the war, a subtle distinction.

7. For a historical overview of the ideological policing of American sexual mores during the Cold War, see John D'Emilio and Estelle B. Freedman, *Intimate Matters: A History of Sexuality in America*, 284–95.

8. Michael Warner (*The Trouble with Normal: Sex, Politics, and the Ethics of Queer Life*, 52–61) argues against the idea that sexual normalcy rests on a distinction between "statistical norms" and "evaluative norms," or between statistical means and standards of judgment.

9. Because homosexuality was increasingly equated with communism, the Mattachine Society (1950–61) dissociated its homophile politics from the Communist Party in 1953. The organization was restructured so that it was no longer based on a "secret society" model like the American Communist Party, and its members moved from radicalism toward assimilative politics stressing the normalcy, respectability, and patriotism of gays and lesbians. On the links between the Communist Party and the Mattachine Society, see John D'Emilio, *Sexual Politics, Sexual Communities: The Making of a Homosexual Minority in the United States, 1940–1970*, 57–91. On the Mattachine Society's rhetoric about national integrity to promote a moderate liberal agenda, see Joan Meyerowitz, "Sex, Gender, and the Cold War Language of Reform."

10. I borrow the distinction between "American" and "Americanism" from Philip Wander ("Political Rhetoric and the Un-American Tradition"), who identifies the Cold War as an ideological struggle between these two concepts of nationhood. Political progressives promoted an ideal of "American" culture that ensures civil liberties and individual rights not limited to the nation-state. The more conservative ideologies of "Americanism," however, were based on nationalistic loyalty to a bounded geopolitical entity. Factions supporting an "Americanist" worldview constituted a cultural and political hegemony during the Cold War.

11. Duncan does not believe that modern poetry creates neat correspondences between the author's sex and the text's "gender." The desire to eliminate "feminine" excesses, such as sentimentality or lyricism, is not unique to male poets. "Even for women, areas of poetic feeling must contend with limits that social attitudes would set within the psyche itself against womanish excess" (*HD* 2.9: 80). Male authors can also exhibit "feminine" flights of fancy, such as the unicorn in Williams's *Paterson V* or the Aesopian ant in Pound's *Pisan Cantos*. But because he presents such sentimental moments in male-authored texts as *exceptions*, and because he discusses *female* poets such as Edith Sitwell or H.D. as more consistently exemplifying sentimental poetics, he does seem to unconsciously conflate sex and gender in a way that reinforces how bodies pose limits to his deconstructive project.

12. For an overview of gender ideologies, countercultural resistance to the Cold War consensus, and homosexual opposition to popular culture's normalizing ideologies of "virility,"

see Robert J. Corber, *Homosexuality in Cold War America: Resistance and the Crisis of Masculinity*, 1–54.

13. Ginsberg inscribed Duncan's personal copy of *Howl* with the following: "FOR [*sic*] Robert Duncan in the hope that *Howl* seems more gracious—mellow—a lament to him as time goes by; or that it drops out of my own affection in the Future" (reproduced in Matt Theado, *The Beats: A Literary Reference*, 242). As Theado notes, the inscription "suggests that the poem was a cause for disagreement between Ginsberg and his fellow poet Duncan." In an interview from the mid-1970s, Duncan reveals that gender and sexuality were at the center of that disagreement. *Howl* exhibited a "pan-sexuality [which] directly came in conflict with my very strong sense of Apollonian dedications. I mean, strong enough for a householder . . . I found it very threatening." Sexuality would become less threatening if writers were to give it "boundaries and various centers." Such "an architecture" would not contain desire but would provide a public structure and visible core missing in work by gay writers like Ginsberg and Burroughs, who try to escape the problem of masculine agency by "melting down, or breaking down, and wanting to disappear" (Duncan in Faas, *Towards a New American Poetics: Essays and Interviews, Charles Olson, Robert Duncan, Gary Snyder, Robert Creeley, Robert Bly, Allen Ginsberg*, 66).

14. Hereafter I do not note Duncan's idiosyncratic phonetic spellings of past participles with [*sic*]. His usual pattern is an elision of the "e" or switching the "ed" to a "t."

15. Robert J. Bertholf ("The Concert: Robert Duncan and Writing out of Painting," 67–68, 89) has paid the most attention to Duncan's household trope. He remarks that the household establishes a sanctuary apart from politics, but I read it as politically deconstructing Cold War distinctions between public and private, work and home. Sherman Paul (*The Lost America of Love*, 169–276) reads love as central to Duncan's politics, but he oddly ends up reading the household trope as a mythopoetic and ahistorical means of arriving at that politics.

16. Elsewhere ("Jack Spicer's Pricks and Cocksuckers: Translating Homosexuality into Visibility") I have written about Spicer's poetics as extending homosexual visibility beyond private coteries.

17. Peter O'Leary's *Gnostic Contagion: Robert Duncan and the Poetry of Illness* provides a strong account of H.D.'s correspondence with Duncan and of the resultant influence of her poetics. However, O'Leary tends to normalize the exchange by insisting on a Freudian oedipality that positions H.D. as mother, Freud as father, and Duncan as child (53). I read Duncan's engagement with Freud and psychosexual identity structures as much more contentious, as is exemplified in one poem he sent H.D., "Apprehensions" (discussed below).

18. See "Sagesse" in H.D., *Hermetic Definition*, 57–84.

19. See Butler, *Precarious Life: The Powers of Mourning and Violence*, 19–49.

## Chapter Four

1. See Althusser, *For Marx* (esp. 221–47), and "The Humanist Controversy" (in *The Humanist Controversy and Other Writings*, 220–305).

2. A handful of crucial texts arguing for the need of queer theory to address intersectionality, identity, and community include: David L. Eng, Judith Halberstam, and José Esteban Muñoz, eds., *What's So Queer about Queer Studies Now?*; Roderick A. Ferguson, *Aberrations in Black: Toward a Queer of Color Critique*; Dwight A. McBride, *Why I Hate Abercrombie and Fitch: Essays on Race and Sexuality*; E. Patrick Johnson and Mae G. Henderson, *Black Queer Studies: A Critical Anthology*; and Jasbir K. Puar, *Terrorist Assemblages: Homonationalism in Queer Times*.

3. All translations are mine, unless otherwise indicated.

4. See Edelman, *Homographesis: Essay in Gay Literary and Cultural Theory*, 3–23.

5. For a classic early critique of Sarduy, see Jean Franco, "The Crisis of the Liberal Imagination and the Utopia of Writing." For praise, see Adriana Méndez Rodenas, *Severo Sarduy: El neobarroco de la transgresión*, esp. 137–48.

6. On the queer theory and performativity's metaphysics, see Brad Epps, "The Fetish of Fluidity."

7. See Bejel, *Gay Cuban Nation*, 128–39.

8. See Julian Bourg, *From Revolution to Ethics: May 1968 and Contemporary French Thought*.

9. See González Echevarría, *La ruta de Severo Sarduy*, 40–42.

10. Sarduy posits that the baroque exemplifies two qualities (*artifice* and *parody*). Each is produced by one of several writing strategies: *substitution, proliferation, condensation, intertextuality* (consisting of *citation* or *reminiscence*), *intratextuality* (consisting of *phonetic grammars, semic grammars,* or *syntagmatic grammars*). He illustrates his discussion with brief examples from several Southern authors, visual artists, filmmakers, and musicians.

11. In many ways, Sarduy's neobaroque, with its emphasis on the proliferation of fragments and partial objects (as I discuss below), is closer to Lezama's baroque than he admits. In "The Baroque and the Neobaroque," he argues that Lezama's baroque—like any version of this aesthetic—is eroticized, but how he characterizes that eroticization points to a different way of understanding Lezama's secret than what I outline above (chapter 2). Sarduy writes that his predecessor's baroque is based on a metaphorical substitution that "expels the 'normal' from the [linguistic] function, and puts in its place another that is totally foreign [*ajeno*], which has the effect of eroticizing the entire work" (*OC* 2: 1388). Eroticization remains tied to a metaphysic that privileges the author as the one who knows the truth. (In my reading of Lezama, no one knows a truth since the "image" where the truth resides compels the continuing production of fragments.) As Sarduy imagines it, his own preferred neobaroque style is not so metaphysical even if it is still difficult. Rather than promoting obscurity through substitution, it is elliptical. Thus it generates a metonymic proliferation that produces a desire like Lacan's or partial objects like Deleuze and Guattari's.

12. See Manuel Díaz Martínez's introduction, "Siempre como siempre," to Sarduy, *Cartas*, 14–15.

13. See Jean-Michel Rabaté, *The Future of Theory*, 10, 71–77. Both Barthes's and Sartre's books have sections titled "What Is Writing?" and Barthes implicitly responds to Sartre though he never mentions him by name. See Susan Sontag's preface to Barthes, *Writing Degree Zero*, vii–xxi.

14. In a graduate course discussion on Barthes and modernist lyric, my student Michael Jonik first used the sharp geometric metaphor of the asymptote to describe this configuration.

15. Carol Maier's translation reads: " . . . in spite of our resistance we are beginning to explore a plane of literalness previously off limits, formulating the question about our own being, about our *humanity* that first and foremost questions the being of our writing" (*WB* 22). Sarduy's original reads: " . . . a pesar de sus resistencias, el hombre se adentra en el plano de la literalidad que hasta ahora se había vedado, formulando esa pregunta sobre su propio ser, sobre su *humanidad* que es ante todo la del ser de su escritura" (*OC* 2: 1137). The primary difference is that Maier's first person plural version ("we" and "our") of the original third person "el hombre" (man) and "su" (his/her) misses Sarduy's point about writing's *impersonality*, about the author's disappearance as a person. In typical antihumanist fashion, his depiction of writing here challenges presumptions about "man" and "humanity." It even questions who "we" are.

16. As Robert Duncan's poetic (chapter 3 above) suggests, anarchistic and liberalist individualism are distinct. The first intrinsically ties the individual to a commonality, while the latter exists in an aporetic relationship with it (see the introduction). Theorizing anarchistic

individualism is beyond the scope of the present project but may be integral for furthering queer theory's and critical theory's examinations of individualism, freedom, and collectivity.

17. A fact not to be overlooked: Sarduy's obsession with the Big Bang—a theory of origins (in Spanish, *orígenes*)—also coincides with his return to Lezama's work. Because he values the *origenista*'s theorization of the baroque, he tempers his youthful dismissal of *Orígenes* and his early adoption of an identity- and agency-based transgression when he was associated with Rodríguez Feo and Piñera's vanguard publication *Ciclón*.

18. Sarduy's Foucauldian epistemic model challenges prevalent ideas about another sense of "revolution" in the 1960s: the scientific. Thomas Kuhn's *The Structure of Scientific Revolutions* (1962) popularized a revolutionary model to explain major epistemological shifts as occurring exclusively in scientific communities through discoverers' individual genius.

19. In *Baroque*, Sarduy explains historical models of planetary rotation alongside analogous developments in the arts. The classicism of painters such as el Cigoli, Raphael, and Tasso reproduces the geo- and heliocentric astonomical models of Galileo and Copernicus, each of whom centers systems through a single heavenly body (Earth or Sun). In contrast, works by baroque visual artists such as Caravaggio and Velázquez, and poets such as Góngora, deploy two centers. Thus, they mirror the elliptical orbits originally theorized by Kepler.

20. Bourg (*From Revolution to Ethics*, 179–203) reads Hocquenghem and the FHAR as revolutionary and opposes their political stance to the period's more reformist French feminism. What I regard as his reformism anticipates later French writers' liberalism, which often causes them to criticize gay antihumanists, particularly Foucault, for failing to affirm the importance of identity for sexual minorities (see Didier Eribon, *Insult and the Making of the Gay Self*). Keith Harvey (*Intercultural Movements: American Gay in French Translation*, 25–91) depicts the FHAR and later French gay activism as having a vexed relationship to liberal ideals of identity-based politics, regardless of any revolutionary cant. In the 1970s, French gay politics struggled with liberal conceptions of self and community, particularly as they were articulated by a foreign minority cultural imaginary that he calls "the American gay." Harvey (55–58) singles out Hocquenghem and the FHAR as militating against a ghettoizing impulse in the American gay scene, an impulse Hocquenghem and others read as camp. Effeminacy, Harvey argues, was rejected by prominent branches of French gay politics because it was "associat[ed] with American cultural otherness" (including capitalism and liberalist ideals of personhood, privacy, and egoism). "At the same time," he continues, "effeminacy 'breaks out' in discourses which reject the American model with force precisely for its *lack* of effeminacy" because of the association of the American gay male with a sense of insulated, liberal personhood (ibid., 90; emphasis in original). Suspicious of both an American liberalism and the FHAR's minority politics, Sarduy, whom Harvey does not mention or analyze, embraces both the feminine and camp to an almost hyperbolic extreme. They are part of his queer ethical strategy of disputing any conceptualization of sexual minority identity, not an unconscious effect of rejecting just a U.S. model. Although much has been written about the transgressive nature of his tropes of femininity and transvestism, a thoroughly historicized account of Sarduy's queer ethic in relationship to French gay politics remains to be written.

21. Deleuze and Guattari (*Anti-Oedipus*, 346–50) explicitly tie such an idea of revolution to the failures of a liberal sexual politics: "No 'gay liberation movement' is possible as long as homosexuality is caught up in a relation of exclusive disjunction with heterosexuality, a relation that ascribes them both to a common Oedipal and castrating stock, charged with ensuring only their differentiation in two noncommunicating series, instead of bringing to light their reciprocal inclusion and their transverse communication in the decoded flows of desire. . . . In short, sexual repression, more insistent than ever, will survive all the publications, demonstrations, emancipations, and protests concerning the liberty of sexual objects, sources, and aims, as long as sexuality is kept—consciously or not—within narcissistic, Oedipal, and castrating co-ordinates that are enough to ensure the triumph of the most rigorous censors" (ibid., 350–51).

22. Alicia Rivero-Potter (*Autor/Lector: Huidobro, Borges, Fuentes y Sarduy*, 100–17) is one of the few critics who suggest that Sarduy generally privileges readers more than authors, especially since his fiction rejects transcendent authorship and has lacunae that allow readers interpretive freedom that effectually makes them co-authors. Due to the erotic relation between author and reader, my reading pushes "co-authoring" in a different direction.

23. It is worth noting that Barthes echoes this passage by Lacan in *Roland Barthes by Roland Barthes* (1975, 168), one year after Sarduy invokes it in *Baroque*.

24. Sarduy plays Barthes and Lezama off one another to make the queerness of literary eroticism more *visible*, even more *physical*. His French and Cuban mentors' names appear together in the 1968 essay "Dispersion/False Notes (Homage to Lezama Lima)," which echoes the language of *Writing Degree Zero* while commenting on his Cuban forebear's baroque poetic. Lezama's image provokes an "expression" and "discovery" that "cause enjoyment" by revealing "the potential multiplicity of its realities" (*WB* 72). "The poet's role is to discover those potentialities, make them visible, reflect them in the concavity of language, and even use them to displace the *truth* of written History" (*WB* 72–73; emphasis in original). Pleasure disrupts history as it is conventionally known and narrated. Thus it provides proof of the writer's commitment. The "word" of Sarduy's baroque poet is revolutionary because it "has been freed of all transitive ballast, of that *about* . . . which is the injury inflicted by information, by its morality, and has thus been restored to its fundamental eroticism, to its truth" (*WB* 72). Here Sarduy invokes Barthes's notion of intransitive writing from "To Write: An Intransitive Verb?" (1966). According to Barthes, writing is produced by a *scriptor*, the subject "constituted as immediately contemporary with the writing," rather than by an author who stands outside the text to deliver some message through it (*The Rustle of Language*, 19). In a review of Sarduy's *Cobra* ("The Baroque Side," 1966), Barthes reads the neobaroque style of that novel as a reminder that "besides cases of transitive or ethical [meaning, "moralistic"] communication . . . there is a pleasure of language, of similar fabric, similar silk as erotic pleasure, and that this pleasure of language is its truth" (ibid., 233). In Sarduy's hands, the baroque is not just *similar* to eroticism; rather, it is an *unadulterated form* of pleasure. He runs with Barthes's ideas and would use the erotic nature of writing to strengthen the link between a Cuban baroque tradition and his queer ethic.

25. Because of their disavowal of structuralism, Barthes felt "rejected by the students, whose cause he supported almost instinctively" (Louis-Jean Calvet, *Roland Barthes: A Biography*, 163). He took umbrage at the facts that students packed halls to hear Sartre lecture, and that they attacked Barthes for offering a seminar to study the student movement's use of verbal language. He wanted to preserve his theory's antiexistentialist integrity, yet he also wished to appeal to the student movement by offering structuralism as a compatible ideological critique. On Barthes's relationship to May '68 and later gay politics, see Calvet, *Roland Barthes*, 163–86.

26. For other passages drawing a strong distinction between *bliss* and *pleasure,* see Barthes, *Pleasure of the Text,* 14, 39, and 52–53.

27. Throughout his career, Sarduy was not remiss at deploying traditional Cuban lyric forms such as *sons* and *décimas*. Privileging style and its pleasures over the clear communication of a message, traditional forms actually work against the same humanist tenets of existentialism and liberalism that alienated him from his homeland.

28. For an analysis of how the first edition of the poem "Big Bang" mirrors French and Spanish, as well as scientific and poetic discourses, see Jacinto Fombona Iribarren, "La poética 'cuántica' de Severo Sarduy: Una lectura de *Big Bang*." On "Big Bang"'s exemplification of the poetic theorized in *Baroque,* see Perla Rozencvaig, "El Big Bang de Severo Sarduy o la explosión poética." The reprint edition from which I cite does not reproduce the French versions of Sarduy's texts or the chapbook's five original illustrations of "machines" by Ramón Alejandro.

## Epilogue

1. Said's turn to philology to articulate his politicized ethic is heartening, but I take issue with his equation of reading's passionate openness with the opportunity "to put oneself in the author's position sympathetically" (*Humanism and Democratic Criticism*, 62). Such sympathy unwittingly ends up endorsing liberalism's sharp divide between identity and difference because the reader ultimately sits in judgment over the text in order to utilize it as a subjective tool. Consequently, the logic of similarity that Said approximates is quite distinct from my own. His hopeful desire for literature's ability to elicit sympathies and resolve identity-based crises implicitly signals his hope for a marked, identifiable end to the sort of vulnerability necessary to produce a continual, dynamic queering of life and nation. For more on my distrust of sympathy as an ethical hermeneutic strategy, see my essay "Reading Emerson in Other Times: On a Politics of Solitude and an Ethics of Risk."

2. See Michael Hardt and Antonio Negri, *Empire* and *Multitude: War and Democracy in the Age of Empire.*

3. On the persistence of the state in cosmopolitical paradigms, see also Bonnie Honig, "Another Cosmopolitanism? Law and Politics in the New Europe."

4. See Jeremy Waldron, "Cosmopolitan Norms."

5. I make this large claim knowing full well that "experience" itself has historically been a slippery and multivalent term (see Martin Jay, *Songs of Experience*). Recuperating different manifestations and representations of vulnerability, though, may go far in defining an ethical and ontological reimagining of experience befitting our contemporary moment.

6. "Whoever demands recognition has already arrived at his destination, is already where he still has to get to; he does not require the recognition he demands. His polemical presumptuousness consists in the fact that he, the one who wishes to be recognized, transforms the others, the ones who are meant to recognize him, into those who have to be recognized. Thus the roles, functions, and positions become involved in an uninterrupted and uncontrollable exchange. Ultimately one cannot decide who it is that is supposed to be recognized here and now, and who it is that is recognizing the other here and now" (García Düttmann, *Between Cultures: Tensions in the Struggle for Recognition*, 111). Ethical work does not necessarily proceed if one speaks from an identifiable point of difference. When a confrontational speech act such as ACT UP's famous slogan (*We're here, we're queer, so get used to it*) enters a general public, its queer difference is immediately domesticated and nullified because its meaning is readily interpretable. When the general public hears the slogan, it recognizes the enunciator as representing an identifiable entity—"*the* queer." This identification dulls the rhetorical force of what García Düttmann calls the slogan's "caesura loaded with tension," its ethical suspension of social logics (ibid., 114).

# REFERENCES


Abelove, Henry. *Deep Gossip.* Minneapolis: University of Minnesota Press, 2003.

Adorno, Theodor W. *Aesthetic Theory.* Edited by Gretel Adorno and Rolf Tiedemann. Translated by Robert Hullot-Kentor. Minneapolis: University of Minnesota Press, 1997. German original, 1970.

———. *Notes to Literature, Volume 1.* Translated by Shierry Weber Nicholsen. New York: Columbia University Press, 1991. German original, 1958.

Agamben, Giorgio. *Homo Sacer: Sovereign Power and Bare Life.* Translated by Daniel Heller-Roazen. Stanford: Stanford University Press, 1998. Italian original, 1995.

———. *State of Exception.* Translated by Kevin Attell. Stanford: Stanford University Press, 2005. Italian original, 2003.

Akam, Everett Helmut. *Transnational America: Cultural Pluralist Thought in the Twentieth Century.* Lanham, MD: Rowman and Littlefield, 2002.

Althusser, Louis. *For Marx.* Translated by Ben Brewster. New York: Verso, 2005. French original, 1965.

———. *The Humanist Controversy and Other Writings.* Edited by François Matheron. Translated by G. M. Goshgarian. New York: Verso, 2003.

Anderson, Benedict. *Imagined Communities: Reflections on the Origin and Spread of Nationalism.* Rev. ed. New York: Verso, 1991.

Antliff, Allan. *Anarchy and Art: From the Paris Commune to the Fall of the Berlin Wall.* Vancouver, BC: Arsenal Pulp Press, 2007.

Appadurai, Arjun. *Modernity at Large: Cultural Dimensions of Globalization.* Minneapolis: University of Minnesota Press, 1996.

Appiah, Kwame Anthony. *Cosmopolitanism: Ethics in a World of Strangers.* New York: Oxford University Press, 2006.

———. *The Ethics of Identity.* Princeton: Princeton University Press, 2005.

Arendt, Hannah. *The Human Condition.* 2nd ed. Chicago: University of Chicago Press, 1998.

———. *The Promise of Politics.* Edited by Jerome Kohn. New York: Schocken, 2005. Originally published 1958.

Auping, Michael. "Jess: A Grand Collage." In *Jess: A Grand Collage, 1951–1993.* Edited by Michael Auping, 31–65. Buffalo: Albright-Knox Art Gallery/Buffalo Fine Arts Academy, 1993.

Badiou, Alain. *The Century.* Translated by Alberto Toscano. Malden, MA: Polity Press, 2007. French original, 2005.

———. *Ethics: An Essay on the Understanding of Evil.* Translated by Peter Hallward. New York: Verso, 2001. French original, 1993.

———. *Manifesto for Philosophy.* Translated and edited by Norman Madarasz. Albany: SUNY Press, 1999. French original, 1989.

———. *Metapolitics.* Translated by Jason Barker. New York: Verso, 2005. French original, 1998.

Balibar, Étienne. *We, the People of Europe? Reflections on Transnational Citizenship.* Translated by James Swenson. Princeton: Princeton University Press, 2004. French original, 2001.

Barbáchano, Carlós. "La Cuba secreta o la íntima historia de un encuentro inacabable." *Cuadernos Hispanoamericanos* 646 (April 2004): 97–105.

Barquet, Jesús J. *Consagración de la Habana: Las peculiaridades del grupo Orígenes en el proceso cultural cubano.* Miami: Iberian Studies Institute/University of Miami Press, 1992.

Barthes, Roland. *The Pleasure of the Text.* Translated by Richard Miller. New York: Hill and Wang, 1975. French original, 1973.

———. *Roland Barthes by Roland Barthes.* Translated by Richard Howard. Berkeley and Los Angeles: University of California Press, 1994. French original, 1975.

———. *The Rustle of Language.* Translated by Richard Howard. Berkeley and Los Angeles: University of California Press, 1989. French original, 1984.

———. *Writing Degree Zero.* Translated by Annette Lavers and Colin Smith. Preface by Susan Sontag. New York: Hill and Wang, 1968. French original, 1953.

Bejel, Emilio. *Gay Cuban Nation.* Chicago: University of Chicago Press, 2001.

———. *José Lezama Lima: Poet of the Image.* Gainesville: University of Florida Press, 1990.

———. "Lezama Lima: Hermetismo poético en una época revolucionaria." *Cuadernos de poética* 8.24 (September–December 1994): 13–31.

Berkman, Alexander. *What Is Anarchism?* Reprint, Edinburgh: AK Press, 2003. Originally published 1929.

Berlant, Lauren, and Elizabeth Freeman. "Queer Nationality." In *Fear of a Queer Planet: Queer Politics and Social Theory.* Edited by Michael Warner, 193–229. Minneapolis: University of Minnesota Press, 1993.

Bersani, Leo. *Homos.* Cambridge: Harvard University Press, 1995.

———. "Is the Rectum a Grave?" In *AIDS: Cultural Analysis, Cultural Activism.* Edited by Douglas Crimp, 197–222. Cambridge: MIT Press, 1988.

Bersani, Leo, and Ulysse Dutoit. *Caravaggio's Secrets.* Cambridge: MIT Press, 1998.

Bertholf, Robert J. "The Concert: Robert Duncan and Writing out of Painting." In *Jess: A Grand Collage 1951–1993.* Edited by Michael Auping, 67–91. Buffalo: Albright-Knox Art Gallery/Buffalo Fine Arts Academy, 1993.

Blasius, Mark. *Gay and Lesbian Politics: Sexuality and the Emergence of a New Ethic.* Philadelphia: Temple University Press, 1994.

Bobbio, Noberto. *Liberalism and Democracy.* Translated by Martin Ryle and Kare Soper. New York: Verso, 1990. Italian original, 1988.

Bourg, Julian. *From Revolution to Ethics: May 1968 and Contemporary French Thought.* Montreal: McGill-Queen's University Press, 2007.

Brenkman, John. "Politics, Mortal and Natal: An Arendtian Rejoinder." *Narrative* 10.2 (May 2002): 186–92.

———. "Queer Post-Politics." *Narrative* 10.2 (May 2002): 174–80.

Brogan, Jacqueline Vaught. *The Violence Within, the Violence Without: Wallace Stevens and the Emergence of a Revolutionary Poetics.* Athens: University of Georgia Press, 2003.

Brown, Wendy. *Edgework: Critical Essays on Knowledge and Politics.* Princeton: Princeton University Press, 2005.

Buckwalter-Arias, James. "Discurso origenista y Cuba postsoviética." *Encuentro de la cultura cubana* 36 (Spring 2005): 54–65.

———. “Reinscribing the Aesthetic: Cuban Narrative and Post-Soviet Cultural Politics.” *PMLA* 120.2 (March 2005): 362–74.

Bunch, Charlotte. “Lesbians in Revolt.” In *Come Out Fighting: A Century of Essential Writing on Gay and Lesbian Liberation*. Edited by Chris Bull, 126–32. New York: Thunder's Mouth/Nation, 2001. Originally published 1972.

Butler, Judith. “Competing Universalities.” In *Contingency, Hegemony, and Universality: Contemporary Dialogues on the Left*. Edited by Judith Butler, Ernesto Laclau, and Slavoj Žižek, 136–81. New York: Verso, 2000.

———. *Excitable Speech: A Politics of the Performative*. New York: Routledge, 1997.

———. *Gender Trouble: Feminism and the Subversion of Identity*. New York: Routledge, 1990.

———. *Giving an Account of Oneself*. New York: Fordham University Press, 2005.

———. *Precarious Life: The Powers of Mourning and Violence*. New York: Verso, 2004.

———. *The Psychic Life of Power: Theories in Subjection*. Stanford: Stanford University Press, 1997.

———. “Restaging the Universal: Hegemony and the Limits of Formalism.” In *Contingency, Hegemony, and Universality: Contemporary Dialogues on the Left*. Edited by Judith Butler, Ernesto Laclau, and Slavoj Žižek, 11–43. New York: Verso, 2000.

———. *Undoing Gender*. New York: Routledge, 2004.

Butler, Judith, and Gayatri Chakravorty Spivak. *Who Sings the Nation-State? Language, Politics, Belonging*. New York: Seagull Books, 2007.

Calvet, Louis-Jean. *Roland Barthes: A Biography*. Translated by Sarah Wykes. Bloomington: Indiana University Press, 1995. French original, 1990.

Casanova, Pascale. *The World Republic of Letters*. Translated by M. B. DeBevoise. Cambridge: Harvard University Press, 2004. French original, 1999.

Caserio, Robert L., Judith Halberstam, José Esteban Muñoz, and Tim Dean. “The Antisocial Thesis in Queer Theory: MLA Convention, 27 December 2005, Washington, D.C.” *PMLA* 121.3 (May 2006): 819–28.

Castronovo, Russ. *Beautiful Democracy: Aesthetics and Anarchy in a Global Era*. Chicago: University of Chicago Press, 2007.

Cavarero, Adriana. *For More than One Voice: Toward a Philosophy of Vocal Expression*. Translated by Paul A. Kottman. Stanford: Stanford University Press, 2005. Italian original, 2003.

Chasin, Alexandra. *Selling Out: The Gay and Lesbian Movement Goes to Market*. New York: Palgrave, 2001.

Cheah, Pheng. *Inhuman Conditions: On Cosmopolitanism and Human Rights*. Cambridge: Harvard University Press, 2006.

Clarke, Eric O. *Virtuous Vice: Homoeroticism and the Public Sphere*. Durham: Duke University Press, 2000.

Cleghorn, Angus J. *Wallace Stevens' Poetics: The Neglected Rhetoric*. New York: Palgrave, 2000.

Connolly, William E. *Identity/Difference: Democratic Negotiations of Political Paradox*. Expanded ed. Minneapolis: University of Minnesota Press, 2002.

Corber, Robert J. *Homosexuality in Cold War America: Resistance and the Crisis of Masculinity*. Durham: Duke University Press, 1997.

———. *In the Name of National Security: Hitchcock, Homophobia, and the Political Construction of Gender in Postwar America*. Durham: Duke University Press, 1993.

Cortázar, Julio. “To Reach Lezama Lima.” Translated by Thomas Christensen. In *José Lezama Lima: Selections*. Edited by Ernesto Livon-Grosman, 138–66. Berkeley and Los Angeles: University of California Press, 2005. Spanish original, 1967.

Crimp, Douglas, ed. *AIDS: Cultural Analysis, Cultural Activism*. Cambridge: MIT Press, 1988.

———. *Melancholia and Moralism: Essays on AIDS and Queer Politics.* Cambridge: MIT Press, 2004.

Davidson, Michael. *Guys like Us: Citing Masculinity in Cold War Poetics.* Chicago: University of Chicago Press, 2004.

———. *The San Francisco Renaissance: Poetics and Community at Mid-century.* New York: Cambridge University Press, 1989.

Dean, Tim. *Beyond Sexuality.* Chicago: University of Chicago Press, 2000.

de Hart, Jane Sherron. "Containment at Home: Gender, Sexuality, and National Identity in Cold War America." In *Rethinking Cold War Culture.* Edited by Peter J. Kuznick and James Gilbert, 124–55. Washington,D.C.: Smithsonian, 2001.

DeLanda, Manuel. *A New Philosophy of Society: Assemblage Theory and Social Complexity.* New York: Continuum, 2006.

Delany, Samuel R. *Times Square Red, Times Square Blue.* New York: New York University Press, 1999.

Deleuze, Gilles. *Essays Critical and Clinical.* Translated by Daniel W. Smith and Michael A. Greco. Minneapolis: University of Minnesota Press, 1997. French original, 1993.

———. *Expressionism in Philosophy: Spinoza.* Translated by Martin Joughin. New York: Zone, 1990. French original, 1968.

———. *Foucault.* Translated and edited by Seán Hand. Minneapolis: University of Minnesota Press, 1988. French original, 1986.

Deleuze, Gilles, and Félix Guattari. *Anti-Oedipus: Capitalism and Schizophrenia.* Translated by Robert Hurley, Mark Seem, and Helen R. Lane. Minneapolis: University of Minnesota Press, 1983. French original, 1972.

———. *Kafka: Toward a Minor Literature.* Translated by Dana Polan. Minneapolis: University of Minnesota Press, 1986. French original, 1975.

———. *A Thousand Plateaus: Capitalism and Schizophrenia.* Translated by Brian Massumi. Minneapolis: University of Minnesota Press, 1987. French original, 1980.

Deleuze, Gilles, and Claire Parnet. *Dialogues.* Translated by Hugh Tomlinson and Barbara Habberjam. New York: Columbia University Press, 1987. French original, 1977.

de Man, Paul. *Aesthetic Ideology.* Edited by Andrzej Warminski. Minneapolis: University of Minnesota Press, 1996.

D'Emilio, John. *Sexual Politics, Sexual Communities: The Making of a Homosexual Minority in the United States, 1940–1970.* 2nd ed. Chicago: University of Chicago Press, 1998.

D'Emilio, John, and Estelle B. Freedman. *Intimate Matters: A History of Sexuality in America.* New York: Harper, 1988.

Dewey, John. *Freedom and Culture.* Reprint, Amherst, NY: Prometheus, 1989. Originally published 1939.

———. *Individualism Old and New.* Reprint, Amherst, NY: Prometheus, 1999. Originally published 1929–30.

———. *Liberalism and Social Action.* Reprint, Amherst, NY: Prometheus, 2000. Originally published 1935.

———. *The Public and Its Problems.* Reprint, Athens: Ohio University Press, 1985. Originally published 1927.

Díaz, Roberto Ignacio. "Wallace Stevens y el discurso en la Habana: palabras de José Rodríguez Feo." *Revista Canadiense de Estudios Hispánicos* 22.1 (October 1997): 3–18.

Dolar, Mladen. *A Voice and Nothing More.* Cambridge: MIT Press, 2006.

Dollimore, Jonathan. *Sex, Literature, and Censorship.* Malden, MA: Polity Press, 2001.

Doolittle, Hilda (H.D.). *Hermetic Definition.* New York: New Directions, 1972.

Duggan, Lisa. *The Twilight of Equality? Neoliberalism, Cultural Politics, and the Attack on Democracy.* Boston: Beacon, 2003.

Duncan, Robert. *Bending the Bow.* New York: New Directions, 1968.

———. *Caesar's Gate: Poems 1949–50, with Paste-Ups by Jess.* Santa Barbara: Sand Dollar, 1972.

———. "A Conversation with Robert Duncan, May 29, 1976." Interview with Robert Peters and Paul Trachtenberg, parts 1–2. *Chicago Review* 43.4 (Fall 1997): 83–105; 44.1 (Winter 1998): 92–116.

———. *Fictive Certainties: Essays.* New York: New Directions, 1985.

———. *Ground Work.* Edited by Robert J. Bertholf and James Maynard. New York: New Directions, 2006.

———. *The H.D. Book:*

Part 1 ("Beginnings"), Chapter 1. *Coyote's Journal* 5/6 (1966): 8–31.

Part 1, Chapter 6 ("Rites of Participation"). In Duncan, *A Selected Prose.* 97–137. Originally published in *Caterpillar* (1967): 6–29 and *Caterpillar* 2 (1968): 125–54.

Part 2 ("Nights and Days"), Chapter 2 ("March 11, Saturday. 1961 [1963]"). *Caterpillar* 6 (1969): 16–38.

Part 2, Chapter 5 ("March 14, Tuesday. 1961 [1963]"). *Sagetrieb* 4.2/3 (Fall and Winter 1985): 38–85.

Part 2, Chapter 6 ("September 2, 1964"). *The Southern Review* (Winter 1985): 26–48.

Part 2, Chapter 9 ("March 22, 1961. Wednesday"). *Chicago Review* 30.3 (Winter 1979): 37–88.

———. *Of the War, Passages 22–27.* Berkeley: Oyez, 1966.

———. "Properties and Our REAL Estate." *Journal for the Protection of All Beings* 1 (1961): 84–94.

———. *Roots and Branches.* New York: New Directions, 1964.

———. *A Selected Prose.* Edited by Robert J. Bertholf. New York: New Directions, 1995.

———. *The Years as Catches: First Poems, 1939–1946.* Berkeley, CA: Oyez, 1966.

Duncan, Robert, and Hilda Doolittle (H.D.). *A Great Admiration: H.D./Robert Duncan, Correspondence 1950–1961.* Edited by Robert J. Bertholf. Venice, CA: Lapis, 1992.

Duncan, Robert, and Denise Levertov. *The Letters of Robert Duncan and Denise Levertov.* Edited by Robert J. Bertholf and Albert Gelpi. Stanford: Stanford University Press, 2004.

Edelman, Lee. *Homographesis: Essays in Gay Literary and Cultural Theory.* New York: Routledge, 1994.

———. *No Future: Queer Theory and the Death Drive.* Durham: Duke University Press, 2004.

Eliot, T. S. *Collected Poems, 1909–1962.* New York: Harcourt Brace, 1963.

Eng, David L., Judith Halberstam, and José Esteban Muñoz, eds. *What's So Queer about Queer Studies Now?* Special issue of *Social Text* 23.3/4 (Fall/Winter 2005).

Epps, Brad. "The Fetish of Fluidity." In *Homosexuality and Psychoanalysis.* Edited by Tim Dean and Christopher Lane, 412–31. Chicago: University of Chicago Press, 2001.

Eribon, Didier. *Insult and the Making of the Gay Self.* Translated by Michael Lucey. Durham: Duke University Press, 2004. French original, 1999.

Esposito, Roberto. *Bíos: Biopolitics and Philosophy.* Translated by Timothy Campbell. Minneapolis: University of Minnesota Press, 2008. Italian original, 2004.

Faas, Ekbert. *Towards a New American Poetics: Essays and Interviews, Charles Olson, Robert Duncan, Gary Snyder, Robert Creeley, Robert Bly, Allen Ginsberg.* Santa Barbara: Black Sparrow, 1978.

———. *Young Robert Duncan: Portrait of the Poet as Homosexual in Society.* Santa Barbara: Black Sparrow, 1983.

Feinberg, Leslie. *Trans Liberation: Beyond Pink or Blue.* Boston: Beacon, 1999.

Fernández Moreno, César, ed. *América Latina en su literatura.* Mexico City: Unesco Siglo XXI, 1973.

Ferguson, Roderick A. *Aberrations in Black: Toward a Queer of Color Critique.* Minneapolis: University of Minnesota Press, 2004.

Ferry, Luc, and Alain Renaut. *French Philosophy of the Sixties: An Essay on Antihumanism.* Translated by Mary Schnackenberg Cattani. Amherst: University of Massachusetts

Press, 1990. French original, 1985.

Filreis, Alan. *Modernism from Right to Left: Wallace Stevens, the Thirties, and Literary Radicalism.* New York: Cambridge University Press, 1994.

———. *Wallace Stevens and the Actual World.* Princeton: Princeton University Press, 1991.

Fombona Iribarren, Jacinto. "La poética 'cuántica' de Severo Sarduy: Una lectura de *Big Bang.*" *Mester* 20.1 (Spring 1991): 39–49.

Foucault, Michel. *The Archaeology of Knowledge and the Discourse on Language.* Translated by A. M. Sheridan Smith. New York: Pantheon, 1972. French original, 1971.

———. *The Essential Works of Foucault 1954–1984*, vol. 1: *Ethics, Subjectivity, and Truth*; vol. 3, *Power.* Edited by Paul Rabinow. New York: New Press, 1997–2000. Selections from French original, 1994.

———. *The History of Sexuality, An Introduction: Volume 1.* Translated by Robert Hurley. New York: Vintage, 1978. French original, 1976.

———. *Naissance de la biopolitique: Cours au Collège de France, 1978–1979.* Edited by Michel Senellart. Paris: Gallimard/Seuil, 2004.

———. *The Order of Things: An Archaeology of the Human Sciences.* New York: Vintage, 1973. French original, 1966.

———. *Security, Territory, Population: Lectures at the Collège de France, 1977–1978.* Edited by François Ewald and Alessandro Fontana. Translated by Graham Burchell. New York: Palgrave, 2007. French original, 2004.

———. *'Society Must Be Defended': Lectures at the Collège de France, 1975–1976.* Edited by Mauro Bertani and Alessandro Fontana. Translated by David Macey. New York: Picador, 2003. French original, 1997.

Foucault, Michel, and Noam Chomsky. *The Chomsky-Foucault Debate on Human Nature.* New York: New Press, 2006. French original, 1974.

Franco, Jean. "The Crisis of the Liberal Imagination and the Utopia of Writing." In *Critical Passions: Selected Essays.* Edited by Mary Louise Pratt and Kathleen Newman, 259–84. Durham: Duke University Press, 1999. Originally published 1977.

García Düttmann, Alexander. *Between Cultures: Tensions in the Struggle for Recognition.* Translated by Kenneth B. Woodgate. New York: Verso, 2000. German original, 1997.

García Vega, Lorenzo. *Los años de Orígenes.* Caracas: Monte Avila Editores, 1978.

Gilroy, Paul. *Postcolonial Melancholia.* New York: Columbia University Press, 2005.

Ginsberg, Allen. *Howl and Other Poems.* San Francisco: City Lights, 1959.

Glave, Thomas. *Words to Our Now: Imagination and Dissent.* Minneapolis: University of Minnesota Press, 2005.

Goldman, Emma. *Anarchism and Other Essays.* Reprint, New York: Dover, 1969. Originally published, 1917.

Goldstein, Richard. *The Attack Queers: Liberal Society and the Gay Right.* New York: Verso, 2002.

González Echevarría, Roberto. *La ruta de Severo Sarduy.* Hanover, NH: Ediciones del Norte, 1987.

Gopinath, Gayatri. *Impossible Desires: Queer Diasporas and South Asian Public Cultures.* Durham: Duke University Press, 2005.

Gosse, Van. *Where the Boys Are: Cuba, Cold War America, and the Making of a New Left.* New York: Verso, 1993.

Green, David. *The Containment of Latin America: A History of the Myths and Realities of the Good Neighbor Policy.* Chicago: Quadrangle, 1971.

Guattari, Félix. *The Three Ecologies.* Translated by Ian Pindar and Paul Sutton. London: Athalone, 2000.

Gunn, Thom. "Homosexuality in Robert Duncan's Poetry." In *Robert Duncan: Scales of the Marvelous.* Edited by Robert J. Bertholf and Ian W. Reid, 142–60. New York: New Directions, 1979.

Halberstam, Judith. *In a Queer Time and Place: Transgender Bodies, Subcultural Lives.* New

York: New York University Press, 2005.

Halperin, David M. *How to Do the History of Homosexuality.* Chicago: University of Chicago Press, 2004.

Hardt, Michael, and Antonio Negri. *Empire.* Cambridge: Harvard University Press, 2000.

———. *Multitude: War and Democracy in the Age of Empire.* New York: Penguin, 2004.

Harper, Phillip Brian. *Private Affairs: Critical Ventures in the Culture of Social Relations.* New York: New York University Press, 1999.

Harrington, Joseph. *Poetry and the Public: The Social Form of Modern U.S. Poetics.* Middletown: Wesleyan University Press, 2002.

Harvey, Keith. *Intercultural Movements: American Gay in French Translation.* Northampton, MA: St. Jerome, 2003.

Heidegger, Martin. "Letter on Humanism." Translated by Frank A. Capuzzi and J. Glenn Gray. In *Basic Writings.* Revised and expanded edition. Edited by David Farrell Krell, 213–65. New York: HarperCollins, 1993. German original, 1947.

Hennessy, Rosemary. *Profit and Pleasure: Sexual Identities in Late Capitalism.* New York: Routledge, 2000.

Hocquenghem, Guy. *Homosexual Desire.* Translated by Daniella Dangoor. Durham: Duke University Press, 1993. French original, 1972.

Honig, Bonnie. "Another Cosmopolitanism? Law and Politics in the New Europe." In Seyla Benhabib, *Another Cosmopolitanism.* Edited by Robert Post, 102–27. New York: Oxford University Press, 2006.

Jarraway, David R. "'Creatures of the Rainbow': Wallace Stevens, Mark Doty, and the Poetics of Androgyny." *Mosaic* 30.3 (September 1997): 169–83.

———. *Going the Distance: Dissident Subjectivity in Modernist American Literature.* Baton Rouge: Louisiana State University Press, 2003.

Jay, Martin. *Force Fields: Between Intellectual History and Cultural Critique.* New York: Routledge, 1993.

———. *Songs of Experience: Modern American and European Variations on a Universal Theme.* Berkeley: University of California Press, 2005.

Johnson, David K. *The Lavender Scare: The Cold War Persecution of Gays and Lesbians in the Federal Government.* Chicago: University of Chicago Press, 2004.

Johnson, E. Patrick, and Mae G. Henderson, eds. *Black Queer Studies: A Critical Anthology.* Durham: Duke University Press, 2005.

Kant, Immanuel. *Basic Writings of Kant.* Edited by Allen W. Wood. New York: Modern Library, 2001.

Keenaghan, Eric. "Jack Spicer's Pricks and Cocksuckers: Translating Homosexuality into Visibility." *The Translator* 4.2 (1998): 273–94.

———. "The Queerness of Poetic Action during Vietnam." *Contemporary Literature.* Special issue: "Contemporary Literature and the State." Edited by Matthew Hart and Jim Hansen. 2009.

———. "Reading Emerson in Other Times: On a Politics of Solitude and an Ethics of Risk." In *The Other Emerson: New Approaches, Divergent Paths.* Edited by Cary Wolfe and Branka Arsić. Minneapolis: University of Minnesota Press, 2009.

———. "A Virile Poet in the Borderlands: Wallace Stevens' Reimagining of Race and Masculinity." *modernism/modernity* 9.3 (September 2002): 439–62.

———. "Wallace Stevens' Influence on the Construction of Gay Masculinity by the Cuban *Orígenes* Group." *The Wallace Stevens Journal* 24.2 (Fall 2000): 187–207.

Keenan, Thomas. *Fables of Responsibility: Aberrations and Predicaments in Ethics and Politics.* Stanford: Stanford University Press, 1997.

Kinsey, Alfred C. *Sexual Behavior in the Human Female, by the Staff of the Institute for Sex Research.* Philadelphia: W. B. Saunders, 1953.

Kinsey, Alfred C., Wardell B. Pomeroy, and Clyde E. Martin. *Sexual Behavior in the Human Male.* Philadelphia: W. B. Saunders, 1948.

Krim, Seymour. "Revolt of the Homosexual." In *Sexual Revolution.* Edited by Jeffrey Escoffier, 469–76. New York: Thunder's Mouth Press, 2003. Originally published 1959.

Kristeva, Julia. *Revolution in Poetic Language.* Translated by Margaret Waller. New York: Columbia University Press, 1984. French original, 1974.

Kuhn, Thomas S. *The Structure of Scientific Revolutions.* 3rd ed. Chicago: University of Chicago Press, 1996. Originally published 1962.

Lacan, Jacques. *Écrits: A Selection.* Translated by Alan Sheridan. New York: Norton, 1977. French original, 1966.

Levinson, Brett. *Secondary Moderns: Mimesis, History, and Revolution in Lezama Lima's "American Expression."* Lewisburg, PA: Bucknell University Press, 1996.

Lezama Lima, José. *La cantidad hechizada.* Madrid: La Vela Latina/Ediciones Jucar, 1974.

———. *Cartas a Eloísa y otra correspondencia, 1939–1976.* 2nd ed. Edited by Eloísa Lezama Lima. Madrid: Editorial Verbum, 1998.

———. *Diarios 1939–40/1956–58.* Edited by Ciro Bianchi Ross. Mexico City: Ediciones Era, 1994.

———. *La expresión americana.* In *Obras completas,* vol. 2: *Ensayos, cuentos,* 277–390. Mexico City: Aguilar, 1977.

———. *La fijeza* and *Dador.* In *Obras completas,* vol. 1: *Novela, poesía completa,* 787-898 and 899–1006. Mexico City: Aguilar, 1975.

———. *Imagen y posibilidad.* Edited by Ciro Bianchi Ross. Havana: Editorial Letras Cubanas, 1981.

———. *Paradiso.* Translated by Gregory Rabassa. Normal, IL: Dalkey Archive Press, 2000. Spanish original, 1966.

———. *El reino de la imagen.* Edited by Julio Ortega. Caracas: Editorial Ayacucho, 1981.

———. *Tratados en la Habana: Ensayos éstiticos.* Santiago: Editorial Orbe, 1970.

Lingis, Alphonso. *The First Person Singular.* Evanston, IL: Northwestern University Press, 2007.

Longenbach, James. *Wallace Stevens: The Plain Sense of Things.* New York: Oxford University Press, 1991.

Love, Heather. *Feeling Backward: Loss and the Politics of Queer History.* Cambridge: Harvard University Press, 2007.

Lumsden, Ian. *Machos, Maricones, and Gays: Cuba and Homosexuality.* Philadelphia: Temple University Press, 1996.

MacFarlane, S. Neil, and Yuen Foong Khong. *Human Security and the U.N.: A Critical History.* Bloomington: Indiana University Press, 2006.

Machover, Jacobo. "La memoria frente al poder. Escritores cubanos del exilio: Guillermo Cabrera Infante, Severo Sarduy, Reinaldo Arenas." *Revista Hispano Cubana* 10 (Spring-Summer 2001): 37–46.

Mackey, Nathaniel. *Discrepant Engagement: Dissonance, Cross-Culturality, and Experimental Writing.* Tuscaloosa: University of Alabama Press, 2000.

Mailer, Norman. "The White Negro: Superficial Reflections on the Hipster." In *The Portable Beat Reader.* Edited by Ann Charters, 582–605. New York: Penguin, 1992. Originally published 1957.

Mañach, Jorge. "El arcano de cierta poesía nueva: Carta abierta al poeta José Lezama Lima." *Bohemia* 41.39 (25 September 1949): 78, 90.

Martin, Randy. *An Empire of Indifference: American War and the Financial Logic of Risk Management.* Durham: Duke University Press, 2007.

May, Elaine Tyler. *Homeward Bound: American Families in the Cold War Era.* New York: Basic, 1988.

McBride, Dwight A. *Why I Hate Abercrombie and Fitch: Essays on Race and Sexuality.* New York: New York University Press, 2005.

McClure, Michael. *3 Poems: Dolphin Skull, Rare Angel, Dark Brown.* New York: Penguin, 1995.

Méndez Rodenas, Adriana. *Severo Sarduy: El neobarroco de la transgresión*. Mexico City: Universidad Nacional Autónoma de México, 1983.

Meyerowitz, Joanne. "Sex, Gender, and the Cold War Language of Reform." In *Rethinking Cold War Culture*. Edited by Peter J. Kuznick and James Gilbert, 106–23. Washington, DC: Smithsonian, 2001.

Michaels, Walter Benn. *Our America: Nativism, Modernism, and Pluralism*. Durham: Duke University Press, 1997.

Miller, D. A. *Bringing Out Roland Barthes*. Berkeley and Los Angeles: University of California Press, 1992.

Miller, J. Hillis. *Topographies*. Stanford: Stanford University Press, 1995.

Montero, Oscar. "The Signifying Queen: Critical Notes from a Latino Queer." In *Hispanisms and Homosexualities*. Edited by Sylvia Molloy and Robert McKee Irwin, 161–74. Durham: Duke University Press, 1998.

Mouffe, Chantal. *The Democratic Paradox*. New York: Verso, 2000.

Muñoz, José Esteban. *Disidentifications: Queers of Color and the Performance of Politics*. Minneapolis: University of Minnesota Press, 1999.

Nadel, Alan. *Containment Culture: American Narratives, Postmodernism, and the Atomic Age*. Durham: Duke University Press, 1995.

Nealon, Christopher. *Foundlings: Lesbian and Gay Historical Emotion before Stonewall*. Durham: Duke University Press, 2001.

Nealon, Jeffrey T. *Foucault beyond Foucault: Power and Its Intensifications since 1984*. Stanford: Stanford University Press, 2007.

Nelson, Deborah. *Pursuing Privacy in Cold War America*. New York: Columbia University Press, 2002.

Newton, Huey P. "Manifesto Issued by the Black Panthers (A Letter from Huey to the Revolutionary Brothers and Sisters about the Women's Liberation and Gay Liberation Movements)." In *Come Out Fighting: A Century of Essential Writing on Gay and Lesbian Liberation*. Edited by Chris Bull, 89–91. New York: Thunder's Mouth/Nation, 2001. Originally published 1970.

Noble, David W. *Death of a Nation: American Culture and the End of Exceptionalism*. Minneapolis: University of Minnesota Press, 2002.

de la Nuez, Iván. *La balsa perpetua: Soledad y conexiones de la cultura cubana*. Barcelona: Editorial Casiopea, 1998.

O'Leary, Peter. *Gnostic Contagion: Robert Duncan and the Poetry of Illness*. Middleton, CT: Wesleyan University Press, 2002.

Paras, Eric. *Foucault 2.0: Beyond Power and Knowledge*. New York: Other Press, 2006.

Patton, Cindy. *Globalizing AIDS*. Minneapolis: University of Minnesota Press, 2002.

———. *Inventing AIDS*. New York: Routledge, 1990.

Paul, Sherman. *The Lost America of Love: Rereading Robert Creeley, Edward Dorn, and Robert Duncan*. Baton Rouge: Louisiana State University Press, 1981.

Pease, Donald E. "The Global Homeland State: Bush's Biopolitical Settlement." *boundary 2* 30.3 (Fall 2003): 1–18.

Perez, Hiram. "You Can Have My Brown Body and Eat It, Too!" *Social Text* 23.3/4 (Fall/Winter 2005): 171–91.

Pérez, Jr., Louis A. *Cuba under the Platt Amendment, 1902–1934*. Pittsburgh: University of Pittsburgh Press, 1986.

———. *On Becoming Cuban: Identity, Nationality, and Culture*. New York: Ecco, 1999.

Pérez, Rolando. "Severo Sarduy." *Review of Contemporary Fiction* 24.1 (Spring 2004): 94–138.

Pérez Firmat, Gustavo. *My Own Private Cuba: Essays on Cuban Literature and Culture*. Boulder, CO: Society of Spanish and Spanish-American Studies, 1999.

———. "The Strut of the Centipede: José Lezama Lima and New World Exceptionalism." In *Do the Americas Have a Common Literature?* Edited by Gustavo Pérez Firmat, 316–32.

Durham: Duke University Press, 1990.

Pérez León, Roberto. *Tiempo de Ciclón.* Havana: Ediciones Unión, 1995.

Phelan, Shane. *Sexual Strangers: Gays, Lesbians, and Dilemmas of Citizenship.* Philadelphia: Temple University Press, 2001.

Pike, Frederick R. *FDR's Good Neighbor Policy: Sixty Years of Generally Gentle Chaos.* Austin: University of Texas Press, 1995.

Povinelli, Elizabeth A. "Sexuality as Risk: Psychoanalysis Metapragmatically." In *Homosexuality and Psychoanalysis.* Edited by Tim Dean and Christopher Lane, 387–411. Chicago: University of Chicago Press, 2001.

Pound, Ezra. *The Cantos.* New York: New Directions, 1970. Originally published 1930–1969.

Prieto, René. *Body of Writing: Figuring Desire in Latin American Literature.* Durham: Duke University Press, 2000.

Puar, Jasbir K. "Abu Ghraib: Arguing against Exceptionalism." *Feminist Studies* 30.2 (Summer 2004): 522–34.

———. "On Torture: Abu Ghraib." *Radical History Review* 93 (Fall 2005): 13–38.

———. *Terrorist Assemblages: Homonationalism in Queer Times.* Durham: Duke University Press, 2007.

Puar, Jasbir K., and Amit S. Rai. "Monster, Terrorist, Fag: The War on Terrorism and the Production of Docile Patriots." *Social Text* 20.3 (Fall 2002): 117–48.

Quinn, Justin. *Gathered beneath the Storm: Wallace Stevens, Nature, and Community.* Dublin: University College of Dublin Press, 2002.

Quiroga, José. *Cuban Palimpsests.* Minneapolis: University of Minnesota Press, 2005.

———. *Tropics of Desire: Interventions from Queer Latino America.* New York: New York University Press, 2000.

Rabaté, Jean-Michel. *The Future of Theory.* Malden, MA: Blackwell, 2002.

Rancière, Jacques. *Disagreement: Politics and Philosophy.* Translated by Julie Rose. Minneapolis: University of Minnesota Press, 1999. French original, 1995.

———. *The Flesh of Words: The Politics of Writing.* Translated by Charlotte Mandell. Stanford: Stanford University Press, 2004. French original, 1998.

Rawls, John. *Political Liberalism,* expanded ed. New York: Columbia University Press, 1996.

Reid-Pharr, Robert. *Once You Go Black: Choice, Desire, and the Black American Intellectual* New York: New York University Press, 2007.

Rhodes, Benjamin D. *United States Foreign Policy in the Interwar Period, 1918–1941: The Golden Age of American Diplomatic and Military Complacency.* Westport, CT: Praeger, 2002.

Richardson, Joan. *Wallace Stevens: The Later Years, 1923–1955.* New York: Beech Tree/Morrow, 1988.

Ricco, John Paul. *The Logic of the Lure.* Chicago: University of Chicago Press, 2002.

Rivero-Potter, Alicia. *Autor/Lector: Huidobro, Borges, Fuentes y Sarduy.* Detroit: Wayne State University Press, 1991.

Robinson, Paul. *Queer Wars: The New Gay Right and Its Critics.* Chicago: University of Chicago Press, 2005.

Rojas, Rafael. *El arte de la espera: Notas al margen de la política cubana.* Mexico City: Editorial Colibrí, 1998.

———. "*Orígenes* and the Poetics of History." Translated by Luis P. Aguilar-Moreno. *New Centennial Review* 2.2 (Summer 2002): 151–85.

Rozencvaig, Perla. "El Big Bang de Severo Sarduy o la explosión poética." *Chasqui* 10.1 (November 1980): 36–42.

Said, Edward W. *Culture and Imperialism.* New York: Vintage, 1993.

———. *Humanism and Democratic Criticism.* New York: Columbia University Press, 2004.

Sarduy, Severo. "Una autobiografía pulverizada: Entrevista." Interview with Mihály Dés. *Quimera* 102 (1991): 32–38.

———. *Cartas*. Edited by Manuel Díaz Martínez. Madrid: Editorial Verbum, 1996.

———. *Gestos*. Barcelona: Seix Barral, 1963.

———. Interview with González Echevarría. Translated by Jane E. French. *Diacritics* 2.2 (Summer 1972): 41–45.

———. "Mudo combate contra el vacío: Conversación con Severo Sarduy." Interview with Ana Eire. *INTI* 43–44 (Spring/Autumn 1996): 361–68.

———. *Obra Completa*. 2 vols. Edited by Gustavo Guerrero and François Wahl. Mexico City: Fondo de Cultura Económica, 1999.

———. "Severo Sarduy: Maquina barroca revolucionaria." Interview with Jean-Michel Fossey. In *Severo Sarduy*. Edited by Julián Ríos, 15–24. Madrid: Fundamentos, 1976.

———. *Written on a Body*. Translated by Carol Maier. New York: Lumen, 1989. Spanish original, 1968.

Sartre, Jean-Paul. *Existentialism and Human Emotions*. Translated by Bernard Frechtman. New York: Citadel, 1987.

———. "What Is Writing?" In *What Is Literature?* Translated by Bernard Frechtman. Reprinted in *Essays in Existentialism*. Edited by Wade Baskin, 303–31. Secaucus, NJ: Citadel, 1965. French original, 1947.

Sedgwick, Eve Kosofksy. *Between Men: English Literature and Male Homosocial Desire*. New York: Columbia University Press, 1985.

———. *Epistemology of the Closet*. Berkeley and Los Angeles: University of California Press, 1990.

Shelley, Martha. "Gay Is Good." In *We Are Everywhere: A Historical Source Book of Gay and Lesbian Politics*. Edited by Mark Blasius and Shane Phelan, 391–94. New York: Routledge, 1997. Originally published 1970.

Shively, Charley. "Indiscriminate Promiscuity as an Act of Revolution." In *Come Out Fighting: A Century of Essential Writing on Gay and Lesbian Liberation*. Edited by Chris Bull, 132–41. New York: Thunder's Mouth/Nation, 2001. Originally published 1974.

Sifuentes-Jáuregui, Ben. *Transvestism, Masculinity, and Latin American Literature*. New York: Palgrave, 2002.

Solanas, Valerie. *The S.C.U.M. Manifesto*. New York: Verso, 2004. Written 1968, originally published 1974.

Sor Juana (Juana Inés de la Cruz). "Primero sueño" ("When I Dream"). In *Poems, Portest, and a Dream*. Translated by Margaret Sayers Peden, 78–129. New York: Penguin, 1997. Spanish original, 1692.

Spinoza, Baruch. *Ethics*. Edited and translated by G. H. R. Parkinson. New York: Oxford University Press, 2000.

Stevens, Wallace. *Collected Poems*. New York: Vintage, 1990.

———. *Collected Poetry and Prose*. Edited by Frank Kermode and Joan Richardson. New York: Library of America, 1997.

———. *The Letters of Wallace Stevens*. Selected and edited by Holly Stevens. Berkeley and Los Angeles: University of California Press, 1996.

———. *The Necessary Angel: Essays on Reality and the Imagination*. New York: Vintage, 1951.

Stevens, Wallace, and José Rodríguez Feo. *Secretaries of the Moon: The Letters of Wallace Stevens and José Rodríguez Feo*. Edited by Beverly Coyle and Alan Filreis. Durham: Duke University Press, 1986.

Stockton, Kathryn Bond. *Beautiful Bottom, Beautiful Shame: Where "Black" Meets "Queer."* Durham: Duke University Press, 2006.

Theado, Matt. *The Beats: A Literary Reference*. New York: Carroll and Graff, 2003.

Treichler, Paula A. *How to Have Theory in an Epidemic: Cultural Chronicles of AIDS*. Durham: Duke University Press, 1999.

Turkle, Sherry. *Psychoanalytic Politics: Jacques Lacan and Freud's French Revolution*. 2nd ed. New York: Guilford, 1992.

Unruh, Vicky. *Latin American Vanguards: The Art of Contentious Encounters*. Berkeley and Los Angeles: University of California Press, 1994.

U.S. Office of Homeland Security. *National Strategy for Homeland Security.* Washington, DC: GPO, 2002.

Vaid, Urvashi. *Virtual Equality: The Mainstreaming of Gay and Lesbian Liberation*. New York: Anchor, 1995.

Vitier, Cintio. *Lo cubano en la poesía*. Havana: Letras Cubanas, 1970.

———. *Para llegar a Orígenes: Revista de arte y literatura*. Havana: Editorial Letras Cubanas, 1994.

Waldron, Jeremy. "Cosmopolitan Norms." In Seyla Benhabib, *Another Cosmopolitanism*. Edited by Robert Post, 83–101. New York: Oxford University Press, 2006.

Wander, Philip. "Political Rhetoric and the Un-American Tradition." In *Cold War Rhetoric: Strategy, Metaphor, and Ideology.* Edited by Martin J. Medhurst, Robert L. Ivie, Philip Wander, and Robert L. Scott, 185–200. Westport, CT: Greenwood, 1990.

Warner, Michael. Introduction to *Fear of a Queer Planet: Queer Politics and Social Theory.* Edited by Michael Warner, vii–xxxi. Minneapolis: University of Minnesota Press, 1993.

———. *Publics and Counterpublics*. New York: Zone, 2002.

———. *The Trouble with Normal: Sex, Politics, and the Ethics of Queer Life*. New York: Free Press, 1999.

Whitman, Walt. *Leaves of Grass: Norton Critical Edition*. Edited by Scully Bradley and Harold W. Blodgett. New York: Norton, 1973.

Whyte, William H. *The Organization Man*. New York: Simon & Schuster, 1956.

Williams, William Carlos. *Paterson*. Edited by Christopher MacGowan. New York: New Directions, 1992. Originally published 1946–1958.

Winnubst, Shannon. *Queering Freedom*. Bloomington: Indiana University Press, 2006.

Wood, Bryce. *The Dismantling of the Good Neighbor Policy.* Austin: University of Texas Press, 1985.

———. *The Making of the Good Neighbor Policy.* New York: Columbia University Press, 1961.

Young, Allen. "Out of the Closets, into the Streets." In *Out of the Closets: Voices of Gay Liberation*. Edited by Karla Jay and Allen Young. 20th anniversary ed., 6–34. New York: New York University Press, 1992. Originally published 1972.

Young, Iris Marion. *Inclusion and Democracy.* New York: Oxford University Press, 2000.

Zambrano, María. *La Cuba secreta y otros ensayos*. Edited by Jorge Luis Arcos. Madrid: Ediciones Endymion, 1996.

———. *Persona y democracia: La historia sacrificial*. Barcelona: Anthropos, 1988.

# INDEX

www.ingramcontent.com/pod-product-compliance
Lightning Source LLC
LaVergne TN
LVHW090939080826
845145LV00003B/808

* 9 7 8 0 8 1 4 2 5 7 3 2 6 *